Axioms for Golf Over 40

- You can't stop the aging process, but you can use diet and exercise to slow it down.

- Strength, flexibility, and endurance are equal components for good golf at any age.

- Older muscles need to be stretched every day, even when you aren't playing golf.

- A half-hour of stretching before you play is far more beneficial than hitting a few extra balls on the range.

- An hour a day of exercise is much better for your game than that new titanium driver.

- Strength training not only improves your distance and accuracy, it also prevents common injuries that plague over-40 golfers.

- Strong arms generate more clubhead speed with less effort.

- Strong legs are the foundation on which to build the swing and the driving force behind all good golf.

- A firm, flexible midsection powers the rotary motion of the golf swing and prevents lower back injury.

- Your swing mechanics improve as you become stronger and fitter after 40.

- Stronger cardiovascular conditioning leads to better, more consistent shots in the later holes of a round.

- What you eat can and does affect what you shoot on the golf course.

- Drinking alcohol on the golf course never helps your game and probably hurts it.

Fitness Commandments for Over-40 Golfers

- **Stretch every muscle you strengthen.** Warm muscles are more receptive to flexibility exercises, and it's important to take advantage of that receptivity. Spend a minimum of 30 seconds stretching each muscle after strength training.

- **Don't overdo it.** You shouldn't take on too much too soon in your fitness program.

- **Continue to practice and play as you build a better golf body.** Your swing goes through some subtle changes as your body changes. Continuing to swing the golf club and play regularly as you make this transformation are important.

- **Don't shortchange your cardiovascular training.** Keeping your heart in shape is just as important to good golf as honing your putting touch. By getting yourself in good cardiovascular condition, you improve the way your body processes oxygen, and you are better able to maintain a consistent rhythm and tempo throughout your rounds.

- **Set an unwavering time and place to work out and stick to it.** The moment you start making excuses for not engaging in golf-specific exercises is the moment you compromise your golf fitness and your game.

- **Don't quit in the off-season.** Whether or not you're playing golf in cold weather, you should still exercise daily.

- **Set realistic fitness goals that correspond to your goals on the course.** If your goal is to lower your handicap from double to single digits in nine months, you should have corresponding fitness goals, such as lowering your body fat percentage below 15 percent and doubling your flexibility and endurance over that same period.

- **Don't run unless you're already a runner.** Forty is not the age to take up running if your body isn't already accustomed to the pounding it takes from running.

(continued)

Golf Over 40 For Dummies®

Cheat Sheet

Fitness Commandments for Over-40 Golfers (continued)

- **Always seek the advice of fitness professionals before embarking on any full-time fitness regimen.** Only a qualified professional can assess your needs and prescribe a program that perfectly matches your body.

- **Take a few golf lessons along the way.** Your game changes as you become stronger and more flexible, and a professional golf instructor can help you work through those changes.

Rules for Stretch Training

- Hold all stretches for at least 30 seconds.

- Never rush into or out of a stretch. Slower is always better during stretch training.

- Never, *ever* bounce a stretch. This is the number one sin among impatient golfers and one of the biggest causes of pulled muscles.

- Stretch for at least 15 minutes before every round.

- Continue to stretch during play, taking advantage of downtime between shots or holes to keep your muscles flexed and ready.

- Stretch every day regardless of your other activities.

Rules for Strength Training

- **Lift enough weight to provide resistance, but not so much that you sacrifice your form.** Good form isolates the muscle group that you're working and limits the likelihood of injury.

- **Slower is always better.** The slower you perform various strength exercises the more benefit you'll gain, even if it means lifting a lighter weight.

- **Fatigue your muscles, but don't strain them.** If your range of motion is small, don't force your body to move in ways that cause pain or discomfort.

- **Increase your repetitions before you increase your weight.** Golf isn't bodybuilding. Your first concern is performing a solid exercise for a maximum number of repetitions. The amount of weight you lift is secondary.

- **Never strengthen the same muscle group two days in a row.** If you lift with your arms and upper body today, strengthen your lower body or work on cardiovascular training tomorrow.

- **Never lift hurt.** Unless you're engaged in a prescribed rehabilitation program under the supervision of a physician or physical therapist, never lift through an injury.

Hungry Minds™

For Dummies®: Bestselling Book Series for Beginners

Golf Over 40

FOR

DUMMIES®

Golf Over 40

FOR

DUMMIES®

by Kelly Blackburn with Steve Eubanks

Hungry Minds™

HUNGRY MINDS, INC.

New York, NY ◆ Cleveland, OH ◆ Indianapolis, IN

Golf Over 40 For Dummies®

Published by:
Hungry Minds, Inc.
909 Third Avenue
New York, NY 10022
www.hungryminds.com
www.dummies.com

Library of Congress Control Number: 00-112135

ISBN: 0-7645-5343-7

Printed in the United States of America

10 9 8 7 6 5 4 3 2 1

1O/SW/QT/QR/IN

Distributed in the United States by Hungry Minds, Inc.

Distributed by CDG Books Canada Inc. for Canada; by Transworld Publishers Limited in the United Kingdom; by IDG Norge Books for Norway; by IDG Sweden Books for Sweden; by IDG Books Australia Publishing Corporation Pty. Ltd. for Australia and New Zealand; by TransQuest Publishers Pte Ltd. for Singapore, Malaysia, Thailand, Indonesia, and Hong Kong; by Gotop Information Inc. for Taiwan; by ICG Muse, Inc. for Japan; by Intersoft for South Africa; by Eyrolles for France; by International Thomson Publishing for Germany, Austria and Switzerland; by Distribuidora Cuspide for Argentina; by LR International for Brazil; by Galileo Libros for Chile; by Ediciones ZETA S.C.R. Ltda. for Peru; by WS Computer Publishing Corporation, Inc., for the Philippines; by Contemporanea de Ediciones for Venezuela; by Express Computer Distributors for the Caribbean and West Indies; by Micronesia Media Distributor, Inc. for Micronesia; by Chips Computadoras S.A. de C.V. for Mexico; by Editorial Norma de Panama S.A. for Panama; by American Bookshops for Finland.

For general information on Hungry Minds' products and services please contact our Customer Care department; within the U.S. at 800-762-2974, outside the U.S. at 317-572-3993 or fax 317-572-4002.

For sales inquiries and resellers information, including discounts, premium and bulk quantity sales and foreign language translations please contact our Customer Care department at 800-434-3422, fax 317-572-4002 or write to Hungry Minds, Inc., Attn: Customer Care department, 10475 Crosspoint Boulevard, Indianapolis, IN 46256.

For information on licensing foreign or domestic rights, please contact our Sub-Rights Customer Care department at 650-653-7098.

For information on using Hungry Minds' products and services in the classroom or for ordering examination copies, please contact our Educational Sales department at 800-434-2086 or fax 317-572-4005.

Please contact our Public Relations department at 212-884-5163 for press review copies or 212-884-5000 for author interviews and other publicity information or fax 212-884-5400.

For authorization to photocopy items for corporate, personal, or educational use, please contact Copyright Clearance Center, 222 Rosewood Drive, Danvers, MA 01923, or fax 978-750-4470.

Hungry Minds™ is a trademark of Hungry Minds, Inc.

About the Authors

Kelly Blackburn is considered a pioneer in the sport of golf when it comes to fitness. She has traveled the PGA Tour circuit for seven years as a professional fitness trainer to more than 20 touring professionals. Blackburn authored *Exercises for Elite Golf Performance* and created www.golffitnesscenter. com. Kelly adapted the individual fitness programs she developed for her professional golfing clients into Kelly Blackburn's Golf Fit System — a program currently available in fitness centers internationally and an in-home system that can benefit all golfers. She combines her touring schedule with golf fitness lectures for corporate outings throughout the United States. Kelly lives in Atlanta with her husband and two boys.

Steve Eubanks is an award-winning golf writer and former PGA golf professional. His other books include *At The Turn; Augusta: Home of the Masters Tournament;* and *Out of the Rough* with Laura Baugh. He is a regular contributor to *Golf World* magazine and CBS Sportsline, and his work has also appeared in *Sports Illustrated, Golf Digest,* and *Links* magazines. Steve lives in Georgia with his wife and children.

Dedication

To Debbie Eubanks and Dave Blackburn who put up with us throughout
this process.

Acknowledgments

I'd like to thank Larry Nelson who believed in me 100 percent eight years
ago and who continues to believe in me as a professional trainer. I'd also
like to thank Tommy Aaron, Hubert Green, Tom Jenkins, Allen Doyle, Walter
Hall, Jim Albus, Bobby Duval and the rest of my "over 40" players that have
given me the opportunity to give them the tools to help them enhance their
performance. For my husband and family that tolerate my absence during
the golfing season to continue my passion, thank you is not enough. To
Laura Baugh, Allyson Grove, Stacy Collins, and Mark Reiter at IMG, thank
you for your patience in accommodating my hectic schedule to complete
this project. And finally, thanks to Bay Hill Country Club and Atlanta Athletic
Club for providing the backdrop for the many photographs in this book.

Publisher's Acknowledgments

We're proud of this book; please send us your comments through our Online Registration Form located at www.dummies.com.

Some of the people who helped bring this book to market include the following:

Acquisitions, Editorial, and Media Development

Project Editor: Allyson Grove

Acquisitions Editor: Stacy S. Collins

Copy Editor: Donna S. Frederick

Acquisitions Coordinator: Stacy Klein

Technical Editor: Dr. Norton Baker

Editorial Manager: Jennifer Ehrlich

Editorial Assistant: Jennifer Young

Cover Photos: ©William Sallaz/Image Bank

Production

Project Coordinator: Jennifer Bingham

Layout and Graphics: LeAndra Johnson, Jackie Nicholas, Kristin Pickett, Jeremey Unger

Proofreaders: Andy Hollandbeck, Angel Perez, Linda Quigley, York Production Services, Inc.

Indexer: York Production Services, Inc.

General and Administrative

Hungry Minds, Inc.: John Kilcullen, CEO; Bill Barry, President and COO; John Ball, Executive VP, Operations & Administration; John Harris, CFO

Hungry Minds Consumer Reference Group

Business: Kathleen A. Welton, Vice President and Publisher; Kevin Thornton, Acquisitions Manager

Cooking/Gardening: Jennifer Feldman, Associate Vice President and Publisher; Anne Ficklen, Executive Editor

Education/Reference: Diane Graves Steele, Vice President and Publisher; Greg Tubach, Publishing Director

Lifestyles: Kathleen Nebenhaus, Vice President and Publisher; Tracy Boggier, Managing Editor

Pets: Dominique De Vito, Associate Vice President and Publisher; Tracy Boggier, Managing Editor

Travel: Michael Spring, Vice President and Publisher; Brice Gosnell, Publishing Director; Suzanne Jannetta, Editorial Director

Hungry Minds Consumer Editorial Services: Kathleen Nebenhaus, Vice President and Publisher; Kristin A. Cocks, Editorial Director; Cindy Kitchel, Editorial Director

Hungry Minds Consumer Production: Debbie Stailey, Production Director

◆

The publisher would like to give special thanks to Patrick J. McGovern, without whom this book would not have been possible.

◆

Contents at a Glance

Cartoons at a Glance

By Rich Tennant

"I really have to exercise more. I went from yelling 'Fore' on every shot in my 20's, to yelling 'Wow' in my 30's, to yelling 'Ow' in my 50's."

page 209

"Betty, you're not going to embarrass me at the club by wearing that hat, are you?"

page 241

"I may not play as well as I used to, but I don't have to remember it as long either."

page 7

"I BIRDIED THE 5TH, 6TH, AND 10TH HOLES. UNFORTUNATELY IT WAS WHILE I WAS PLAYING THE 3RD, 7TH, AND 12TH HOLE."

page 27

"I don't know what the big deal is. I've been playing golf over 40 since I was 20."

page 75

"Don't laugh – it's added 30 yards to his drive."

page 157

"What? It helps me with my balance."

page 133

Cartoon Information:
Fax: 978-546-7747
E-Mail: richtennant@the5thwave.com
World Wide Web: www.the5thwave.com

Table of Contents

Introduction

● ●

*A*s the great athlete and entertainer Muhammad Ali said upon announc-
ing his retirement from boxing, "Getting old is a drag, but it sure beats
the alternative." No truer words have ever been spoken. Nobody likes to
admit that they're getting old, especially those people in the forty-something
age bracket who still consider themselves active and athletic. Even though
the forties are the prime of life (and despite proclamations of being in better
shape than during the teen years), no one is immune from the effects of
aging. No matter how fit or active you are, and no matter how youthful you
look and feel, the body changes after your 40th birthday in ways that affect
all your physical activities. Even golf, the last bastion of sport for the middle-
aged weekend warrior, is a different game after 40. Your muscles respond differently to stimuli from the brain; your reflexes, coordination, and dexterity
change; your metabolism and stamina are different; and your concentration
skills (hopefully) mature.

These changes aren't good or bad; they're just different. And because your
bodies and minds change with age, you have to make changes in the way you
approach certain activities. Golf is no exception. If you want to continue to
lower your scores and improve your game after your 40th birthday (and I
assume that's the case because you've chosen to open this book), you have
to change the way you prepare, practice, and play, and you have to be willing
to accept that these changes are a natural fact of life. You don't have to be
held hostage to the consequences of aging, especially when it comes to activities you love, such as golf. There's no reason that the average golfer cannot
become longer, more accurate, and shoot lower scores after turning 40, 50,
or even 60. It's all a matter of preparation and practice. And this book is
designed to help you figure out how to do both.

This isn't a golf primer. Because of the specific needs of golfers over 40, I
assume a certain level of golf knowledge when preparing this text. That
shouldn't discourage beginners over 40 from taking up golf. In fact, many of
the millions of people who play golf for the first time every year are well past
40 when they take up the game. That's great! I hope those people find this
book helpful. But there are some terms and basics of the game that I assume
you already recognize. If you don't know a backswing from backspin, a tee
from a green, or a sand wedge from a sandwich (at the turn,) don't be dis-
couraged. I recommend that you read this book as a companion to *Golf For
Dummies,* 2nd Edition (Hungry Minds, Inc.) by Gary McCord, a book for the
golf novice of any age. The combination of these two books can set you on
course for an enjoyable life as an over-40 golfer.

After spending some time practicing the things that you discover in this book, expect to

- ✔ Increase your strength, both on the golf course and off
- ✔ See a measurable increase in the distance that you hit the golf ball and an appreciable difference in your accuracy
- ✔ Improve your flexibility
- ✔ Improve your stamina
- ✔ Lower your scores
- ✔ Enjoy golf more than ever before

How to Use This Book

Many of the examples and exercises in this book are better explained visually, so you can find plenty of pictures in these pages. The models in the pictures range from Senior Tour players, such as Larry Nelson and LPGA players like Laura Baugh, to club pros and amateurs of varying ages and body types, all with two things in common: They've seen 40 pass by, and they want to do whatever it takes to continue to improve their golf games.

You may not be as flexible or as strong as the people in these photos, but that shouldn't discourage you. The stretching and strengthening exercises in this book are designed for golfers of all ages, abilities, and body types. Just because you aren't as flexible as Laura Baugh or Larry Nelson doesn't mean that you aren't gaining tremendous benefit from the exercises.

I also include useful anecdotes from tour players, club pros, good amateurs, and high-handicap golfers who have experienced the benefits of the principles I outline. These examples can give you real-world feedback on what to expect.

You can skim this book, jumping from chapter to chapter to find the references that are most salient to your golf game, or you can read it from cover to cover. No matter what route you take, always keep the book with you as you begin your new golf training regimen. This book isn't a literary masterpiece; it's a how-to manual, a *Popular Mechanics* for golfers over 40. If you treat it as such, returning to these pages often to check your progress, you may find it to be an invaluable guide to your continued enjoyment of the game.

How This Book Is Organized

I divide this book into seven parts, each containing two or more chapters. Here's a closer look at how the parts break down.

Part I: Playing into Your Prime

The body and mind change after you turn 40. This part outlines those physiological and psychological changes, how they affect your golf game, and what you can do about them.

Part II: The Basics and Beyond after 40

The basics of the golf swing have undergone some changes over the years. Players and teachers have modified the swing to compensate for improvements in technology, changing course conditions, and different training methods. No one would teach a younger player learning the game today with titanium clubs exactly the same way a golfer in the 1920s or '30s (playing with hickory-shafted clubs) learned the game. That same principle applies as you grow older. As your bodies change, the basics of the game need to be tweaked to compensate for those changes.

Part III: Problem Areas: Fighting Them with Fitness

You're never too old to get into shape for golf. This part outlines exactly the type of exercises that you need to incorporate into your routine to improve your game.

Part IV: Improving Balance and Endurance

The golf swing is like a personal ballet, as beautiful and fluid as it is difficult to attain. As with all things athletic, balance and endurance are critical components to good golf. As you age, those components become more challenging. This part explains why and offers you ample ways to improve your balance and conditioning.

Part V: Golf Isn't a Contact Sport: Avoiding Injury

Because golf doesn't require running, jumping, catching, throwing, or coming into physical contact with your fellow competitors in an aggressive way, many people assume that you can't injure yourself on the golf course. Those are the people you find lying in bed complaining of back spasms or who end up with their arms in slings. Golf works the body in ways that leave you prone to injury if you don't take the necessary precautions. This part shows you how to avoid those injuries and stay fit for golf well past 40.

Part VI: Taking Golf Fitness to the Next Level

Working out isn't a one-time thing, and there are no secrets to good golf. This part outlines the programs you should institute on a regular basis to lower your scores.

Part VII: The Part of Tens

In this part, I include self-evaluation tests, drills, programs and mistakes to avoid as you move forward. These chapters are quick and easy to read, but they're critically important. If you spend a lot of time going through this part, your scores will reflect it.

Icons Used in This Book

This book uses several helpful icons (the little pictures in the margins) to guide you to the information that you need. Here's a look at what each icon represents.

This icon tells you that you're about to read about the experiences of a tour pro.

These are time-tested points of importance from someone who trains the very best in the game. Pay particularly close attention to these sections.

If you don't follow these instructions, the trouble you may find will make a pot bunker look easy.

 This stuff is so technical, it makes titanium look obsolete. You can skip over these tidbits if you don't want to know all the technical details.

 This icon denotes advice from golf pros of all ages and talents as well as clues you in to some exercise secrets that can improve your game.

 This icon gives you information that bears repeating. Bears repeating.

Where To Go From Here

You're holding a book that can change the way you look, feel, act, and (most importantly) score on the golf course. To take it from here, get out your clubs and put on your gym shorts. It's time to change your golf game forever.

Part I
Playing into Your Prime

The 5th Wave   By Rich Tennant

"I may not play as well as I used to, but I don't have to remember it as long either."

In this part . . .

1 explain the effects of aging on the body and how the physical and mental changes you experience after 40 can impact your golf game. I also make the case for fitness and show you why it's imperative that you take steps now to improve your strength, flexibility, and endurance or else suffer the consequences later. Those consequences include shorter distance off the tee, less consistency with the irons, lower endurance, and higher scores. You don't have to fall into that trap. Understanding the effects of aging on your golf game and taking steps to counter those effects can help to make you a better golfer, not to mention a healthier, happier, and more positive over-40 athlete.

Chapter 1

Oh, How Golf Changes after 40

● ●

● ●

"From the time that I turned 40 until now have probably been the best years of golf for me."

— Loren Roberts

For a half-century golf has been called the "game of a lifetime." Nobody seems to know where the expression originated, but it's true. Golf is a game that you can play from the time that you're old enough to walk until you're too old to stand. People from nine to 90 enjoy the game and continue to play it with the same enthusiasm they've always had. But that doesn't mean golfers who play the game their entire lives will always play well. A time comes in everyone's life when the body doesn't respond the way it used to — movements that were easy to perform in younger years are tougher to reproduce.

In that respect, golf isn't unique. If you've ever been to an Old Timers' baseball game, you've seen the depressing effects of aging on athletic skills. Legends of the game look like slow-moving amateurs with limps, aches, and overly expansive midsections. The same is true with football, basketball, hockey, soccer, swimming, and most any other sport you can name. No matter how great the athletes in those sports were in their teens, twenties, and thirties, they find that when they hit their forties they have trouble competing against players half their ages.

Fortunately, golfers can prolong that decline. Just look at Ben Hogan, the great golfer of the 1950s who is still considered one of the greatest who ever played. Hogan had his greatest successes after his 40th birthday. Payne Stewart, the 1999 U.S. Open champion who is tragically killed in a plane crash in 1999, also had his best year at age 42, and Tom Watson continued to win PGA Tour events at 48 years old. In fact, Watson even finished in the top

10 at the PGA Championship in 2000 at the age of 50! No one questions the talent and tenacity of Hale Irwin, who dominated the Senior PGA Tour for three seasons and still plays well against the youngsters, and Tom Kite has remained competitive with younger players, such as Tiger Woods and David Duval into his early fifties.

Contrast that with players like Fred Couples, who admitted to being semi-retired at 41 and Ben Crenshaw, who, by age 46, had more rounds in the 80s than any active player on the PGA Tour.

So, what was the difference? Why was Tom Watson still winning at age 48 while Ben Crenshaw, two years younger than Watson, was shooting 80? Why did Fred Couples resign himself to semi-retirement at the same age Ben Hogan was when he won three major championships?

Some of the answers lie in genes and the different ways people age. But you can't attribute all these differences to luck or heredity. In an overwhelming majority of the cases, the players who remained competitive long after their 40th birthdays were the ones who recognized the adverse affects of aging and went to work to curtail those effects. Stewart, for example, spent more time in the PGA Tour's *fitness trailer* (a rolling gym that travels with the tour each week) in the two years after he turned 40 than he did in 15 previous years on tour. The same was true of Tom Watson who rarely darkened the door of the gym in the '70s and '80s, but who became a fitness-trailer regular throughout the '90s after his 40th birthday.

Like most successful over-40 golfers, Watson, Stewart, Irwin, Kite, and others saw the handwriting on the wall, and they did something about it.

Everything Is Different after 40

Life certainly doesn't end at 40. You don't go to sleep the night before your 40th birthday feeling great only to wake up decrepit and senile the next morning. Age is much subtler than that, especially when it comes to golf.

Many over-40 golfers swear their game is better today than it was 20 years ago — that they're longer off the tee and hit their irons 10 yards longer at age 40 than they did at 20. In some instances that's true. New equipment and technology have helped average golfers hit longer, straighter shots, and improved grasses and course conditions have enabled superintendents to keep golf courses in better shape. Those factors combine to give older golfers the illusion that they are stronger and longer at 40 than they were at 20.

The truth is that everything about your body changes as you grow older. For example,

✔ Your eye-hand coordination diminishes.

✔ Your physique changes.

✔ Your strength, flexibility, and endurance all decline.

✔ Your mental stamina isn't what it used to be.

Feeling changes in your body

Everyone knows that you aren't as strong, fast, or flexible in older age as you were when you were younger, but not many people understand exactly what happens to the body as you age.

Strength and power actually begin to decline when you enter your late twenties. You start losing muscle mass at about age 28, and by age 65 you lose a minimum of 20 percent of your strength and 50 percent of your cardiovascular capacity.

These changes mark the beginning of a negative downward spiral. Less muscle means less active tissue in the body to burn calories, so your metabolism slows. A slower metabolism often leads to a loss in cardiovascular fitness, which results in less blood flowing to the muscles. This creates a reduction in *stroke volume,* which is the amount of blood the heart actually pumps. Lack of blood weakens and tightens already deteriorating muscles, and reduces the blood and oxygen flow to the brain. So, in addition to weaker, stiffer and more easily fatigued muscles, you also lose your ability to concentrate and stay focused.

In addition, collagen, the structural basis for tendons also deteriorates with age, which means that your tendons become more rigid at the same time your muscles are stiffening. As if things needed to get any worse, your tendons compensate for this loss of collagen by *cross bridging,* or connecting with other tendon fibers. That cross bridging enables tendons to retain their strength, but it also causes them to be less flexible.

The effects of these processes show up in your mid- to late-30s when you realize that you can't run that 100-meter dash like you used to or shoot a jump shot like you once could. Your reaction time has slowed, and your muscles take longer to respond. The mind remains willing, but the body simply won't react.

Recognizing differences in your golf game

Noticeable declines in golf performance, however, usually come later. Golf isn't a reaction sport like baseball or tennis. Nobody throws a golf ball at you and expects you to hit it, nor do you have to run from one shot to the next. But that doesn't mean your golf muscles aren't deteriorating or that your flexibility is the same as it always was. After you hit 40, the weakening and tightening of the muscles starts to show in golf. The results are

- Less flexibility and decreased *turn* (rotation of the shoulders and the hips during the swing)
- Weaker arms and torsos
- Fatigue in the critical golf muscles, which leads to inconsistent swings and slower clubhead speed
- A loss of dexterity or *touch* around the greens
- An increase in back and joint-related injuries

Getting Inspiration from the Pros

As bleak as this picture seems, I do have some good news. If you choose to put forth the effort, you can stop most of these bad things from happening to you, and you can, indeed, become a stronger, better golfer at age 40 than you were at age 20. It's all a matter of doing the right things for your body, modifying your game to fit your age, and sticking to a golf-specific workout regimen that can improve every aspect of your game. (Reading this book certainly won't hurt, either.) Consider the following inspiring examples of two PGA pros.

When former U.S. Open champion Hubert Green (see Figure 1-1) turned 52, he realized he had a serious problem. With an unorthodox swing that had always been lightning quick, Green all but retired from the regular tour in his early forties. But after his 50th birthday he found new life, as many former champions have, on the Senior PGA Tour. The only problem was, Hubert's swing was still just as quick at age 52 as it had been when he was 22. As a result of this whipping action, injury and erratic play always loomed close on Hubert's horizon.

Six weeks into the season, Hubert contacted me and said he wanted to get his game and his body back in shape. It was a risky move. Everybody's body reacts differently to working out, and when you haven't worked out in 30 years, anything's possible. Hubert may respond well and improve his game, or his body may react badly to the early stages of the workout program, which could have led to an abysmal season.

Figure 1-1:
U.S. Open
and PGA
Champion-
ship winner
Hubert
Green.

Fortunately, things worked in Hubert's favor. After starting a strength and conditioning program I designed for him that included a heavy dose of flexibility training, Hubert added 13 yards to his average driving distance and increased his accuracy by 5 percent. He climbed into the top 10 on the money list and had his first multiple-win season as a senior.

Working out was hard work, but Hubert isn't complaining about the results.

Former Masters champion Tommy Aaron encountered a situation similar to Green's. With a long, fluid swing and a tall, thin frame, Aaron (see Figure 1-2) never thought that working out — especially working out with weights and going through stretching exercises — would help his golf game.

Figure 1-2:
Masters
Champion
Tommy
Aaron.

Two months shy of his 60th birthday, Tommy saw the light. He approached me about establishing a workout regimen for the first time in his life. At the time, he couldn't touch his toes from a standing position. Three years later, he had doubled his strength and flexibility. In 2000 at age 63, Aaron became the oldest man in history to make the cut at the Masters.

In light of those examples, you may be wondering whether a health and fitness program can turn a 40-year-old, middle-of-the-road golfer into a Senior Tour champion? The answer is absolutely not. But a good diet and golf-specific exercises can improve your golf scores and keep you playing your best at 40 and beyond.

Gary was right all along

At age 65, Gary Player is now credited as the godfather of the modern golf fitness movement. In the 1960s and '70s, when Gary Player was one of the three best players in the world along with Arnold Palmer and Jack Nicklaus, many players made fun of Gary for his devotion to working out. Nicklaus openly said that Gary's weight lifting and sit-ups would eventually hurt his golf game. But Gary remained undaunted, hitting the gym every day and preaching the virtues of exercise to a group of golfers who pointed at him and snickered before retreating to the locker room for drinks.

My, how things have changed. All those people who made fun of Gary for drinking his carrot juice and lifting his dumbbells are now in the gym beside him, pumping iron, jogging, biking, and eating healthier foods. Even Nicklaus works out!

In January of 2000 at the Senior Skins Game, Gary Player set a milestone, becoming the first professional golfer to win at least one professional event in six different decades. Looks like Gary was right all along.

Chapter 2

Keeping the Golf Body Fit after 40

· ·

In This Chapter

▶ Sizing up your body's strengths and weaknesses

▶ Discovering the four critical elements of fitness

▶ Recognizing the pitfalls of neglecting fitness after your 40th birthday

· ·

"Golf is such an up and down game, and all parts of your game usually don't peak at the same time. But when they do, all kinds of guys can shoot really low scores. There were some times in the past when things looked like they were coming together, but the last nine holes I just ran out of gas. That's when I decided to do something."

— Larry Nelson

*N*o matter what you read or hear, you can't stop the aging process. Fatigue, wrinkles, sags, and aches and pains are a natural part of growing older, and no drugs, diet, workout regimen, or herbal supplement can stop that. In golf, the effects of aging manifest themselves in lost distance off the tee, less accuracy with iron shots, a loss of touch in the short game, as well as physical tiring during a round and soreness afterward. You may not be experiencing all these problems, but chances are pretty good that you have already discovered at least one or two. And, you can rest assured that more are on the way.

But don't give up. Just because you can't stop the aging process doesn't mean you can't do everything in your power to retard its effects. Yes, you will have body parts that ache as you age, and you will notice losses in strength, coordination, and feel, especially after you turn 40. But you can take steps to minimize the effects of aging on your golf game. In order to take those steps, you must first figure out some things about your body, and how aging affects you.

Evaluating Your Body Type

All over-40 golfers are different, with different body types, different metabolisms, different physical abilities, and different aches and pains. These differences not only impact how over-40 golfers look and feel, but also how they swing the golf club.

Before you can fully understand the effects of aging on your body, you need to analyze your body type. Which of the following body types best describes you?

- ✔ *Ectomorph:* Someone who is typically small-boned and thin, with very little body fat and a high metabolism, who struggles to gain muscle mass and weight. Most over-40 ectomorphs gain some weight in their abdominal regions, but they never put on the pounds like other people their age. They generally have no trouble with endurance and energy, but lose strength quite rapidly after 40. Golfing professionals like Laura Baugh (see Figure 2-1), Tommy Aaron, and Joe Inman fall into this category.

- ✔ *Mesomorph:* Usually a big-boned person with substantive muscle mass and a large frame. Mesomorphs are naturally strong, and they lose strength at a slower pace than other body types. They also tend to gain fat as they age. Strength training isn't a big problem for mesomorphs, but inactivity usually leads to a few extra pounds (in all the wrong places) and a substantial decrease in their cardiovascular conditioning. They may tire more easily than they used to, even if they haven't lost much strength. Golfers Greg Norman and Larry Nelson (see Figure 2-2) are prime examples of this body type (although both those players are in excellent physical condition).

Figure 2-1:
Ectomorphs like Laura Baugh are naturally small with little body fat.

Figure 2-2:
Larry
Nelson.

✔ ***Endomorph:*** A heavy person, with substantial body fat and low muscle tone. These people are prone to dramatic weight fluctuations, and they can get winded and tire quickly. Strength and speed are questionable as well. Although endomorphs may be strong and fast in their teens, twenties and even into their mid-thirties, by the time they hit their forties, they are losing strength at an alarming rate while their reflexes are slowing substantially. Golfers like Craig Stadler (see Figure 2-3) and Billy Casper are examples of the endomorph body type. (Even Jack Nicklaus qualifies as an endomorph, although Nicklaus goes to great lengths to control his weight and maintain his strength through diligent training.)

Not every over-40 golfer fits neatly into one of these categories. But if you're honest in your self-evaluation, you know which body type best describes you, and you can tailor your golf training to your specific physical makeup. If, for example, you have an ectomorph body, you can improve your golf game by gearing your physical training around strength and muscle development coupled with lots of stretching exercises. If you fit more comfortably into the mesomorph category, you can tailor your workout to include more endurance and cardiovascular exercises (see Chapter 12), with targeted strength and flexibility exercises complementing the regimen. Endomorphs should focus on fat-burning aerobic exercises along with strength-building programs that turn excess fat into strong muscle.

No two golfers look exactly alike, even on tour. Your workout needs are just as specific and unique as your golf swing. Treat those needs with the same personal care you would any other aspect of your game. Seek professional advice about your body type and what kind of workout program makes the most sense for you.

Figure 2-3:
Craig
Stadler.

© Kevin Clark/1995

When I was designing workout programs for Hubert Green and Larry Nelson, I had to take two very different approaches because the needs of the two players varied so much. Hubert was the quintessential ectomorph, with a lightning quick swing and a high metabolism. Weight gain wasn't an issue for Hubert, but flexibility and strength training were major concerns. With Larry on the other hand, strength wasn't quite as big a concern, but endurance was a huge issue. Proper diet and cardiovascular conditioning, coupled with stretching exercises fit Larry's needs perfectly.

Don't assume that because you have a particular body type that you are doomed as a golfer. David Duval was a 240-pound doughboy with 25 percent body fat when he was in college. But through a high-protein, low-fat diet coupled with strength and aerobic training, David dropped to 180 pounds and lowered his body-fat percentage to single digits, becoming one of the most fit golfers on tour. The same premise held true for LPGA Hall of Famer Nancy Lopez who struggled with weight gain after her 40th birthday. Lopez worked with a trainer on a diet and exercise regimen to keep her weight in check while increasing her strength and endurance.

Testing Your Body's Fitness Level

Before you can start the process of building a better over-40 body for golf, you must be honest with yourself about where you are now and where you want to be in the future. Just as a 10-handicap golfer cannot realistically expect to qualify for the U.S. Open, an out-of-condition golfer cannot expect to wave a magic wand and become fit for the game. Honest self-evaluation is the first and most important step in setting up a program to improve your game. Answering the following questions gives you a good platform from which to start.

Which of the following statements best describes you?

❏ I haven't gained any weight in the last ten years, but I'm not as strong or as flexible as I was when I was younger.

❏ I have to watch my weight more now than I did when I was in my twenties or thirties, but I haven't lost much strength. If anything, I'm stronger than ever, just not as fit as I used to be.

❏ I've always had trouble with my weight, and that problem seems to get worse with every passing year. I'm not as strong as I used to be and I tire much quicker these days.

Which joints ache after golf? Can you rate your joints from 1-10 starting with those that hurt the least up to those that hurt the most?

Ankles and knees ____

Hips ____

Shoulders ____

Elbows and wrists ____

The morning after a full day of golf, what muscles are sore? Can you rate your soreness in the following muscles from 1-10?

Torso (abdominals, lateral obliques, and back muscles) ____

Forearms ____

Legs ____

Others (shoulders, upper arms, neck, and lower legs) ____

What aches and pains do you have today that you didn't have 10 or 15 years ago? _____

Which of those aches and pains is noticeably worse after you play golf?

_____

What extra precautions are you currently taking to avoid exacerbating your aches and pains during and after golf?

How much time and effort are you willing to set aside to retard the aging process and improve your golf game?

Mark this test and refer back to it as you work your way through the other parts of this book. The test will help you in tailoring your routine to your specific needs and goals.

Priming Your Body for Golf

Like all athletes in the top level of sports, professional golfers make the game look easy. Their swings seem as fluid and effortless as running water, and they look as though they are on a leisurely stroll as they pound drives more than 300 yards and hit high soft iron shots. The truth is, under-40 professionals, such as Tiger Woods, David Duval, Sergio Garcia, and Ernie Els as well as over-40 professionals, such as Loren Roberts, Greg Norman, and Larry Nelson make the game look easy, not because they aren't exerting themselves, but because they're strong and fit enough to make a complicated athletic move (the golf swing) look simple. Very few amateurs can devote that amount of time, energy, and money to their golf games, but that shouldn't stop those amateurs — especially those over 40 — from making positive changes in their games by improving their strength and conditioning.

Over the years conditioning for athletes has become an exact science. The workout regimen for basketball teams isn't the same as the program designed for swimmers, football players, or tennis stars. Each sport requires certain physical skills. Trainers must develop programs that enhance the specific skills needed for a particular sport.

Golf is no different. Even with the advancements in equipment and course conditioning, golf is still a game of balance, discipline, and touch. Enhancing and improving those specific skills — especially in an over-40 body — requires a balanced regimen with four equally important components: strength, flexibility, endurance, and diet. The rest of this chapter takes a more in-depth look at each of these critical fitness components.

Building strength

Not that long ago many people commonly assumed that strong muscles were slow muscles, and anyone who worked out with weights ran the risk of becoming a muscle-bound brute incapable of swinging a golf club or having the delicate touch necessary for short chips, pitches, and putts. Big, strong muscles were bad in golf, or so said the conventional wisdom.

Even in the days when this thinking was prevalent, there were exceptions. Because the in-club gym idea hadn't caught on in country clubs in the '50s and '60s, Gary Player and his friend and workout partner, amateur Frank Stranahan carried their own free weights with them on tour, much to the chagrin of their fellow tour players. But while others sat in the clubhouse bars and scoffed, Player won eight major championships, while Stranahan became the top amateur golfer in the nation and regularly beat the world's best professionals in head-to-head competition.

Today the value of strength in golf is almost universally recognized, especially for those over 40.

Strength in all major and minor muscle groups (see Figures 2-4 and 2-5) plays a critical role in the golf swing:

- ✔ Strong abdominals and *external obliques* (the trunk muscles along your sides where "love handles" normally develop) are essential for good posture at address. This becomes especially critical for golfers over 40 because of the increased risk of back and neck injury resulting from poor posture.

- ✔ Shoulder, arm, and upper back strength are crucial in the takeaway, the downswing, the follow-through, and the short game. Your swing is initiated with the shoulders and hips rotating away from the target. The *pectoralis major* (the chest muscle) aids in moving the target arm away from the target. The forearms and wrist engage to keep the club in a cocked position. The triceps extend to keep the target arm straight, while the biceps flex the opposite or non-target arm. The rotator cuff muscles work to stabilize the shoulder girdle and turn with the shoulders and arms. The rotator cuff of the non-target arm pulls the club back and externally rotates the arm. The hamstrings and external obliques assist hip rotation during the backswing, creating a stable stance and good posture. The weight shifts from an almost equal distribution at address to upwards of 85 percent on the rear foot due to the redistribution of the upper body.

- ✔ The lower back is a source of much pain and misery in golfers over 40. The coiling of the upper body around a resistant lower body, coupled with the twisting of the back during the downswing and follow-through, can have devastating results. Even in a properly executed golf swing, back muscles pull at the *lumbar,* and, if a golfer isn't strong, the discs are susceptible to strain and injury. Nothing can guarantee that you won't have back problems, even if you do everything right, but a strong lower back is less likely to become an injured lower back.

- ✔ Strength in the legs and hips is also crucial. Strong hamstrings provide a solid base at address while the *adductors* (inner thighs) and *hip flexors* initiate both the backswing and the downswing. The *gastrocnemius* — commonly called the calf muscle — drives the lower body through the swing, while the *ankle flexors* are critical for balance.

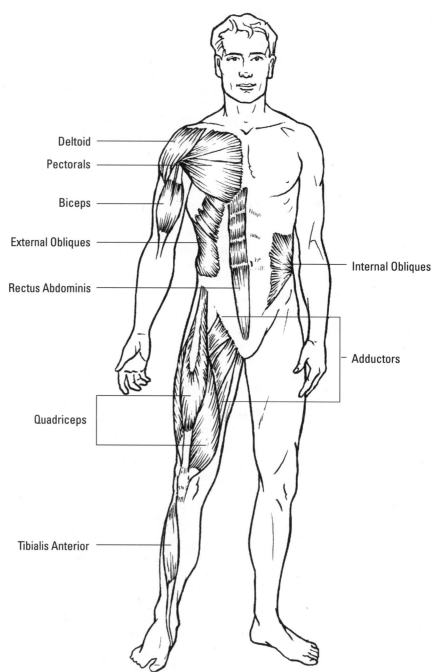

Deltoid

Pectorals

Biceps

External Obliques

Rectus Abdominis

Internal Obliques

Adductors

Quadriceps

Tibialis Anterior

Figure 2-4:
Your golf
muscles —
front view.

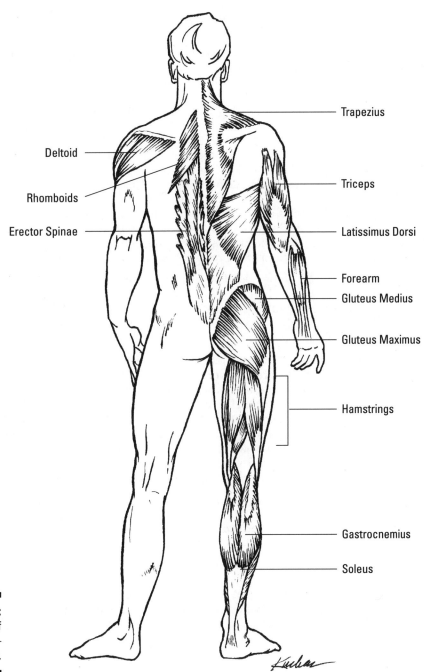

Figure 2-5:
Your golf
muscles —
back view.

Maintaining flexiblity

Golf requires flexibility in all parts of the body. Tight muscles restrict and slow down the motion needed to effectively swing the golf club, and 40-year-old muscles aren't as naturally flexible and supple as 20-year-old muscles. That means over-40 golfers must work harder just to maintain the same level of flexibility they had in their twenties and thirties.

Keeping flexible requires a great deal more than simply warming up with a few bouncing stretches at the first tee before a round. Golfers who want to improve their games after 40 need to take flexibility training as seriously as hitting practice balls or working on the putting green. Here are some reasons why.

- Stiff muscles and tendons in the trunk and lower body inhibit proper setup (see Chapter 4) and cause golfers to slouch. You can't make a proper golf swing from a poor setup, and you can't set yourself in the proper position at address without some degree of flexibility.

- Making a proper shoulder turn (see Chapter 5) is impossible if your *deltoids* (the shoulder muscles), pectoralis major, *obliques* (the stomach muscles), and latissimus dorsi (the upper back muscles) are stiff and unresponsive. The backswing is a turn of the upper body around the relatively stable lower body. Upper body flexibility makes that turn possible.

- The biceps, triceps, wrist and elbow flexors must also be flexible in order for the arms to work properly in the swing. You may have heard the phrase *releasing the golf club.* This term refers to the point in the swing when the wrists, elbows, shoulders, and hands work together to generate the greatest clubhead speed at the exact moment the club makes contact with the ball. In order for those body parts to work in this synchronized fashion, each muscle group in the arms and shoulders must be flexible. Stiff arms lift the club and make a slashing, violent, and technically incorrect swing. Supple arms swing the golf club fluidly.

- The hip flexors and adductor muscles must also remain flexible if you want to swing the club efficiently. Because the lower body initiates the downswing and provides the stable base on which the entire swing is structured, having a full range of motion with these muscles is critical.

- Making a good golf swing also depends on flexible back and abdominal muscles. These opposing muscle groups are stretched to their limit in golf, and over-40 players must go to great lengths to stretch these muscles properly. If you don't, poor golf is the least of your worries. You can fix a bad swing. A bad back can last forever.

Staying conditioned

It's a cruel irony of life, but if you are like a majority of Americans you have more leisure time and more disposable income to devote to golf after you turn 40. The problem is your body doesn't have the stamina to take advantage of it. You may have the time and desire to play 36 holes on Saturday, but instead you play 14 good holes, two lackluster holes, and two bad holes before retiring to the couch for an afternoon nap.

This scenario may sound cruel to some, but research bears this idea out. After you hit 40, your body begins to slow down, and you have to exert as much as 25 percent more energy than you did when you were 30 to complete the same task. You may not think of golf as a test of stamina and conditioning, but conditioning is critical to consistently good golf scores. Here's why:

- ✔ **Golf is a game of rhythm and timing.** Winded golfers with racing hearts can't make the same rhythmic swings they did at a relaxed state. Well-conditioned golfers don't have that problem. They remain as strong and consistent on the 18th hole as they were on the first.

- ✔ **Cardiovascular conditioning improves blood flow throughout the body.** The improved blood flow helps over-40 muscles remain flexible and consistent at the beginning, middle, and end of a round.

- ✔ **Being in good shape is good for your brain.** Cardio-intensive workouts improve the flow of oxygen throughout the body, with the brain as a primary benefactor. Because golf is a game of intense concentration where "getting into the zone" is the ultimate goal, anything that improves a golfer's ability to focus is a plus. Cardiovascular training does that. When focus and concentration come into play during the closing holes of a round, the best-conditioned golfers have an advantage.

- ✔ **An old adage exists among competitive golfers that says, "Tired muscles choke, and fit muscles don't."** That's a bit of a simplification, but still true. Fatigued muscles tend to contract and tense up — not what an over-40 golfer needs in the closing holes of a tightly contested match.

Eating the proper diet

All athletes must watch what they eat, especially golfers over 40 who have much different metabolisms than their 20-year-old counterparts. For some reason, most golfers don't consider diet an integral part of their games. You need to look no further than the restaurant at most clubs to understand golfers' dietary leanings. Burgers, fries, an obligatory salad for show, and plenty of beer dominate the menu.

Over-40 golfers who are serious about improving their games must factor in how much a good diet can help. Consider these reasons:

- ✔ **Golf isn't an aerobic sport. Your heart rate and your intake of oxygen don't accelerate into a fat-burning zone when you play golf. But most people dismiss the toll your body takes during a typical round.** Doing so is a mistake. Walking through 18 holes of golf (which can easily exceed 3 miles) can drain the body of up to 800 calories. You wouldn't strike out on a 3-mile hike without proper nourishment. So, you shouldn't go to the golf course without the proper fuel, either.

- ✔ **Just as good cardiovascular conditioning is important to maintaining a consistent rhythm and repetitive swing throughout the round, diet is equally critical (see Chapter 19).** The proper balance of complex sugars, carbohydrates, and proteins in your system keeps your body going without a great deal of variance — no highs or lows, no jitters or sluggishness.

- ✔ **A properly nourished golfer is less likely to be adversely affected by weather elements, such as sun and heat.** Plenty of water and the proper food can keep you going when the competition falls away.

These factors are important for all golfers, but they are critical for golfers over 40 because of the changes you go through as you age.

The comeback kid

If the world hadn't been watching Tiger rewrite the history books, the season Larry Nelson had on the Senior PGA Tour in 2000 would have been the hot topic in locker rooms around the country. Nelson had the best year of his career, with six victories and almost $3 million in official earnings. This benchmark performance came six years after Nelson hit bottom, when his tour earnings were less than $40,000 and he had slipped into such poor physical condition that he couldn't even touch his toes.

So, what changed in those six years after Nelson's 47th birthday? Diet and exercise. Nelson realized that he had fallen out of golf shape, and that he needed to retool his conditioning before embarking on a senior career. He contacted me and asked for help on his overall fitness, with his ultimate goal as being ready to play the Senior PGA Tour. It took almost three years, but Larry did, indeed, improve his strength, flexibility, and endurance through a steady fitness regimen, not a stop-and-start, on-again, off-again program.

The key to Larry 's fitness success comes, not because of the individual weight lifting, stretching, or diet programs, but because he is consistent and diligent in working his individual program on a daily basis. Fitness in golf is like fitness in any other sport: It's not a short-term solution. The best players in the world recognize that and do what it takes to keep up with their workouts, no matter how hectic their schedules are.

Part II
The Basics and Beyond after 40

The 5th Wave   By Rich Tennant

"I BIRDIED THE 5TH, 6TH, AND 10TH HOLES. UNFORTUNATELY IT WAS WHILE I WAS PLAYING THE 3RD, 7TH, AND 12TH HOLE."

In this part . . .

The basic fundamentals of golf — the grip, the stance, the takeaway, the downswing, and the finish — are golf's Holy Grail, constant, sacred, and untouchable. Although those fundamentals remain consistent from the days when Harry Vardon was winning championships at the turn of the 20th century through Tiger Woods's championship reign at the turn of the 21st century, most honest instructors and earnest observers of the game will admit that the fundamentals "evolve" as players age.

Any objective look at the greatest champions of the game — players, such as Ben Hogan, Sam Snead, Gene Sarazen, Arnold Palmer, Gary Player, and Jack Nicklaus — shows you that these players modified their fundamentals as their bodies aged and their physical abilities changed. In this part, I show you that if tweaking the fundamentals to accommodate age helped the greatest players in history, those same modifications can improve your golf game as well.

Chapter 3

Grasping Your Grip

• •

In This Chapter

▶ Knowing the importance of the grip

▶ Figuring out how to hold the club for the best results

▶ Considering some ways your grip changes as you get older

• •

> *"The fundamentals of the golf swing are like the foundations of a house; they must be laid on firm ground. My whole theory of golf is to get a good foundation, and then you can build as many stories on it as you want. In many cases developing a solid foundation requires change, specifically for people who have been playing a number of years in a way that feels good to them, but with some basic flaw in their foundations that inhibits their growth as players."*
>
> — Johnny Miller

The most basic fundamental in golf is the grip because the hands connect the golfer to the club. When you say that idea out loud it sounds almost too simple, but in the complexities of the golf game, many people forget the importance of the hands, and how to place them on the club. Ben Hogan once wrote that "good golf begins with a good grip," and he worked for years to perfect what he considered the correct way to position his hands on the club.

However, Jack Nicklaus says he never tied himself in knots concerning the way he holds the club. Nicklaus instead concentrates on using his hands, unconsciously, to translate body leverage into clubhead speed. "I believe the hands function best, in terms of squaring the clubface at impact, when they work instinctively during the swing — when they behave reflexively rather than through conscious direction."

Despite their very different approaches, Nicklaus and Hogan had one thing in common: As they got older, they both made slight modifications to their grips. Hogan weakened his grip in the latter stages of his career because he had tremendous hand and arm strength, and because of the fact that he had always fought a *hook* (a shot that often dives left off-line and sometimes out of play). Nicklaus may have never tied himself in knots over the grip, but he did strengthen his grip in the 1990s in order to "unconsciously" and "reflexively" generate more clubhead speed and hit stronger shots as his body aged.

In this chapter, I show you how to make similar adjustments in your game to accommodate for the losses in strength, flexibility, and coordination that are a natural part of aging. The first fundamental to consider tweaking is the grip.

The Goal of the Grip

Plenty of mystical golf hyperbole has been written over the years, including everything from "connective" proclamations like "Be the ball," to projective teachings like "Swing the clubhead, not the handle." These concepts all have their place, just not in this book. As a practical matter, the only connection you have with the ball is through the club, and the only connection you have with the club is through the hands. That makes the grip the A-number-one fundamental of golf on which all others are based. So what is the function of the golf grip, and why has every golf instructional author devoted at least one chapter to the subject?

The answer depends on whom you ask, and you can get some pretty different opinions from the best players in the world. Hogan considered the grip the source of all energy transfer from the body to the ball, while Nicklaus thinks of it simply as a way of putting your hands on the club so that the wrists can hinge without much effort. Both players were considered the best of their generations, so who was right?

They both were. Hogan and Nicklaus were different people with different golf swings, and very different strengths and weaknesses. Hogan was a small man, about 150 pounds at his heaviest, with strong, East Texas working-class hands. He also had a slashing swing that required great precision and diligence to perfect. Nicklaus' hands were so naturally weak that even in his prime he would have to pass an unopened jar of mayonnaise to his wife Barbara to open. Jack's strength lay in his powerful legs and the high, flowing arc of his swing. His hands simply needed to hang on.

Even though Hogan and Nicklaus took different approaches to their respective grips, they (and every other championship golfer of note) can agree on one principle: It doesn't matter if a golfer employs the interlocking grip (used by players like Nicklaus), the overlapping (or *Vardon grip* as it is commonly called), or the *10-finger grip* (a baseball grip where all your fingers are in contact with the club), the purpose of the grip is to position the hands on the club so that the player can generate maximum clubhead speed without sacrificing accuracy and consistency. By the way, if you want more detailed explanations of the various types of grips, check out *Golf For Dummies,* 2nd Edition by Gary McCord, published by Hungry Minds, Inc.

Coming to grips with your grip

Over the years, conventional golf grips — such as the interlocking and Vardon grips — have become the universal standard of all great players. Rarely will you find a good player using a baseball or 10-finger grip, and you will never find a champion at the highest level using a *split grip* (where the hands are apart from each other on the club) or other odd variations. According to four-time major champion Nick Price, "You can always find players who have unconven-

tional grips, and many of them do well. But these golfers must build idiosyncrasies into their swings to compensate for their poor grips. A player who has a sound grip and who checks it regularly will never have to worry about it hurting his swing; the proper grip can only help his swing. Certainly most golfers would be able to swing the club more efficiently if they gripped the club correctly."

The "correct" grip always remains in the eye of the beholder, but there is no doubt that the grip can and should change as the body ages. Just as your over-40 body won't let you get away with eating and drinking as much as you could when you were 20, your post-40 golf game won't let you get away with the same grip you used when you were younger. And the reason for that is the toll the aging process takes on your hands.

Coping with Your Aging Hands

You have 28 small bones in your hand and wrist, which are moved by a series of flexor and extensor tendons (which you can think of as a series of marionette strings under your skin that allows you to close and open your fingers) triggered by three major nerves. Each hand also has 16 working joints, each with a different range of motion and each cushioned by a small layer of cartilage. In short, the hand is a complex, sensitive, and vulnerable body part.

Because of the sheer number of bones, joints, tendons, ligaments, and nerves in your hands and wrists, you have a greater chance of suffering the effects of age in those areas than in other parts of the body. Bone loss, tightening of the ligaments and tendons, as well as a loss of cartilage and natural inflammation are all conditions that occur after 40, and each can have a devastating impact on the hands. Age-related maladies in the hands, wrists, and fingers are broad and varied, ranging from general soreness and stiffness to severe, and sometimes crippling, joint problems. The following are the most common hand problems for golfers over 40.

✔ **Tendonitis: An inflammation of the tendons caused by strain or overexertion.** Tendonitis is marked by a constant aching in the hand that elevates into a stabbing or stinging pain during the golf swing. This is the most common (and most painful) hand ailment golfers over 40 are likely to experience. Although various treatments for the symptoms of tendonitis are available, the only cure is resting the afflicted area. That means no golf for a few weeks, and as little lifting and strenuous exercise in the hand and wrist region as possible.

✔ **Carpal tunnel syndrome: A painful condition brought on by one of the ligaments in the hand (the *transverse carpal ligament* for those who want to be technical about it) compressing against one of the main nerves in the hand.** This problem — which is normally associated with repetitive movements, such as extensive typing, but is also common among over-40 golfers — results in numbness, tingling, and pain in the hand, wrist, and fingers. Corrective treatments for carpal tunnel syndrome range from rest for the afflicted hand and medication to reduce inflammation to surgery to cut the ligament and decompress the compressed nerve.

✔ **Arthritis: The most severe and sadly the most incurable ailment of the hands and wrists is arthritis.** Arthritis is a swelling or inflammation of the joints that can range in severity from mildly painful and annoying to crippling and disfiguring. Doctors have no complete cure for arthritis, but you can try anti-inflammatory medications that minimize the symptoms as well as exercises that strengthen the hand and stretch the ligaments and tendons around the swollen joints. (See the section "Strengthening Over-40 Hands" later in this chapter for details about these exercises.)

One of the biggest mistakes golfers over 40 make is ignoring pain in the hands and wrists, writing it off as just part of getting older. Because so many ailments have similar symptoms, always get expert medical advice for any pain, numbness, or swelling in your hands and wrists. Self-diagnosis can do you more harm than good, and simply "playing through the pain" may lead to severe and irreparable damage. Only a doctor can determine if the pain that you're experiencing is a minor problem that can be cured by resting the injured area or a major problem that requires aggressive treatment.

Changing Your Grip after 40

Of course, you can't completely stop the degenerative effects of aging in your hands, but you can do plenty of things to minimize the maladies that age inflicts on your hands without sacrificing distance, accuracy, or feel. The first is to retool the position of your hands on the golf club.

Almost every golf instructor universally advocates a neutral or palms-facing grip (see Figure 3-1), regardless of whether the golfer holds the club with the fingers interlocking or overlapping.

Figure 3-1:
Close-up of
neutral grip.

"The reason the square grip (or neutral grip) is best is because the hands will always tend to return to this palms-facing position at impact. What most golfers don't understand about the grip is that the easiest way to ensure square contact with the ball is to adopt a grip with which the palms of both hands are square to the target. This means that, if you took the grip and opened both hands, both palms would be at right angles or square to the target line, an imaginary line from the ball to the target." — Johnny Miller

Miller adopted the neutral grip when he was a student at Brigham Young University, and it served him well through his thirties. But consciously or subconsciously, Miller modified his grip after he turned 40 to counteract a loss of strength in his hands and to prevent possible injury.

With the palm-facing or neutral grip, you can see *two* knuckles of the left hand, and the line or "V" formed between the thumb and the hand pointing toward your chin. This is what Miller called *square,* and it is the grip taught by most instructors. It is not, however, perfect for over-40 golfers.

Moving your left hand

The neutral grip allows strong players to square the club at impact without the hands becoming too active. But as you lose strength, as the tendons in the hands tighten, and the joints become more sensitive to the trauma of hitting a golf ball, you need to strengthen that neutral grip. Move your left hand more on top of the club so that *three* knuckles of the left hand are visible, and the "V" between the thumb and hand points to your right shoulder (see Figure 3-2).

Figure 3-2:
Close-up of
stronger
left-hand
grip.

For over-40 golfers this stronger grip accomplishes several things:

- ✔ It allows hands that aren't as strong as they once were to hinge on the backswing and release the club through impact.

- ✔ It enables you to relax your grip pressure without sacrificing control. Having a relaxed grip is not only important in generating clubhead speed at impact; it also cuts down on injury. The more grip pressure you apply, the greater chance of straining tendons and ligaments in your hands. A stronger left hand allows for less pressure and fewer injuries.

- ✔ It puts the left thumb in a stronger position, which makes the club more secure at the top of the backswing, reducing the club's chances of slipping in the hands.

In order to feel the effects of this stronger over-40 grip, take your right hand off the club and make a few swings with only the left hand. Doing so gives you a feel for the wrist angle this new grip creates, as well as the strong position of the club at the top of the backswing. It also allows you to feel the pressure differences with the new grip and to feel how relaxed the grip can be with the left hand in a stronger position.

The inherent problem with changing any fundamental in golf is the tendency of some golfers to overdo it. When you take on the challenge of changing something as basic as the grip, that tendency can have devastating consequences. Strengthening the left hand makes sense for golfers over 40 for all the reasons that I describe earlier in this chapter as long as the guidelines are followed to the letter. If, for example, you strengthen your grip to a point where all four knuckles of the left hand are visible instead of only three, you limit the ability of the wrist to hinge properly on the backswing, and you risk further damage to your swing by causing other parts of the body to compensate for this overly exaggerated grip.

Keeping an eye on your right hand

A similar problem occurs with the right hand. In both the neutral grip and the stronger over-40 grip, the right hand remains reasonably neutral with the "V" of that hand pointing to your chin or left ear. This position keeps the right hand from overpowering the swing, kicking in and casting the club from the top of the backswing like a fly-fishing rod or hinging the wrists too quickly on the backswing. When you strengthen the left hand, you must also make sure that your right hand remains neutral. See Figure 3-3 for an example of the worst grip in golf.

Figure 3-3:
Close-up of strong right-hand grip.

Johnny Miller calls this a "Harley Davidson grip," saying of golfers who play with such a grip, "When they waggle the club, they look like one of those leather-jacketed cats revving up a powerful cycle. Very early Brando, and they last just about as long as players."

Miller couldn't have put it better. This strong right-hand grip is the kiss of death in golf. Even before you take the club away from the ball, the outcome is inevitable. Your hands cannot hinge properly. You will end up lifting and throwing your club at the ball, and your shot will be short and crooked, not a combination that lends itself to good scores.

Sticking with the knuckle count as the basic rule for the over-40 grip, you should always see two knuckles of the right hand (and not from the underside of the shaft) at address. This position ensures that the right hand doesn't become overly active in the swing, but remains the perfect companion to its newly positioned stronger partner, the left hand.

When he was 17 years old, Hal Sutton's father took his prodigy son to Austin, Texas, to take a lesson from the legendary teacher Harvey Penick. As Hal remembers it, "I hit about 50 balls, and Harvey just watched. Then he said, 'People are going to tell you that your left hand grip is too strong. Don't listen to them. It's not too strong.' I've taken thousands of golf lessons since that one, but I still remember every word (Harvey) said."

Sutton continues to use that strong left hand grip he had when he was 17, and he continues to win with it at the age of 43. In fact, Sutton checks his grip as part of his standard pre-shot routine, lifting the club and making a visual check of the position of both hands before addressing each shot during a round. Building that same sort of visual check into your pre-shot routine goes a long way toward keeping your grip consistent for years to come.

Strengthening Over-40 Hands

Changing your grip can help your golf game after 40, but doing so won't retard the effects of aging on your hands. For that, you need to incorporate strength training into your daily routine. Where the hands are concerned, I recommend two types of strength exercises:

- ✔ *Flexor exercises:* where resistance is applied as the hand closes into a fist
- ✔ *Extender exercises:* where resistance is applied as the hand opens and the fingers extend.

Squeezing a ball for resistance

The most common *flexor exercise* for the hand involves squeezing a ball. This is also one of the most misused and misunderstood of all strength exercises. The squeeze ball exercise is not a power lift. You aren't trying to apply pressure to the ball until it explodes!

The keys to performing this exercise correctly are the following:

- ✔ **Picking a ball that offers a medium range of resistance, not a tennis ball that you can't squeeze at all or a foam ball that provides no resistance.** A racquetball or gel-filled ball is the most appropriate to use.
- ✔ **Squeezing and releasing the ball slowly, isolating various fingers with each repetition (see Figure 3-4).**

Figure 3-4:
Close-ups of
squeeze ball
exercise at
the start and
finish
positions.

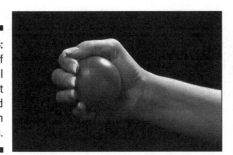 

✔ **Repeating the exercise doing 10 to 20 repetitions.** Aim for three sets of 10 to 20 repetitions with a rest of 30 seconds between each set. During the rest period, extend and spread your fingers to stretch your hand. Just because you can squeeze the ball 100 times without stopping doesn't mean that you should. Your hands get a better workout if you take a break between sets.

✔ **Working both hands equally.** Don't fall into the old golf trap of thinking the left hand should be considerably stronger than the right. In strength training (as in life), both sides deserve equal time.

Stretching a rubber band for strength

The *extender exercise* is equally simple, but almost never practiced. All you need is a sturdy rubber band and ten minutes. Here's how it works.

1. **Wrap a short, strong rubber band around your thumb and a finger so that the band is relaxed when the hand is closed (see Figure 3-5).**

Figures 3-5:
Close-ups of
rubber band
pull at start
and finish
positions.

2. **Open the hand slowly, stretching the rubber band between the thumb and finger, then close the hand just as slowly so that you feel resistance in both directions.**

3. **Repeat the exercise 20 to 30 times with each finger of each hand until all fingers have worked through the same number of repetitions. Extend and release slowly to make the exercise more effective.**

4. **Do this exercise once every day.**

Applying these fundamental changes to your grip and exercising your hands can go a long way toward keeping you strong and competitive into your forties, fifties, sixties, and beyond.

Chapter 4

Getting into Position: The Over-40 Setup

"If you set up correctly, there's a good chance you'll hit a reasonable shot, even if you make a mediocre swing. If you set up incorrectly, you'll hit a lousy shot even if you make the greatest swing in the world."

— Jack Nicklaus

*E*very touring professional agrees that the setup is the most important aspect of golf — more important than the backswing, follow-through, swing plane (see Chapter 6), *weight shift* (the movement of body weight during the swing), visualization, or be-the-ball hypnosis. If you have a good setup — good stance, good ball position, and good alignment — you're more than halfway there. Nicklaus says the setup is "90 percent of good shot making," while Nick Price says, "The swing is a chain reaction, and the golfer who gets the first links in the chain — the grip, the stance, and the setup — right has a much better chance of getting the later links right."

No matter what percentage of importance you apply to the setup, the undeniable fact is that you can't make the most efficient use of your body during the golf swing if you set yourself up in a bad position from the start. Even if you've been able to manipulate the swing to get away with some setup flaws in the past, as you grow older, those extra motions in your swing come back to haunt you. When you're over 40, how efficiently you move becomes more critical, and the only way to ensure that you have the most efficient swing possible is to start from a good setup.

Just as you should consider strengthening your grip (see Chapter 3) as you lose strength and feel in your over-40 hands, you should also make some modifications to your setup as your body changes with age. And as I explain in this chapter, these minor setup changes prepare you for the natural swing changes that occur as you grow older.

Nicklaus is right: By setting a good pre-swing base, you give yourself a chance to make a mistake or two in your swing and still get away with it. From a poor setup, or even a setup that worked when you were younger but now contains some fundamental flaws, you have no chance of executing good golf shots, no matter how perfectly you swing the club.

Setting Up Your Setup: The Basics

Many people are confused by the term *setup*. Some assume it simply refers to the *stance* — how the feet are positioned or how much the knees are flexed, while others think of setup in terms of ball position or pre-shot routine. Some of these assumptions are partially right and some are totally wrong. The *setup,* as most professional players and golf instructors see it, refers to three distinct areas: stance, ball position, and alignment.

✔ **Stance: This is how your feet and body are postured before the swing.** Although many people overcomplicate it, the golf stance isn't much different from the stance you use in other sports. Whether you're jumping for a rebound, reading a quarterback, or preparing to return a serve, the following items hold true:

• You're taut but relaxed, full of energy, and ready to explode like a lion.

• Your body is bent slightly forward at the waist, but with your back relatively straight.

• Your head is up, but not abnormally so.

• Your feet are shoulder-width apart or a little wider.

• Your weight is evenly distributed and centered between the ball and the arch of your feet.

• You're not slouching or slumping.

• Your bottom is above or slightly behind your heels, but not abnormally so.

• Your arms are free to move. You have only mild tension in your hands.

This is exactly the same position you need to be in to hit a golf ball — no contortions, no checklists, no odd angles. The stance to hit a golf ball is, purely and simply, a standard athletic position.

✔ **Ball position: You control where the ball is positioned in the stance because golf is not a reaction sport where the ball is thrown or hit at you.** You can play the ball off your front foot, your back foot, or in the middle of your stance; you can even play it five feet away and take a running start at it like Adam Sandler did in the movie *Happy Gilmore* (although that technique is not recommended, especially for those over 40 who risk looking foolish *and* hurting themselves with such a stunt). Antics aside, ball position is a crucial part of the setup and one that should be given due notice.

✔ **Alignment: If you're not lined up toward the green, chances are better than average that you won't hit it.** Still, many golfers line up yards off line in the hopes of either pulling, pushing, hooking, or slicing the ball back to the intended target. It's amazing how many golfers line up incorrectly and then stand in stunned amazement as their shots fly into the trees. This is a foolhardy approach to golf, and one that you should forever banish from your mind. A great stance, good ball position, and the perfect golf swing mean nothing if your alignment is off. If you line up toward your intended target, you have at least a chance of hitting your ball there. It's that simple, and too often, that idea is simply forgotten.

You can't control many things in golf — wind, bad bounces, good putts that somehow stay out of the hole — but the one thing you can control is how you set up to a particular shot. You may not have the greatest swing in the world, but that problem shouldn't stop you from doing everything in your power to make sure your setup is perfect.

Simplifying Your Setup as You Age

No matter how well-conditioned you are, your body has changed with age and will continue to change as you grow older. Because of those changes, you need to consider a few slight, subtle modifications to your setup.

Slow, steady, and successful

For years Jack Nicklaus was criticized for being a slow player when, in fact, Nicklaus' rounds didn't take any longer than any other player on tour. As he described it, "I walk very fast up to the ball, make a fairly fast decision about what I want to do when I get there, but then sometimes I set up to the shot slowly, because the setup is the only aspect of the swing over which you have 100 percent conscious control. It is the single most important maneuver in golf."

Nicklaus won 18 professional majors (including a Masters title at age 46 and a sixth place finish at the Masters at age 58). When it comes to the importance of the setup, all golfers would do well to keep Nicklaus' approach in mind.

It's awfully easy to tie yourself in a knot when you tinker with your setup, however. Over the years, instructors have thrown out so many mental images and visual cues that understanding how the average golfer can become confused is simple. For example:

- Do you set your feet at a 90-degree angle to the target line or do you open the lead foot up a few degrees?

- Do you imagine yourself sitting on a barstool, leaning forward to address the ball, or do you place your weight on the balls of your feet and bow to the ball as if you were impaled on a sharp stick?

- Should your head be up or down? Your left arm rigid or hanging loosely at your side?

- Should your hips and shoulders be completely parallel to the ground or at a slightly upward angle?

- What about your knees? How much flex is too much? How much is not enough?

- What about the ball? Should you have it positioned off your front foot? Your back foot? In the middle of your stance? Do you change ball position with each club? After you get the ball positioned in your stance, should your feet be aligned at the target? Five degrees left of the target? Should the shoulders be aligned left of the target and the hips and feet at the target? Or is it the other way around? And which one of these things should you remember first?

If you tried to incorporate every tidbit of advice ever given about the setup, your head would probably explode before you reached the first tee. Despite what the editors of dozens of instructional-based golf magazines want you to believe, the setup is not that complicated. In fact it's quite simple. It's just not easy.

The setup isn't easy because the golf ball sits still. Unlike in other sports, the ball isn't moving at you, and you don't have to react to it. You have plenty of time to think about every calculation and possible change that has ever rolled through your noggin. And therein lies the problem. As Nicklaus points out, the good news is that you have 100 percent conscious control over your own setup. The bad news is, you have 100 percent conscious control over your own setup. As a result, you're more likely to overthink the process, to tie yourself in a thousand Gordian knots before you ever take your first swing.

That is why you need to simplify the setup, making a few minor changes to accommodate your over-40 body, and focus on a few critical cues that can get you into a comfortable and correct position to make a good golf swing.

Modifying your stance after 40

As you age, your balance and equilibrium change from what they once were. That's not to imply that you are stumbling through life. In fact, the changes in your equilibrium may be so subtle that you don't recognize them. If you don't believe it, try riding a roller coaster a few dozen times, a feat that was probably no big deal when you were a teenager, but one that is likely to leave you dazed and confused today.

Because of subtle changes in your balance, the hard and fast rule that your feet must be shoulder-width apart to hit a golf ball no longer exists. In fact, most over-40 professionals such as Laura Baugh and Larry Nelson (see Figure 4-1) set up with their feet slightly wider than shoulder-width. Doing so allows them to make good solid golf swings without worrying about being unstable or unbalanced.

Figure 4-1:
Laura Baugh and Larry Nelson at address.

A slightly wider stance provides a sturdy base on which to turn. But be careful. A stance that is too wide can actually restrict your backswing and force you to cast the club like a fishing rod or lunge at the ball like a woodchopper with an ax. It's a delicate balance between a slightly wider over-40 stance and one that is too wide.

Figure 4-2 shows the modern stance with the feet shoulder-width apart, the recommended over-40 stance with the feet slightly wider than shoulder-width, and a stance where the feet are too wide and the golfer has no chance of making a good swing.

Figures 4-2: Steve demonstrating three stances of varying widths.

Another game-killing mistake many over-40 golfers make when taking their stances is the *arched back* or *question mark syndrome*. These two odd-looking stances usually come from golfers trying too hard to work through a mental checklist instead of remembering the basics. As a result, they contort their bodies in all manner of unnatural ways.

- ✔ The *question mark stance* (see Figure 4-3) derives its name from the idea that golfers contort their spines in such a way that they look like question marks. As you can imagine there is no way to turn the shoulders and make a sound golf swing from this position. All golfers with the question mark stance can do is lift the club with their hands and make a slashing stab at the ball. The results that come from this stance aren't pretty.

- ✔ Another equally devastating mistake is the *arched back stance* (see Figure 4-4). You can almost see this golfer going through a mental checklist: Okay, bottom out, head up, hands high, left arm straight, now relax and swing! Sadly, this golfer has no chance of hitting a good golf shot from this stance. He has doomed his chances before ever taking the club back.

The odd thing about both the question mark stance and the arched back stance is that they both require more effort than it takes to make a good athletic stance (see Figure 4-5). Your body doesn't naturally gravitate toward such skewed twisting. In fact, if you forget the checklists, and think only about being an athlete, you're more likely to strike a good pose at address than repeating some of the bad positions shown in this chapter.

Figure 4-3:
Steve demonstrating the question mark stance.

Figure 4-4:
Steve demonstrating the arched back stance.

Varying ball position

Despite what you've read or heard in the past, you won't find some magical spot in the stance from where you can hit all golf shots perfectly. Such a spot simply doesn't exist. Players have their own ideas about where you should place the ball in the stance, but those ideas have come out of many hours on the practice tee. Some players say they change the position of the ball in their stance depending on which club they hit. Others play the ball in one spot for every shot. The universal rule of ball position is that there is no universal rule.

Figure 4-5:
Steve
demonstra-
ting the
correct
stance.

No strain to gain

The basic idea governing ball position is that you shouldn't have to strain to reach the ball at address, because if you do, you'll have to strain to reach it at impact. Think of the *Happy Gilmore* example cited earlier in this chapter. In this farcical tale, a former hockey player becomes a championship golfer by taking a running start at the ball before every shot. That is the ultimate strain!

The fact is that you need to position the ball somewhere comfortably between your feet, but far enough away from your body that your arms and the club naturally rest behind it at address.

Striking the right spot

Another generally accepted idea about ball position says that the ball should be positioned so that you can hit it as your swing reaches maximum speed at the bottom of the *swing arc* (the imaginary circle the clubhead would form during the swing). If the ball is too far forward in the stance (more toward the left foot), the swing will have already passed the bottom of its arc before the ball is struck and the ball will be hit on the upswing. If the ball is too far back in the stance (toward the right foot), contact will come before the swing reaches its maximum speed at the bottom of the arc. The ball will be struck at a sharp angle on the downswing. Neither of these outcomes is very good.

Although no one can point to the exact spot where every golfer should play the ball, it is commonly held that if the club is swung properly, the ball should be played somewhere between the middle of the stance forward to the left foot. Anything farther forward than the left toe is generally believed to be too far forward, and anything back of center is commonly considered too far back. (Figure 4-6 shows three examples of ball position at the moment prior to impact.)

Figure 4-6:
Laura, Larry, and Steve the moment before impact.

Altering alignment: Aim, ready, aim again

If you aren't aiming at your target, you're probably not going to hit it. Unfortunately for most golfers (no matter what their age), that simple truth gets left in the clubhouse when they make their way to the first tee. Sure, they think they're aiming down the middle of the first fairway, but they probably aren't. Instead they're running through their mental checklists — eye on the ball, head still, left arm straight, knees bent, bottom out — only afterward making a cursory glance down the fairway at their intended target. This pattern of thinking, they assume, passes for aiming. In fact, it's the equivalent of firing a gun with your eyes closed.

Aimless golfers can't help it. The mental checklist procedure is all they know because it's all they practice. On the occasions when they do hit range balls, *target* is the last thing on their minds. They work on swing plane and slow takeaways with no regard to where they're aiming their body or club. As long as the ball goes out there, preferably *far* out there, they're happy.

Good players are exactly the opposite. They never hit a shot in practice or on the course without a distinct target line. These are the players who do the following:

- ✔ Always start their pre-shot routines from behind the ball, picking out their intended target line and shaping the shot in their minds.

- ✔ Spend time in the pre-shot routine squaring the club to the target at address.

- ✔ Look at the target at least twice as long as they look at the ball before the swing.

- ✔ Normally hit their shots on line, even when they don't hit the ball perfectly.

Many over-40 players fall into the subconscious trap of lining up closed or right of their intended target, then compensating for that alignment problem by sliding forward during the downswing, trapping the ball with a clubface that has been closed at an odd angle and pulling the ball back left of where the body was aligned to get it back on line. The reasons for this problem are twofold. First, working yourself into a closed stance is easy because of the optical illusion created by looking down the target line with your eyes parallel to the line rather than facing the target straight on with your eyes perpendicular to the line. Secondly, a certain lure goes along with the pulled shot because it generally goes farther. When you slide forward (called *coming over the top of the shot* in golf vernacular) you deloft the club. Suddenly a 5-iron takes on the loft of a 3-iron, or a 7-iron becomes a 5-iron. As a result you may miss the target badly, but, gosh, you hit that 7-iron 175 yards! You animal! Who cares if you're in the water and about to make double bogey, you hit it long!

Don't fall victim to this seductive trap. You can't control how much or how often you're going to pull the ball. The added distance of a come-over pull can be a great temptation, but don't go for it. Doing so ruins your scores in the long run.

Maintaining Your Setup and Avoiding Bad Habits

Bad habits don't happen overnight. You don't go to sleep one evening with perfect posture and alignment only to wake up the next morning with an entirely new setup. The changes are gradual just like the changes in your body occur slowly over time. This section takes a look at some things you can do to check and maintain your setup as you age and keep bad habits from creeping in.

Keeping a good stance

You should constantly check your stance to ensure that you haven't slipped into any bad habits. Some of the best ways to do that include the following:

- ✔ Standing in front of a full-length mirror and marking (in removable grease pencil) certain spots where your head, shoulders, feet, and bottom fall in the reflection. Doing so allows you to go back to the mirror and check yourself against a pre-established standard.

✔ If you have access to a 2 x 4 and a saw, cut the 2 x 4 to match the width you want between your feet at address and keep the board with you when you practice. This allows you to periodically check the width of your stance against a standard measurement.

✔ Have someone videotape you on the driving range. Nothing beats the tape in terms of capturing you in real time as you go through your routine and setup.

Eyeballing ball position

Over time, working the ball forward or backward in your stance without realizing your mistake is very common. The best way to gauge whether or not that problem is happening is to have a friend take still photos of your ball position at address when you are comfortable that you have the ball in the right spot. By having those photos available, you can periodically check to see if you have moved your ball position.

Checking alignment

Video and still photography aren't very useful in checking your alignment because capturing a distant target, the golfer, and the clubface in one frame is very difficult. You do have plenty of other methods at your disposal, however.

For instance, consider the following:

✔ The most common and still most effective method is the *two-club-troth*. This is where you line two parallel clubs on the ground, both pointing down the target line. By lining your body up with one of the clubs and the clubface up with the other, you can make a quick and easy check of your alignment.

✔ Many players line up the stripes of *range balls* (practice balls on driving ranges are often stripped to distinguish them from other balls on the course) so that they point toward the target. This is a good visual cue for clubface alignment, but it does little to help line up the body.

✔ Still other players place tees and other items in front of the ball on a line toward the target. This is another visual cue that helps the player line up the clubface.

The setup is more than half your battle. If you work the drills in this chapter and get yourself in a good athletic position to make the golf swing, you have a great chance of becoming an exceptional over-40 player.

Chapter 5

Tuning Up Your Turn

> *"The secret in golf is to have a backswing so sound that on the course you don't think about the downswing. Of course, that doesn't happen too often. Yet, I have experienced many moments when I have only thought of a position in my backswing and the ball has come off the clubface properly. The correct backswing will set up the conditions that make it much more likely that the right things will happen later."*
>
> — Nick Price

How you start your swing plays a tremendous role in how you finish it. After gripping the club correctly and setting up to execute a shot, the first move you make as you turn the shoulders to swing is the most important one. Not only do you set the path of your swing in the first milliseconds of the backswing, you also determine which muscles control the swing and how much energy transfers from your body to the club. In this chapter, I break down exactly which muscles you use during the turn and provide some key exercises to help over 40-golfers strengthen those muscles as they get older.

Muscling into the Turn

Every muscle group between your navel and your neck is at work during the backswing. And although no one group is more important than any other in this process, understanding the role of each major upper body muscle group as it relates to the turn is key.

Many very good players, including Bobby Jones, felt that the left arm or shoulder initiated the backswing. This was the feel they liked to get and the one thought that helped them start the turn. But, their idea was only partially correct.

Integrating your entire upper body

A pushing action with the left side initiates the backswing turn, but it isn't just the arms and shoulders that are at work. The *Trapezius muscle,* which runs along your upper back, plays a key role in initiating the turn, as does the *Latissimus Dorsi* (the muscle that originates from the spine and attaches to the bone of the upper arm), or lat muscle as it's often called. Both these muscle groups are instrumental in turning the shoulders. The *biceps* come into play as the club comes off the ground and turns on plane while your forearms slowly rotate the clubface open on the backswing.

The external *oblique muscles,* which run down your sides, also play a key role in the backswing, and must be flexible in order for you to make a complete shoulder turn. Many players assume they aren't making a complete shoulder turn because their shoulders aren't flexible, when actually it's the obliques that are restricting their turn. *Upper* and *lower abdominals* (in your midsection) also play a key role in keeping your trunk sturdy throughout the turn. Without a strong and flexible midsection, your natural tendency is to pick up the club rather than turn it back (See the section "Avoiding common mistakes" later in this chapter for more on picking up the club.)

Seeing why bigger isn't always better

If power and speed in golf were based solely on strength, then the biggest, burliest muscle-bound golfers would hit the ball farther than everyone else, and golfers of smaller stature would be at a distinct disadvantage. But that is not the case at all. Take, for example, Gary Player. He's only 5 feet 7 inches tall and weighs 145 pounds after a hearty meal, yet he has won 95 professional tournaments worldwide and is one of only five men in history to win all four professional majors. Player is proof positive that smaller golfers can generate tremendous power.

So how do they do it? How do over-40 golfers such as Player, Ben Crenshaw (who is 5'9", 155 pounds), Mark McCumber (5'8", 155 pounds), and Chi Chi Rodriguez (5'7", 130 pounds) keep up with taller, heavier, and stronger players? What about women? How does someone as petite as 41-year-old Cindy Flom power drives past her husky male pro-am partners on a weekly basis? In fact, how is it that most LPGA Tour players hit the ball farther than most bigger and stronger male amateurs?

The answer is simple: All these players have harnessed the power of what's called the *X Factor,* building swings that maximize the leverage of a strong shoulder turn and a sturdy base. They build tension by coiling their bodies with a full turn, and they unleash tremendous energy when they unwind that coil.

Finding Your Power through the X Factor

Okay, golf isn't rocket science, brain surgery, or even calculus, and anything in golf that requires a calculator with a function key is gobbledygook. Fortunately the X Factor is simple. The only reason it's referred to in mathematical terms is because you can actually calculate it, just like you can calculate your handicap.

In golf, the formula is:

X = Shoulder Turn – Hip Turn

If you think of your shoulders and your hips as dials on a compass, you can see how this formula works. A full shoulder turn of 90 degrees on the backswing, where a line across the shoulders would be perpendicular to the ground, minus a hip turn of say, 30 degrees, where the left heel has come off the ground and the hips have turned slightly, would give you an X Factor of 60 — which is pretty good (see Figure 5-1). Any X Factor more than 50 isn't bad for an over-40 golfer. If your other fundamentals are sound, an X Factor of 60 should allow you to generate a fair amount of clubhead speed at impact.

Figure 5-1:
Steve at top of backswing with good X Factor; Steve picking the club straight up with zero X Factor.

A shoulder turn of 80 degrees, which is still good for over-40 golfers, minus a hip turn of 20 degrees, which would likely mean both feet remaining firmly planted on the ground, still generates an X Factor of 60. That means the golfer who turns his shoulders only 80 degrees but keeps his hips more firmly planted creates the same amount of energy as the golfer who turns her shoulders 90 degrees but turns her hips 30 degrees.

Avoiding common mistakes

Do you see where this illustration is headed? A huge wind-up on the backswing doesn't necessarily translate to clubhead speed on the downswing. You can turn your shoulders 100 degrees, wrapping the club around you like Gumby, but if you also turn your hips 60 degrees, you have created an X Factor of only 40. That means you have built up less energy than the player with the shorter 80 degree backswing who keeps his or her hips firmly in place.

The other fatal flaw among many amateurs is picking the club up with the hands and assuming that this passes for a backswing (refer to Figure 5-1). It's very possible to take the club as far back as many professionals without turning your shoulders at all. All you have to do is pick the club up with your hands, and you can create an X Factor of zero. If you do make contact with this swing, the results won't be pretty.

The one principle to remember about the turn in golf is that it isn't how far you turn your shoulders on the backswing, it's how big an X Factor that you can create that really matters.

Using the X factor to improve distance

Not surprisingly, the best X Factor in the game belongs to the best player in the world, Tiger Woods. In fact, the X factor is the source of Tiger's seemingly inhuman length off the tee. Tiger has the uncanny ability to turn his shoulders well beyond 90 degrees and sometimes beyond 100 degrees with very little movement in his hips. This X Factor creates enormous energy that Tiger unleashes in the form of 350-yard tee shots and 200-yard 7-irons. Like most things in the game today, nobody has mastered the X Factor better than Tiger.

By the same token, older golfers are also maximizing the X factor to improve their games. Take 45-year-old professional Laura Baugh, for example. The LPGA rookie of the year in 1973 and the youngest player to win the U.S. Women's Amateur when she was only 16, Laura earned a reputation on tour as an accurate but not particularly long hitter. For years she assumed that her lack of distance was due to her lack of stature. She was a size 2 for most her adult life, so it seemed only natural that she wouldn't hit the ball as far as others did.

The history of the X factor

Ben Hogan believed that the backswing sequence was so crucial to the success of the swing, that he listed it as one of only five "fundamentals" of golf. According to Hogan, the backswing was triggered first by the hands moving the club back, followed by the arms, then the shoulders turning, all parts working in concert to swing the club back around a steady center and a sturdy right leg. The left hip would follow the shoulders back, but the hips wouldn't move at all until the hands were above the hips and the backswing was at least half completed.

Hogan's theory, born of countless hours of thoughtful research and millions of practice shots, stated that the downswing was simply a reverse of the backswing sequence. The hips would move first, initiating the downswing, followed by the shoulders, arms, and hands. Many experts have grappled with this idea over the 50 years since Hogan first set it out in his two books, *Power Golf* and *Five Lessons,* but none has been able to discount it. Hogan's fundamentals of a turning sequence for the backswing followed by an unwinding reverse-sequence for the downswing and follow-through are still considered gospel among many professionals and top-ranked amateurs.

In pure physiological terms, Hogan was more right than he could have ever known. Although he often referred to the "large" muscles of the back and shoulders and the role they played in effectively swinging the golf club, Hogan was ahead of his time in outlining and demonstrating the proper role of the back, shoulders, abdominals and obliques in the golf swing and the turning action they created. He also provided a classic living example of leverage and power created by turning the upper body around a relatively stable lower body. Hogan wasn't a big man. In fact, he was known as "Bantam Ben" because of his size, but Hogan produced tremendous power and efficiency in his swing through his turn. In the 1950s he didn't have a name for this principal. Today it's known as the *X Factor.*

Then Laura saw a videotape of her swing, and she realized that her lack of distance wasn't because of her size. "I had this awful reverse weight shift," she said. "My hips were way out of position, and even though I was taking the club back a long way, it wasn't doing me any good. I realized that if I was going to be competitive, especially as I got older, I needed to gain some distance."

Laura went to work on her swing, focusing on keeping her hips steady while maintaining her full shoulder turn. Her X factor doubled and the results were dramatic. Laura gained upwards of 40 yards off the tee and she leapt into the top 20 in driving distance on the LPGA Tour for the first time in her career after her 40th birthday (see Figure 5-2).

"I work out and stretch every day, and with this new swing I'm really long," she says. "It's a big advantage when you're hitting shorter clubs into par fours and reaching par fives in two. I'm only sorry I didn't recognize the swing changes I needed to make sooner."

Figure 5-2:
Laura
Baugh at
top of
backswing,
front and
side views;
after impact,
front and
side views.

Laura's epiphany isn't unusual, and there's no magical secret to her success. She recognized the need to increase her X factor in order to achieve greater distance as she aged, so she began stretching. She also worked on turning her shoulders around relatively stable hips. You can make those same changes, regardless of your age. By incorporating the stretching exercises found in this chapter with a deliberate focus on increasing your X factor, you can achieve similar results to those Laura experienced after her 40th birthday.

Stretching to Improve Your Turn

Swinging a golf club correctly takes a complete effort from many muscles. Your right side is no less important than your left during the backswing. Your arms and hands are no more vital than the stomach and back. That's why over-40 golfers must work on stretching and strengthening the big muscle groups that turn the golf club. Two simple exercises can help you accomplish that.

Doing the turn drill

The purpose of the turn drill is to get your muscles accustomed to stretching the X Factor to it fullest. Follow these simple steps to perform this stretch.

1. **Place a club behind your lower back so that the grip and the shaft are wedged between your elbows and across your back.** The clubhead should be on your left side, and the grip of the club on your right.

2. **Assume a mock address position and slowly turn your upper body so that the clubhead points to the ground while your feet remain firmly planted and your hips stay relatively stationary (see Figure 5-3).** Laura Baugh works many hours to stay flexible enough to make this turn. Don't feel bad if you can't quite replicate her flexibility right away.

Figure 5-3: Laura showing backswing stretch with club behind her.

3. **After fully extending the stretch as far as you comfortably can, hold for a count of ten.** Slowly turn out of the stretch and simulate a slow motion follow-through to your finish position (see Figure 5-4). Hold the finish for a count of ten. This follow-through gives you a feel for the large muscle groups working through the swing while allowing both sides of the body to be stretched equally.

This exercise is a slow action! Take at least three or four seconds to fully complete your turn. Rushing this stretch not only negates the desired effect, but may also result in your hurting yourself. As with all stretches, take it slowly and feel the sensation in every muscle group.

Figure 5-4:
Laura
demonstra-
ting follow-
through
stretch with
club behind
her.

Trying a standing stretch to expand your X factor

From a standing position either in your home or on the golf course, you can do another great stretch for all the torso, arm, shoulder, and neck muscles. It's a great warm-up exercise before a round, but also a stretching drill that you can incorporate into your daily routine.

In order to perform this stretching and strengthening drill, follow these steps.

1. **Hold the head of the club in your left hand and the grip in your right, with the club directly in front of you and your arms fully extended.**

2. **With your knees slightly flexed, slowly turn your arms, shoulders, and head 90 degrees to the right so that you are staring to your immediate right.**

3. **Take the stretch a little farther, trying, if you can, to look directly behind you, turning your shoulders and head 180 degrees while keeping your hips as still as possible. Hold this position for a count of ten (see Figure 5-5).**

4. **After turning as far to the right as you can, slowly turn back to the front and repeat the stretch on your left side. Hold the opposite side for a count of ten.**

You should feel this stretch in your back, sides, and abdomen, and, if you work at it regularly, you can improve the strength and flexibility of those muscles.

Figure 5-5:
Laura with club in front turning the stretch.

Building a bigger X Factor after 40 is far more important in golf than how far you take the club back or how strong your hands and arms are. By working all the muscles in the upper body, you have a good chance of improving your distance, accuracy, and overall flexibility.

Chapter 6

Improving Your Downswing and Follow-Through

"I'm a believer in the short swing because so little can go wrong with it. A player with a long swing is more likely to take the club back on one plane and bring it back down on another. I am conscious of the swing being one, complete, fluid movement. I keep my head down as I hit through the ball, while my follow-through is long but controlled. If you are all over the place on the follow-through, your swing is unlikely to have been well-balanced."

— Laura Davies

*W*hen you get to the downswing, you're 90 percent home. Of course, that last 10 percent is pretty important because that's when you actually hit the golf ball, but if you've done everything right so far, you have a great chance of hitting a good golf shot.

Think of your golf swing as an engine, the grip and setup are the assembly and tuning process, the backswing is the fuel needed to fire the engine, and the downswing is the moment of ignition. If you have a well-built engine that is properly tuned and given the right fuel, when you turn the key the spark plugs fire, fuel ignites, and the engine purrs. But if your car's engine is faulty or tuned improperly, or if you've filled the tank with faulty fuel, the engine will spit and sputter or not start at all. The same idea is true in golf. If you have built your swing on a solid foundation and go through the proper sequence, the "ignition process" should go smoothly. If not, your down-swing will stall, and the quality of your shot will be in serious jeopardy.

After you initiate the downswing, there is little more you can consciously do. From the moment you change directions in your swing until the time you make contact with the ball, you can't control your motion or even think about it. You simply don't have time. The whole process takes no more than one second.

The sequence that you use to take the club back — hands moving first, followed by arms, shoulders, and finally hips — you should *reverse* on the downswing with the hips initiating the change of direction, followed by the shoulders, arms, and finally the hands releasing the club through impact.

Some very good players have different ideas about the feel of this downswing motion. Johnny Miller says he feels the change of direction in his knees, with the left knee moving toward his intended target (the fairway or the green), while Jack Nicklaus feels it in his feet and legs. Others feel the downswing start with a pushing action in the calf muscle of the right leg. One thing isn't in question: More than 95 percent of the best players in the world agree that the lower body initiates the downswing.

Hitting (from) below the Waist

The biggest muscle groups in the body are below the navel, and these muscles generate the power and clubhead speed needed to hit long, accurate golf shots. Physiologically, the action works this way:

✔ From the top of the backswing, the *abductor* (the outer muscle of the upper thigh or the muscle that draws a part of the body away from the midline) and *adductor* (the inner muscle of the upper thigh or the muscle that draws a part of the body toward the midline) muscles along with the *hip flexors* (the front of the hip that allows you to raise a bent leg, for example) move the hips in a lateral and counterclockwise fashion through the shot. This movement is an unwinding of the hips from their taut position at the top of the backswing. This action also pulls the upper body into a position to hit the ball. The shoulders follow the hips, and the arms drop toward the ball. The right arm folds into a pre-release position with the right elbow staying close to the right side as the entire upper body follows the lower body's lead.

✔ At the same time, the right *gastrocnemius* (calf muscle) is pushing off, moving the body's weight off the right foot and onto the left foot. This weight shift occurs at the same time the hips are rotating, which adds to the lateral shift through the shot.

✔ The *hamstrings, quadriceps,* and *gluteus* muscles support the directional change of both the upper and lower body, along with the weight shift, and the rapid movement of the arms, hands, and club through impact.

✔ The *adductors* and *ankle flexors* (allows the ankle to rise upward, point downward, and roll inward and outward) also help propel the body into the follow-through, with the right leg continuing to bend and turn through impact.

All these actions look and feel different for different players, but if executed properly one thing is consistent: The lower body initiates the downswing and moves the upper body into the proper position to hit the ball. If you look at professionals like Laura Baugh and Larry Nelson (Figure 6-1) it is obvious that their lower bodies pull their shoulders and arms into position. The same is true with less-skilled amateurs.

Figure 6-1:
Laura (left),
Larry
(center),
and Steve
(right)
initiating the
downswing.

Determining Your Swing Plane

Plenty of confusion exists in golf about the *swing plane,* the angle at which the club shaft travels around the body during a swing. To understand the swing plane and what body parts affect it, you have to take a bit of a math lesson.

The swing plane is, technically, a geometric plane. Ben Hogan thought of it as a sheet of glass running from the ball through his neck and onward above his shoulders. He felt that if he could swing the club without breaking the glass, he had kept the club on the proper plane. In principle he was absolutely right. If your clubhead could somehow draw a line in space along its path during the swing, the points along that path would lie on the swing plane. Connect the dots and draw an imaginary plane (or a sheet of glass if that's easier to visualize) and you have your swing plane.

For good players, the swing plane has no bumps or wrinkles. Just as Hogan never broke his sheet of glass, most good players (and all great players) return the club to the ball on the same plane that it was taken away. The swing then remains on that same plane throughout the follow-through. That is not to say that all swing planes look alike. Hogan had a very flat swing, as does Gary Player. Nicklaus has always had a very upright plane (although Jack's has flattened somewhat with age). The point is, some swing planes are upright (see Figure 6-2), and some are flat (see Figure 6-3), but all good swing planes are consistent on the backswing and follow-through.

Figure 6-2:
Steve at backswing and follow-through with an upright plane.

Breaking the plane: When your hands get out of line

Breaking the plane at the top of the backswing is a common flaw among amateurs and a particularly common occurrence among golfers over 40. Golfers commonly refer to this problem as *throwing the club from the top, coming over it from the top,* or *letting the right side take over at the top.*

All these descriptions imply the same action, a violent motion where the hands and right shoulder initiate the downswing with a throwing or pushing action. This action breaks the swing plane, as the hands are taken outside the imaginary sheet of glass. This action also spells disaster for the golf shot. When the hands (instead of the lower body) take over on the downswing, all the hard work you go through to get yourself into a good position is for nothing. You waste the energy that you create on your backswing, and the shot flies short and crooked, a deadly combination for any golfer regardless of age.

Most golfers who have played more than two or three rounds know the feeling of throwing the club from the top, and most are frustrated by it. You *know* you didn't mean to grab the club so hard with your right hand. You weren't *trying* to come over it with your right side. If only you could cut your right hand off at the wrist, or have someone shoot novocaine into your right shoulder so that you wouldn't use it so much at the top of the swing. These are the typical comments (minus the expletives, of course) that golfers over 40 make after they have changed their swing planes in midswing and hit an awful shot as a result. What they don't realize is that they are swearing at the wrong body parts.

Figure 6-3:
Steve at backswing and follow-through with a flat plane.

Making up for tired legs

The hands take over at the top of the backswing only when the legs are too tired, too weak, or too untrained to initiate the downswing. If the lower body does its part, the hands and arms will fall into place. If the lower body does not initiate the downswing properly, the hands automatically take over. That's why breaking the swing plane is so prevalent among golfers over 40. As your legs get weaker or as your lower body tires with age, your upper body compensates during the golf swing by throwing the club with your right shoulder, hand, and arm. Your shoulder, hand, and arm aren't to blame for this mistake. They're just trying to keep you from whiffing the ball completely. Your tired legs are the real culprits.

Nicklaus said, "Sometimes when I've laid off golf for a while, my legs aren't in any condition to work correctly in my forward swing. Then I'm in the same boat as the fellow who rides in a car or sits in an office all week and wonders why his shoulders 'come over' the ball on Saturday mornings."

That's *you* that Jack is talking about. Your over-40 legs probably aren't as spry as they were 20 years ago, and after sitting a desk all week and not exercising your lower body very much, you cannot expect to hop on the first tee and drive your legs through your opening tee shot. However, you can do some simple exercises to keep your over-40 lower body ready for golf.

Key Exercises to Strengthen Your Lower Body

A complete lower body strength and flexibility program like the one I outline in Chapter 10 is the best possible scenario for keeping yourself in prime golf shape, but even those exercises don't guarantee that your lower body will initiate the downswing. For that you need to work on the following drills that simulate the lower body's action during the swing.

Cross-armed swing

You don't have to be at the golf course to strengthen the lower body's role in the golf swing. In fact, you don't even have to have a golf club. One of the best ways to focus solely on the action of the hips, legs, and feet is to stand in front of a mirror with your arms crossed over your chest and simulate a golf swing (see Figure 6-4). Because your arms aren't involved in this drill, feeling the lower body initiate the downswing is easy. This drill also provides a good way to condition the lower body to move through the shot without the complications of actually having to hit a ball. You can work on this drill in your office, your bedroom, or your shower, and you should practice it as often as possible (every day is ideal, but three or four times a week works fine) to keep the lower body primed after 40.

Figure 6-4: Larry with arms crossed from top of swing to follow-through.

Resistance drill

Because so many of the best players in the world have differing opinions on just what the lower body feels like during the downswing, you are probably wondering what you should feel in your swing. The answer is simple: It depends. (Hey, I said the answer was simple, not crystal clear.) You may feel your hips rotate and shift, or you could sense the motion in your quadriceps, knees, calves, or feet driving through the shot. The feel of this motion is completely subjective. No two people are likely to feel exactly the same things.

However, there is a drill that can help you identify your particular feeling. It requires a golf club and the assistance of another person, but the drill itself is very simple. After you take the club to the top of your backswing, have a friend or playing partner hold the club at the top as you simulate the start of the downswing with your lower body (see Figure 6-5). The resistance of the club being held back magnifies the sensations you feel in the lower body as you start this move and helps you to identify what you feel as the lower body initiates the downswing. Hopefully, you can replicate that feeling on the course.

Figure 6-5:
Kelly and Larry with Kelly holding the club at the top of the Larry's swing.

Three Stretches to Warm Up Your Legs

Over-40 golfers regularly make the mistake of totally forgetting to warm up the lower body before playing. You've probably been guilty of this. You're running a little late to the course, so you sit anxiously in your car as you speed toward the clubhouse. You then sit in a golf cart on your way to the first tee. After you step out onto the tee you go through a few warm up drills, mostly focusing on the arms, shoulders, or back before taking a few practice swings and flailing away at your first tee shot. When the ball sails off in the wrong direction, you wonder how on earth you could make such an awful swing.

Over-40 legs need a little warm-up time before they are called on to initiate the downswing. Just as you probably wouldn't hit your first shot of the day without a couple of practice swings, you shouldn't make your first practice swings without first stretching and loosening the lower body.

Doing three simple stretches before you take your first swing can go a long way toward warming up your lower body and cutting down on mistakes caused by legs that aren't ready to play. The first stretch works your calves and your Achilles. Follow these steps to do this stretch.

1. **With a club on the ground for balance (holding the clubface toward you so that the club doesn't slip) place your right foot a couple of feet behind you, keeping your heel on the ground (see Figure 6-6).**

2. **Tuck your hips underneath you and slowly press downward through the right heel, keeping a slight bend in the knee until you feel a good stretch.**

3. **You will feel this stretch first in your calf muscle and *Achilles tendon* (the long tendon at the rear of your ankle).** As you progress into the stretch, you will feel the sensation progress into your quadricep and hip flexor.

4. **Hold this position for a count of ten and then slowly return to the start position.** Repeat the stretch for the opposite leg. Rushing the stretch will not help you. Take your time and move slowly into and out of the stretch.

The following steps explain how to do a stretch that works your hamstrings and glutes.

1. **Keeping the club in the same position (out front as a guide with the clubhead facing you), place your right foot behind you a couple of feet, tuck the hips, and sit back into your right heel.** Make sure to keep your left leg extended but your knee slightly bent as you slowly lower yourself onto your right leg. Sit back as though you were going to sit in a chair and keep your chest and head upright (see Figure 6-7).

Figures 6-6:
Laura
working
through the
calf stretch.

2. **You will feel this stretch in your left hamstring and gluteus muscles.**

3. **Hold this position for a count of ten and slowly return to the start position.** Repeat the stretch for the opposite leg. Take your time and move slowly into and out of the stretch.

Figure 6-7:
Laura
working
through the
hamstring
and glute
stretch.

This stretch works your abductor and quad muscles. The following steps explain how to do it.

1. **Holding the club in front of you for balance, bend your right knee and slowly lift the right foot off the ground keeping your knee pointed downward (see Figure 6-8).**

2. **After lifting your foot as far as you can, reach behind you with your right hand and grab your right foot.** Slowly and gently push your hip forward while pulling your foot toward your buttocks until you feel the stretch in your right quad and abductor muscles.

3. **Hold this position for a count of ten and slowly return to the start position.** Repeat the stretch for the opposite leg. Always take your time and move slowly into and out of the stretch.

Never rush any stretches. All movements into and out of a stretch should be slow and fluid. Stretching isn't a race. Also, despite what you may have heard in the past, you should never, ever *bounce a stretch* (that's when you extend a stretch by bouncing your body and using momentum to reach a little farther — a terrible thing to do). Don't risk pulling an over-40 muscle just to prove you can take a stretch a little deeper. Doing so is counterproductive and dangerous.

Figure 6-8:
Laura working through the quad and abductor stretch.

Your lower body plays an important role at a crucial point in the golf swing. Keeping all the muscles below your navel properly stretched and trained can go a long way toward keeping your shots long and straight on the golf course after you turn 40.

Incorporating the Head and Hands through Impact

After you initiate the downswing with the lower body, the arms follow with the hands hinged and ready to smack the ball with all the clubhead speed you can generate. The two levers formed by the right arm — the cocked elbow and the cocked wrist — are ready to throw the club at the ball with all the speed your body can muster, which is considerable if you have done everything right so far.

Hogan likened the release of the golf club to pitching a baseball underhanded toward the target. That analogy is as good as any. Your elbow and wrist extend as the shoulders continue to turn, and your arms continue to rotate through the shot. Most players refer to this as *releasing the club through impact.*

Hanging onto your shots too long

Occasionally, you hear a professional or top-notch amateur say she *hung onto a shot.* That phrase implies that she didn't effectively release the club. But that language is a misnomer.

Just as throwing the club with the hands from the top of the swing is more a fault of the lower body than the hands themselves, hanging onto the club through impact and somehow not fully releasing the hands and arms isn't the fault of the hands and arms. It is a sure sign that the golfer's head has moved.

Keeping a steady head

Nicklaus probably put it best when he said, "I regard keeping the head very steady, if not absolutely stock still, throughout the swing as *the* bedrock fundamental of golf. It is inviolable as far as I'm concerned."

There's not much ambiguity in Nicklaus's position, nor will you find too many people who disagree with him. Swinging the golf club around a steady center (in this case, your head) is the most critical fundamental to making consistent swings and a key component in generating clubhead speed and momentum.

Consider for a moment a slingshot — not the Y-stick-and-rubber-band kind, but the two-strings-and-a-pouch kind that David used to kill Goliath. The principles of this kind of slingshot are the same as the golf swing. By swinging the rock around a steady center, you build up centrifugal force, and when you finally let go of one of the strings, the rock flies farther and straighter than you could have ever thrown it with your bare hands.

The golf swing operates under the same premise. By swinging the club around a steady center, you gain the added benefit of leverage and centrifugal force. This allows professionals and good amateurs to move the clubhead at more than 100 miles per hour through impact. It also allows them to return the clubface squarely to the ball. Any head movement, laterally or up and down, changes the center of the swing and disrupts this process.

WARNING!

You probably know that keeping your head still is important in the golf swing, but revisiting this fundamental, especially after you turn 40, never hurts. As you grow older, your swing isn't as long or as loose as it once was, and because of that, you may have a tendency to sway back and forth during your swing in an attempt to somehow make up for a loss in flexibility. That is a fatal error in golf. Any time you deviate from the fundamental principle of swinging around a steady center, you jeopardize all aspects of your swing.

As you can see from the downswings of Laura Baugh (Figure 6-9) and Larry Nelson (Figure 6-10), the best over-40 players in the game keep their heads perfectly still through impact in order to hit the ball long and straight. If you do the same, your game will show dramatic improvement.

Figure 6-9:
Laura from top of swing through impact.

Figure 6-10:
Larry from top of swing through impact.

Practicing Some Still Head Drills

You can't see your own head during a golf swing, so it's almost impossible to tell if you have subconsciously worked yourself into a sway or dip where your body moves laterally during the swing or your head bobs up and down. But here are some easy drills that you can use to test your steady center.

- **Marking a mirror:** If you have a full-length mirror and a grease pencil, one way to practice keeping your head still is to stand in front of the mirror and draw a box or circle around the reflection of your head. If you can consistently swing a golf club without your head exiting the lines of the box or circle, you can feel comfortable that you are keeping a steady center. The only problem with this drill is its impracticality on the golf course. Even if you could take a full-length mirror with you to the driving range, when you're hitting golf balls you're looking down, not up at your reflection. This drill is good for the home or office, but it does have its limitations.

- **Taking the video test:** The best real-time test for whether or not you are keeping your head still is to have your swing videotaped as you hit practice balls. If the camera is held steady, you can quickly tell if your head is moving from the landmarks in the background. For example, if a telephone pole or bagstand in the distance was clearly visible behind your left ear on the backswing, but completely obscured by your head on the downswing, you have a problem. Videotaping your swing can be cumbersome — unless you're one of the few people who owns a tripod, you'll have to enlist the help of a friend to tape your swing — but doing so is, by far, the best way to check the stability of your head as well as other fundamentals of your swing. (See Chapter 4 for details on how videotaping can help you check your setup.)

Putting It All Together: The Finish

No single visual image has done more damage to aging golfers than the young golfer with the high fluid finish, his or her body forming the perfect reverse C from heels to head. Trying to achieve this bowed-back finish has ruined more over-40 backs than anything else in golf. And sadly those injuries have been for nothing.

The bowed-back, reverse-C finish as a fundamental is dead and gone! None of the top players today even try to contort their bodies into this unnatural position. They know that if they tried it their days on tour would be numbered.

Laura and Larry both finish their swings standing perfectly straight (see Figure 6-11), no overarching bows in the back, no contortions or alphabetical letters being formed. This is the perfect over-40 finish. Try to match their technique to avoid getting hurt.

Figure 6-11:
Laura and
Larry in
finish
positions.

The fundamentals of golf don't magically change just because you turn 40. They remain what they have always been. But, your body does change and will continue to change as you grow older. A few tweaks in the way you approach the fundamentals after 40 can be the difference between remaining in top form on the course and falling off your game. After you have mastered the basics, the next step is to tone and tune your over-40 body for the specific motion golf requires.

Part III

Problem Areas: Fighting Them with Fitness

The 5th Wave   By Rich Tennant

"I don't know what the big deal is. I've been playing golf over 40 since I was 20."

In this part . . .

You hear a lot of talk these days, especially among over-40 professionals, about *golf fitness* or being in *golf shape*. Pros have discovered that training the body for golf requires more than hitting practice balls. Such training also includes a balanced dose of strength and flexibility work that targets specific golf needs. The over-40 golf body has some particular deficiencies that you can correct through fitness training. And, as a bonus, these golf-specific training programs also improve your overall health.

New state-of-the-art equipment can carry your game only so far. To win the battle of the aging golf game you must improve the machine that swings the club: your body. This part shows you how to achieve that.

Chapter 7

Rejuvenating Noodle Arms

> *"I've heard golfers say that as we grow older we should give in gracefully to the physical limitations of age, but I believe the very opposite. We ought to resist them with every fiber of our being. The widespread tendency among those over 40 to let nature take its course and to allow muscles and reflexes to deteriorate seems not only sad to me, but easily avoidable. True, at that stage of life the golfer cannot act as though he were 20. He won't be able to neglect his physical conditioning for long periods of time and then, by a crushing load of work and practice, suddenly force himself back into shape. He will have to pay regular attention to keeping himself in form."*

— Paul Runyan, former Senior PGA Champion and World Senior Champion

The world is full of weekend warriors. Health club owners around the country see them everyday: Men and women who wake up one day and decide they are overweight, out of shape, and in dire need of a good hearty workout. Off to the gym these people trot. There, all the nifty equipment, glittery lights and sweaty hard bodies energize them as they lift weights, jog on treadmills, ride stationary bikes, and climb stair machines. Oh, how they love this feeling of physical accomplishment! Of course, the next day every-thing from their toenails to their eyelids hurts, and they spend the rest of the week gingerly hobbling through their daily routines.

This kind of workout is awful. It does more damage than good to your body and can ruin your golf game by tightening muscles that need to remain flexi-ble and supple while straining sensitive areas of the body that need to be developed gradually. Many over-40 golfers give up on the entire fitness process after one workout because of the detrimental impact it has on their games. They lift as much weight as they can in their first workout session, then wonder why they can't take a club back above their waist the next day. They moan and complain never realizing that their soreness and stiffness was self-inflicted. As a result, they forget about fitness, spouting the defeatist mantra that has plagued golf for decades: "Golfers shouldn't lift weights, especially with the arms," they say. "It's bad for your game."

That statement is, quite simply, baloney. The golf swing is an athletic move that requires strength and flexibility. Even if you are over 40 and have never lifted weights in your life, a strength and flexibility program is available that can improve your golf game by increasing your muscle efficiency, elasticity, and stamina. That program, as I explain in this chapter, includes a combination of light weight lifting, resistance training, and stretching of every muscle group that you use in the golf swing.

Debunking the Myths about Arm Strength

Despite evidence and testimony from professional golfers of all shapes, sizes, ages, and genders extolling the virtues and benefits of strength training, a pervasive myth still exists among many amateurs that working out with weights, especially for the arms, somehow destroys your ability to swing a golf club. This myth lingers for several reasons:

- ✔ **Lifting weights tightens the muscles being exercised, so it has always been assumed that lifting weights with your arms hinders flexibility and feel in the muscles needed to turn and release the golf club.** Although the basic premise of this argument is true, the conclusion is flawed. Coupled with flexibility exercises, a strength program for the arms actually enhances the turn and release of the club. Trimming fat and toning the various muscle groups also enhances your ability to control your swing and to feel subtle changes in the motion of the swing needed to execute pitches, chips, and putts.

- ✔ **Golfers have long assumed that lifting weights builds large slow muscles that get in the way as you try to make a fluid turn.** This idea is nonsense. People who put forth this argument mistake strength training and bodybuilding. The two activities are separate and distinct, especially when it comes to golf. No one expects 45-year-old golfers to transform themselves into Mr. or Ms. Olympia, nor should they try. But that doesn't mean over-40 golfers shouldn't work out regularly to build strength and stamina in their arms.

- ✔ **Some golfers believe that one arm or side should be stronger than the other, and they believe that lifting weights may somehow upset that delicate balance.** This notion is also bunk. Both your left and right arms play equally important roles in the golf swing, and both need to be strengthened and stretched equally.

✔ **The final myth says that players who lift weights with their arms grip the club too tightly, which hinders the smooth release of the club through impact.** Again this belief is hooey. Someone who works out with weights is actually less likely to grip the club too tightly, because of the added strength in the arms.

Some truths about golfers who have incorporated strength training into their routines include the following:

✔ **They improve their distance off the tee by an average of 10 to 15 yards.** This idea only makes sense because stronger golfers can generate more clubhead speed.

✔ **They are more accurate.** Strength training, coupled with flexibility, allows the muscles to function more efficiently, which translates into greater control.

✔ **They are remarkably more consistent.** Stronger muscles are able to repeat the motions required in the golf swing more consistently than weaker muscles.

✔ **They have more stamina, because stronger, more efficient muscles don't tire as easily as weaker muscles.**

Establishing Rules for Over-40 Strength Training

In order to develop and maintain a successful strength program for your arms or any other part of your body, you need to establish some goals and guidelines for approaching the process. Golf-specific strength training should not only help you with your golf game, it should also improve your general health, and help you to avoid injury. With those objectives in mind, the following are some ground rules to observe before embarking on any strength-related program.

Take it slowly

It doesn't matter if you haven't worked out for a few years or if you've never worked out at all, you must enter this process very slowly. The purpose of strength conditioning is to get your body into better long-term shape for golf, not to build a perfect physical specimen in the matter of a few months. If you were to try to incorporate all the exercises in this book into one massive training session, you would be so sore and fatigued that you wouldn't be able to pull a golf club out of your bag, and swinging it would be completely out of the question.

The last thing you want to do is work yourself so hard in the opening days and weeks of your program that you can't hit balls or play golf. Doing so defeats the purpose of your workouts! Strength training is an imperceptibly gradual process. During your first few weeks, you may not complete all the repetitions of a single exercise. That's okay. As long as you make gradual progress each time you work out, you're making positive strides. One more repetition each time you exercise is enough.

Start all weight training on machines

Dumbbells, or free weights as one may refer to them, look easier to use because they're simple, but for a beginner, *weight machines* (stacked weights attached by cables and pulleys to specific exercise machines) are the way to go. These machines, designed for very specific exercises, put you in the right position to perform the exercises so that a particular muscle is isolated. Machines also balance the weight for you and provide a fluid motion with cables, bars, or chains connecting the weights. Companies like Nautilus, Cybex, Paramount, Life Fitness, and Reebok produce all sorts of these machines that focus on individual muscle groups. If you ever been in a gym you've seen plenty of them. Chest press machines, leg extension machines, overhead press machines, and biceps curl machines are just a few examples.

Don't be intimidated by the machines. They may look like looming monsters, but they're actually easier to use and much more efficient than free weights for those just beginning a strength training program. If you take your time and find out how to use the machines properly, you'll be in a much better position to progress to free weights later in your workout life. But even after you move on to free weights, never abandon machines entirely. Mixing in free weights with machine workouts allows you to develop different parts of a particular muscle and work on balancing the weight yourself. This also gives the body a constant challenge instead of becoming complacent with the same routine.

Lighter is better

This is strength training for *golf,* and you are over 40. It's not a weight-lifting contest, and you're not a teenager. Always work with lighter weights, and in the beginning stick to extremely light weights. Repetition and fluidity of motion are much more important than how much weight you lift. When it doubt, err on the side of lighter.

Start with one set and progress to three

In the beginning of your workout life, perform only one set of each exercise with enough repetitions in that set to fatigue the muscle. A good number for any lift is one set of 20 reps. For the first few weeks, you may want to try only 10 reps. The point is, you want to build your workout around one set of numerous reps with a light weight. Doing so increases strength and endurance in the muscles without injuring them or building tremendous bulk.

After several weeks, you can consider modifying your workout to include three sets of progressively fewer reps, adding more weight with each set and adding stretching exercises in between. For example, instead of one set of 20 reps, modify your program to start with 12 reps in the first set of an exercise, then add a rest period of 30 seconds, stretching the worked muscle. Then you can progress to another set of 10 reps with a slightly heavier weight, followed by another 30-second stretching interval. The third set can include eight reps with even heavier weight followed by stretching afterward.

Research by physicians, physiologists, and health experts has shown that this progressive sequence with intermediate stretching exercises between each set increases strength by as much as 20 percent. The program is not for beginners, but it is a goal you can ultimately work toward.

Never lift hurt

This process of building strength is not supposed to be painful. The objective is to make you a stronger, more efficient golfer. If you have an injury in a specific muscle or muscle group, you should never aggravate that injury by lifting weights or doing any strength training that isn't mandated as part of a rehabilitation program. Lifting while you're hurt does not help you. All it does is prolong your recovery process.

Always seek professional guidance before embarking on any strength-training endeavor. Every person has different strength-training needs, and designing one blanket program that fits everyone is impossible. A professional fitness trainer (one who specializes in golf-specific fitness is optimum) can start you out slowly, showing you the proper technique and giving you advice on weight, repetitions, and the speed at which you should try to progress. Strength training is no different than taking a golf lesson. You should seek out the guidance of experts before designing your personal strength training program.

Arming Yourself for Better Golf after 40

Strong arms make better golf swings. It's just that simple. Research has shown that golfers who regularly employ arm-related strength training in their routines have a lighter grip pressure, and make fewer hand- and arm-related mistakes during the swing than golfers who do not strengthen their arms on a regular basis. In this section, I explain three muscles in your arms and give you some simple exercises to strengthen and stretch those muscles that directly affect the golf swing.

Biceps

Many people falsely assume that the *biceps* (powerful muscle in the front of the upper arm) have very little impact on the golf swing. In fact, the biceps play a critical role in setting the club properly on the backswing. The left bicep is instrumental in putting the club on the correct swing plane (see Chapter 6) as the shoulders turn the club back, and the right bicep flexes and the right arm bends into a 90-degree angle at the elbow at the top of the backswing. Because of those roles, strengthening and stretching the biceps is critical to improving your game, especially as you grow older. The following exercises can help:

✔ **Machine curls:** The most common bicep exercise is called the curl, which is simply a contracting and extending of the biceps with weight providing resistance. On a machine, this exercise is self-explanatory. You sit down, designate the amount of weight you wish to lift (not too much!), and slowly go through your repetitions (see Figure 7-1). Keep in mind to insure correct posture and always contract the abdomen to support your back. Depending on your fitness level, begin with one set of 10 repetitions, increasing to a maximum of 20 repetitions over a two- to three-week period. Ultimately your goal is the 12-10-8 format mentioned earlier in this chapter. See the section, "Start with one set and progress to three" for details. Don't forget to stretch between sets.

Figure 7-1:
Kelly curling weight on a machine.

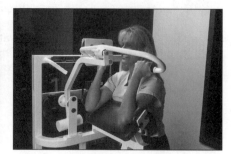

You'll find that curls not only work your biceps but also your forearms and wrists, as lifting the weight without using these muscles is impossible. However, do not fall into the *white knuckle syndrome.* This is where you grip the bar so tight your knuckles turn white. Curling with an open or lighter grip only reminds you to grip your club lighter as well. A lighter grip also means that your biceps are doing most of the work.

Strength training isn't a race! Just like all stretches, all lifts should be slow and steady in both directions. Despite what you may see during Olympic weight-lifting competitions, never jerk a weight up or drop it down after a lift. You're trying to exercise the muscle in both directions and the only way to do that is through slow, steady repetitions. A good rule is to lift the weight for two counts and lower for four counts.

✔ **Free weight curls:** After working out with the machine for a few weeks, you can mix some free weight curls into your program. You can do these curls from both standing and sitting positions, with several variations for each.

• From a sitting position, you can work one arm at a time, by resting your elbow on your thigh and curling the dumbbell up from an angle between your legs (see Figure 7-2). In doing this exercise, be sure to work both arms equally with the same amount of weight. Depending on your fitness level, begin with one set of 10 repetitions increasing to a maximum of 20 repetitions over a two- to three-week period. Ultimately your goal is the 12-10-8 format mentioned earlier in this chapter. Remember to stretch between sets.

Figure 7-2:
One-arm
curl from
seated
position.

- You can also curl free weights from a standing position (see Figure 7-3). Starting with the weights at your side you can work either one arm at a time or both together. The same principles apply. Be sure to work both arms equally and give equal time to stretching both arms. Depending on your fitness level, begin with one set of 10 repetitions increasing to a maximum of 20 repetitions over a two- to three-week period. Ultimately, you can work toward the 12-10-8 format mentioned earlier in the chapter. Always stretch between sets.

- A variation of the standing curl is called the *hammer curl.* In this exercise, the hands are rotated palms facing as the biceps contract and extend (see Figure 7-4).

Figure 7-3:
Standing
two-arm
straight curl.

Figure 7-4:
Standing
hammer
curls.

Letting your back and shoulders overtake your biceps in thrusting the weight up from this standing position is very easy. Always concentrate on the muscle group you are working and avoid letting larger muscles take over.

✔ **Bicep stretches:** This is one of the most difficult muscle groups to isolate in a stretch. In fact, the most effective way to stretch the biceps requires the assistance of a strap. In Figure 7-5, you can see Laura using something called a Golf Fitness Stretch Trainer, which is specifically designed to assist in these types of stretches, but a belt or even a towel will suffice.

To properly stretch the bicep, fully extend your arm with the palm up. Then, placing the band across your hand at the spot where you would grip a golf club, slowly and gently apply pressure, pulling the strap back and the hand down until you feel the stretch in your bicep. (You will also feel this stretch in your forearm.) Hold this stretch between 15 and 30 seconds for each arm.

Figure 7-5: Laura stretching biceps with Golf Fitness Stretch Trainer.

Triceps

The *triceps* (large muscles in the back of the upper arm) are also misunderstood in golf. Not only do the triceps support the lead arm during the backswing, they also play an instrumental role in generating clubhead speed on the downswing. Keeping these muscles strong and flexible is imperative. Consider these exercises:

✔ **Machine extensions for triceps:** Just like the bicep curls, the machine-based tricep extensions are pretty self-explanatory. You sit at the machine, bend your elbows upward, and place your palms on the hand grips. Then add the desired weight and slowly and steadily press downward, keeping the elbows close at your sides (see Figure 7-6). Depending on your fitness level, begin with one set of 10 repetitions increasing to a maximum of 20 repetitions over a two- to three-week period. Ultimately your goal is the 12-10-8 format mentioned earlier in the chapter. Remember to stretch between sets.

Figure 7-6:
Tricep
extensions
on the
machine.

Be aware of any twinges you feel in either elbow during this exercise. You shouldn't strain a joint in exercising your triceps, so be careful. If something hurts that shouldn't, stop immediately. Remember the white knuckle rule as well.

✔ **Free weight overhead extensions:** Sitting in an upright position, you can work the triceps with a single dumbbell simply by lifting the weight over your head with both hands holding one end of the dumbbell. Then slowly drop the weight behind your head, keeping your elbows tightly tucked next to your ears (see Figure 7-7). You finish the exercise by extending the weight back to its original position above your head. Depending on your fitness level, begin with one set of 10 repetitions, increasing to a maximum of 20 repetitions over a two- to three-week period. You want to work toward the 12-10-8 format mentioned earlier in the chapter. Be sure to stretch between sets.

✔ **Cross-tricep extensions:** Another free weight exercise that isolates one tricep muscle at a time is the cross-tricep extension. In this exercise, you lie on your back with one arm across your abdomen and the other arm fully extended and holding a dumbbell directly above your chest. Keeping your upper arm perfectly still, you bend the elbow, slowly bringing the weight across your chest to the opposite shoulder. With the elbow now pointing in the air, you reverse the process, straightening the arm and bringing the weight back up above your chest (see Figure 7-8).

Depending on your fitness level, begin with one set of 10 repetitions increasing to a maximum of 20 repetitions over a two- to three-week period. Ultimately your goal is the 12-10-8 format mentioned earlier in this chapter. Don't forget to stretch between sets and repeat this exercise with both arms.

Figures 7-7: Laura demonstrating overhead extensions.

Figure 7-8: Cross-tricep extensions.

✔ **Tricep stretches:** The tricep is another difficult muscle to isolate in a stretch, but not quite as tough as the bicep. Although there are unassisted tricep stretches that get the job done, the best stretch for this muscle is an assisted stretch (one which requires the aid of some device, such as a golf club, towel, belt, or a stretch training device). In Figure 7-9, Laura is using the Golf Fitness Stretch Trainer. In Figure 7-10, she is using a golf club. You can use a towel or a belt or any other device that allows you to assist in stretching this hard-to-reach muscle.

To accomplish this stretch, place the desired stretching device in one hand and hold one arm directly over your head, bending it at the elbow until your hand is behind your head. Move the opposite hand behind your back to grab the other end of the device. Slowly pulling with the lower arm, you'll find the tricep stretch in the upper arm. Rotate the hips forward while contracting the abdomen to support the low back and hold the stretch for 15 to 30 seconds on each side.

Figure 7-9: Laura stretching the tricep with the Golf Fitness Stretch Trainer.

Figure 7-10: Laura stretching the tricep with a club.

Forearms

The forearms have long been thought of as the harbingers of clubhead speed, where all the power is generated at impact and where all the secrets of golf ultimately lie. That's not totally accurate, but the forearms are vitally important to your swing. The next few exercises explain how you can make sure they are strengthened and stretched as you age:

- **Forearm curls:** Very few gyms have forearm curl machines, so this is one exercise where free weights are your only option. Fortunately, the exercise is simple. From a seated position place your forearms on your thighs so that your wrists extend off your knees. With weights in each hand — palms up — slowly and simply curl your wrists, keeping the rest of your body as still as possible (see Figure 7-11). Depending upon your fitness level, begin with one set of 10 repetitions increasing to a maximum of 20 repetitions over a two- to three-week period. Ultimately your goal is the 12-10-8 format mentioned earlier in this chapter. Don't forget to stretch between sets.

- **Wrist curls:** This exercise is the same as the forearm curl exercise, except for the placement of your hands (see Figure 7-12). This time, grip the weights with your palms down. You won't have as large a range of motion from the reverse side, but you are working a different muscle, so exercising an equal number of sets and reps, both palms up and palms down is important. Depending upon your fitness level, begin with one set of 10 repetitions increasing to a maximum of 20 repetitions over a two- to three-week period. Ultimately your goal is the 12-10-8 format mentioned earlier in the chapter. Remember to always stretch between sets.

Figures 7-11:
Forearm
curls.

Figure 7-12:
Wrist curls.

▶ **Forearm stretches:** To stretch the forearms, repeat the same exercise that you used to stretch the biceps. (See the section "Biceps" earlier in this chapter.) You'll feel the stretch in both your biceps and your forearms each time you perform this stretch. The only difference is the muscle group that you're concentrating on stretching. This stretch is also very difficult to find, but that doesn't mean that it isn't important. All stretches are important, especially after strength training. The forearms are no exception.

Strong arms must also be flexible arms. You should place equal importance on the strengthening and stretching components of all these exercises. No one exercise is more important than any other one.

Chapter 8

Saggy Shoulder Solutions

. . . .

. . . .

"I want to turn my shoulders as far as they will possibly go short of forcing my right knee to collapse or stiffen or my weight to move to the outside of the right foot, or my left heel to rise more than about an inch from the ground. Take it from me that a swing in which the shoulders turn through 90 degrees or more, even though the club falls short of horizontal at the top, will be a lot more powerful than a swing in which the club drops way below horizontal, but the left shoulder fails to turn past the ball on your backswing."

— Jack Nicklaus

Most golfers grossly overestimate their capabilities when it comes to the shoulder turn. (Check out Chapter 5 for more on the mechanics of the turn.) Because they don't regularly videotape themselves hitting balls, they believe they're turning their shoulders a full 90 degrees with occasional forays into the 100 and 110 degree range when, in fact, their shoulder turn is nowhere close to being that full.

Everybody would love to wind up with the same powerful backswing as Tiger Woods or the turn Nicklaus had in his heyday, but very few people have the physical makeup to achieve that degree of shoulder turn. You can certainly improve your shoulder turn (I give you some exercises later in this chapter to help with that), and you should definitely strengthen and stretch your shoulder muscles to enhance that turn and ward off possible injuries, but you also need to be realistic. Tiger and Jack are the best who ever played. You can certainly improve, but don't set your expectations too high.

Getting Your Shoulders into the Swing of Things

The shoulder is the Grand Central Station of the golf swing with cartilage and numerous muscles, tendons, and ligaments intersecting and fusing together around a universal ball-and-socket joint.

The bones of the shoulder joint are stabilized by a ring of cartilage surrounding the *glenoid* (the area where the end of the *scapula,* the socket, meets the head of the *humerus,* the ball). This cartilage is a cushion, like a strong sponge, that keeps the bones from rubbing against each other. The ligaments actually hold the bones together, and the tendons connect those bones to all the surrounding muscles. The biceps tendon, for example, attaches the biceps muscle to the shoulder and assists in stabilizing the joint.

The shoulder itself has four short muscles that originate on the scapula and pass around the shoulder joint. The tendons of those muscles fuse together to form what's known as the *rotator cuff.* Your rotator cuff provides lateral motion in your shoulder, allowing you to pass the salt across the kitchen table or reach across your chest to pick up the television remote.

The shoulder is a complex area of the body where a lot of activity is initiated. In the golf swing all the components of the shoulder fire at once. Different muscles in the shoulder work to turn the club back on the backswing, rotating the club open on the way back and then closed on the downswing. The shoulder lifts the club, releases the club at impact, and swings the club through on the follow-through. It supports a chain reaction of monumental proportion, and as such the shoulder needs to be in good health, have great strength, and be incredibly flexible.

Over-40 shoulders can certainly accomplish all the tasks needed to swing the golf club, but older bodies have some inherent problems that complicate the process. A couple of those problems include the following:

✔ That spongy cartilage that acts as a buffer between the *humerus* (the large bone of the upper arm) and the scapula can become worn or even chipped. This problem can result from a major injury, such as a sudden jolt in the shoulder region, but it more often develops because of simple repetitive wear and tear over the years. Constantly carrying heavy objects or throwing things too hard and too often are examples. The act of striking a golf ball causes a minor trauma to the shoulder area that, over time, can cause serious damage.

✔ Over-40 tendons are stiffer and harder than their younger counterparts, and muscles lose their elasticity and strength with age. This makes a complex joint like the shoulder susceptible to injury from seemingly routine activities. (See Chapter 14 for more on preventing common injuries in your shoulder and rotator cuff.)

Throughout most of 1998 and parts of 1999, 41-year-old British Open champion Tom Lehman struggled with his game when he injured his shoulder playing with his 5-year-old son. At the time Lehman thought his injury was no big deal, just a slight strain. After all, he was just rolling around on the floor with his son. He did that sort of thing all the time. Six months later, Lehman was still suffering the effects of a strained rotator cuff. It was a full 14 months before Lehman was back in form, even though the incident that initiated the problem seemed so minor that he completely dismissed it.

The best way to prevent injuries in the shoulder region and to keep that part of your body fit for golf is to develop strength and flexibility in the muscles and tendons that make up the shoulder. A good workout beats rehab every time. Don't fall victim to saggy shoulders that hinder your game.

Strengthening Exercises for Shoulders

One quick shoulder exercise isn't going to cut it when it comes to training your body for golf after the age of 40. These muscles are too important to your game, and this region of the body is too susceptible to injury for you to give a half-hearted effort. And because most gyms don't spend a great deal of money and space on machines to tone every small muscle in the shoulder area, in this section I outline a set of exercises to get you started on a shoulder-strengthening regimen.

Front shoulder raise

If you touch the front of your shoulder, you find what's known as the *anterior deltoid.* This muscle allows you to lift a glass of water off a table or to raise your hand to wave to a friend. The anterior deltoid muscle also sets the golf club on plane during the backswing and keeps it there after your swing changes directions.

You won't find many machines designed to strengthen this particular muscle, so dumbbells are your best option in an exercise called the *front shoulder raise.* Sitting on the edge of a bench or on an *exercise ball* (an oversized inflated ball recommended by many trainers for various exercises) as Laura is doing in Figure 8-1, hold the weights in both hands with your palms down and your arms straight but resting on your legs. Exhaling as you lift, slowly raise your arms, keeping them straight with slightly bent elbows, and bringing the weights to eye level directly in front of you. Without stopping or pausing, but also without rushing the motion, lower the weights back down until your arms are once again resting on your legs. Depending on your current fitness level, repeat this exercise 10 to 20 times without pausing.

This is a fluid motion, not jerky with different starts and stops. Your arms must remain straight at all times, and your back shouldn't arch in either direction. If you feel the need to thrust the dumbbells up, or if you have difficulty controlling the speed at which you bring them back down, choose lighter weights. This isn't a weight-lifting contest. The objective is to pick a weight you can control that provides some measure of resistance to the exercise without straining the muscle or injuring the joint.

Figure 8-1:
Laura on a workout ball doing the front shoulder raise.

 You should not feel any catches or hear any pops or cracks as you go through this or any of the shoulder exercises in this chapter. If you do feel or hear something abnormal, stop exercising immediately. Your shoulder could already have some minor damage and any further lifting could aggravate the problem. The pain you feel may seem minor, but you should consult an orthopedic specialist if you have any concerns about your shoulders. This area of your body is too vital to too many things to take any unnecessary chances.

Side lateral raise

 If you touch the outside of your shoulder, in the area between the biceps and triceps, you find what's known as the *posterior deltoid*. This muscle allows you to hold your arms out to your sides. If you make a wide sweeping motion with your arms, taking them over your head and returning them to your sides, you can feel the range of motion the posterior deltoid controls. This muscle is crucial to your turn back and through the golf swing. The posterior deltoid muscle also absorbs the brunt of trauma at impact, as slight as that may be. Keeping this muscle strong is critical to your long-term success as an over-40 golfer.

If you can master the front shoulder raise without much trouble, the strength training drill for the posterior deltoid — the *side lateral raise* — should be a piece of cake. Sitting on your bench or ball with dumbbells in both hands, rest your arms at your sides with your palms facing your body. Exhaling as you lift, slowly raise your arms out to your sides, bending your elbows without arching your back. Then, without rushing or pausing, slowly lower your arms back to your sides. Depending on your current fitness level, repeat this exercise 10 to 20 times without pausing (see Figure 8-2).

Figure 8-2:
Laura on ball working side lateral raise.

The posterior deltoid may not be as strong as the anterior deltoid or it may be stronger, so you may have to change the amount of weight you use when you change exercises. Doing so is much better than struggling through a lift with bad form just because you're too lazy or have too much pride to go down a few pounds in the weights you lift. Strength training is a lot like the golf swing: You can get away with bad form in the short run, but in the end it will always come back to bite you.

Overhead presses

The one machine exercise for the shoulders that is universal to most gyms involves the overhead or military press machine. Like most machine lifts, this one is pretty self-explanatory. Sitting on the provided bench and gripping the handles, you lift the weight by slowly straightening your arms directly over your head, then slowly lowering your arms back down to the ready position. Depending on your current fitness level, repeat this exercise 10 to 20 times without pausing (see Figure 8-3).

TOUR TALK

The Shark's story

Greg Norman dismissed the pain he was feeling. An avid — some would say obsessed — fitness fanatic, Norman was 43 years old in 1998 when he first noticed a twinge in his left shoulder. He didn't consider it any big deal. After all, he hit 500 golf balls a day, lifted weights, stretched, biked, fished, and generally maintained a lifestyle that personified active and healthy. Norman assumed the catches he felt were nothing more than age pains, the natural aches that a 43-year-old felt when he engaged in those kinds of activities.

Boy, was he wrong. By the time Greg missed the cut at the Masters and jetted back to Florida, he knew there was a serious problem. His doctor knew it too. A small tear in his rotator cuff had become aggravated; it enlarged when Greg ignored the pain and continued his regular workout and ball-striking regimen. The subsequent surgery sidelined Norman for six months and could have easily ended his playing career altogether. Had he caught the problem earlier, surgery would have probably still been his only course of action, but it wouldn't have been nearly as severe, and the rehabilitation process would have been much easier.

The lesson of Greg Norman is a simple one: Don't mess around with pain in the shoulders. Check it out early and often. You'll be glad you did.

WARNING!

You should practice this exercise only on balanced lifting machines. Attempting to balance free weights over your head in this manner can result in serious injury.

Figure 8-3:
Laura at an overhead press machine.

Stretching: The Key to Keeping Shoulders Strong

I recommend following all lifting exercises with long, deep stretches that slowly extend the muscles that you've just trained. The purpose of stretching immediately following a lift is to reduce the amount of lactic acid, which causes soreness in the muscles and to increase muscular recovery. The shoulder muscles are no different. You should stretch your shoulders every time that you strengthen them.

But you should also stretch your shoulders *before* every round of golf, every practice session — you even need to stretch before taking your first practice swing. The shoulders are too valuable to your golf game (and your everyday life) to risk injury. Warming them up with a few good stretches before any demanding activity, such as golf simply makes good sense.

The following are some easy stretches you can do to strengthen all the shoulder muscles mentioned in this chapter.

Shoulder/chest stretch

A good stretch for all the muscles in your shoulders and chest is the *chest/shoulder stretch.* For this stretch, you need a towel, a belt, a Golf Fitness Stretch Trainer (a professionally designed strap that assists in stretching), or any other article that can be easily held behind your back. Holding your towel or belt behind your back in both hands, slowly extend the arms backward, until you feel the stretch in the anterior deltoids (in the front of your shoulder) and chest muscles (see Figure 8-4). Hold the stretch for 15 to 30 seconds without bouncing or jerking. You probably won't have a big range of motion with this stretch in the beginning, which is fine. The purpose is to slowly stretch the muscles over a long period of time. As you progress in your golf fitness, you will find this stretch becomes easier and fuller.

What you don't want to do is slump forward or bend at the waist in an attempt to get the arms higher. Doing so defeats the purpose. As long as you feel the stretch in your shoulders, you're gaining positive benefits from the motion.

You can also use a golf club (see Figure 8-5) for this stretch, which is a great warm-up drill before a round, and a good habit to get into if you're standing around waiting while on the course.

Figure 8-4: Laura stretching the shoulders with the Golf Fitness Stretch Trainer.

Figure 8-5: Laura stretching the shoulders with a golf club.

Shoulder rotation stretch

A golf club is also what I recommend using for one of the best rotator cuff and posterior deltoid stretches. In the *shoulder rotation stretch,* simply hold the golf club directly in front of you with your left hand on the hosel (or clubhead) and your right hand on the grip, then slowly rotate the club, lowering the clubhead down toward your navel while crossing the grip across your torso (see Figure 8-6). You'll feel this stretch in the rotator cuff. Hold for 15 to 30 seconds and repeat to the opposite side.

This stretch is great for pre-round warm-ups as well as post-workout cool-downs.

Figure 8-6:
Laura using a golf club to do the shoulder rotation stretch.

Perform all stretches slowly and steadily, especially rotation stretches, where the shoulder is concerned. You need to do shoulder stretches with a particularly slow emphasis. Rushing this kind of stretch can lead to disastrous consequences. No matter how late you are to the first tee, never, ever sling the shoulders around in a stretching motion. If you do, you may be sidelined longer than you know.

The shoulders are complicated and critical, one of the most important muscle groups in all of golf and also one of the most sensitive. Work them hard, but work them with care.

Chapter 9

Getting Rid of Junk in the Trunk

"It always seemed logical for me to work on my abs and back to insure that I had a good strong body. That's what turns in golf. I've never understood how other players don't recognize that. I see so many people let their tummies get away from them and then all of a sudden they wonder why they're having back problems. It's simple. You can't let yourself go, especially as you get older and expect everything to continue working like it always has. If you don't work at staying fit something is eventually going to break."

— Laura Baugh

Through all the talk about shoulder turns, swing planes, hip rotation, X Factors, and clubhead release through impact, one principle underlines every fundamental in golf: Nothing is possible without a strong and flexible torso.

The *torso* (made up of the muscles in your chest, sides, abdomen, and back) is the center of all action in the golf swing. It is the axis on which the shoulders and arms turn, and therefore, the foundation on which all other action and reaction in the golf swing is built. You can't turn your shoulders, for example, without twisting the torso. The same principle applies to hip rotation. Without full use of the torso, the hips can't provide resistance on the backswing or create any clubhead speed when initiating the downswing. Strong shoulders, flexible biceps, and a good concept of swing plane (see Chapter 6) will be of no use if your torso is weak, injured, or inflexible.

Signs of a weak and inflexible torso in golf include the following:

✔ Picking the club straight up with the hands on the backswing and making a desperate stab on the downswing

✔ Falling away from the shot in an off-balance tap dance after impact. You've seen this move. Rather than finishing the swing in balance with all the momentum of the swing moving toward the intended target, the golfer falls backward away from the intended line of the shot.

You've all seen golfers who suffer from these afflictions. They do their best to grip the club around their expansive midsections before picking the club straight up to make a weak throw at the ball. Their shoulders never turn, their hips never drive, their lower body never initiates anything, and their swing planes look like sonic waves. They finish their swings, not in a strong upright position, but off balance and falling away from the target, with their feet shuffling to keep them upright.

Many people marvel at just how bad this kind of golf swing looks, but the golfers who swing this way have no choice. Their torsos are so weak and inflexible that they must swing the club using muscles ill-equipped for such a task. It's like trying to throw a ball without using your shoulder, or kicking something without using your hip. You can still do it, just not very well.

Understanding the Torso's Role in the Golf Swing

The torso or trunk is made up of many different muscle groups that do many different things during the golf swing.

✔ The upper, side, and lower abdominal muscles stabilize the torso during the setup and provide support for the back. They also connect the hips with the upper body and stretch as the shoulders turn.

Weak abdominal muscles lead to poor posture, a compromised turn, no midsection support for the downswing, reduced clubhead speed, and a back that is susceptible to injury.

✔ The back itself has several functions with the lower or *lumbar* back bracing the hips as the shoulders turn. Farther up the back, the *latissimus dorsi* (or lat muscle as it's informally called), helps initiate the shoulder turn on the backswing. The *trapezius muscle,* which runs from the tops of the shoulders to the spine, supports the upper back and provides stability to the turning shoulders.

✔ The *external oblique muscles* located on your sides where love handles tend to appear, are stretched in both directions during the backswing and downswing, and the *pectoralis major* — the chest muscle — pulls the arms close together at address, keeping the arms on plane throughout the swing while balancing the muscles of the upper back.

Tuning up Your Torso

Just as many golfers used to believe that lifting weights with the arms somehow destroyed all feel and flexibility in that part of your body (see Chapter 7), many golfers are still skittish about developing their chest, back, and abdominal muscles. They think that by making this part of the body stronger, they will somehow inhibit or destroy their golf swing. This kind of thinking is backward and destructive.

As players such as Greg Norman, Larry Nelson, Tom Watson, and Hale Irwin have clearly demonstrated, strength and muscular development in the chest, back, and abdominal regions not only doesn't hurt your game, it makes you longer, stronger, more accurate, and much less prone to injuries.

Coupled with stretching exercises (which I get to later in this chapter) to enhance and expand your ability to rotate during the golf swing, coordinated strength training drills for your chest, back, and midsection can improve your body and your golf game in the following ways:

- ✔ **Improving your posture.** Strong trunks don't slump, and as you develop strength in your torso you'll find the proper setup is much easier and much less stressful on your over-40 joints.

- ✔ **Making your swing more efficient.** Turning your shoulders around a strong torso is much easier than trying to manipulate the club with your hands and arms because of a weakness in some area.

- ✔ **Eliminating pressure from your back.** Strong abdominals and back muscles allow you to put the spine in a neutral position (no curvatures or contortions in your backbone), which eliminates stress from the vertebrae and cuts down on potential injuries.

- ✔ **Increasing your clubhead speed and distance.** Stronger trapezius and latissimus dorsi muscles rotate the club through impact faster than weaker trunk muscles.

Be just as diligent in strengthening your torso as you are in any other aspect of physical training or any practice you devote to your golf game. A few minutes in the gym working on your trunk can mean as much to your over-40 game as an hour on the range, so take the following exercises seriously. Strengthening your trunk enhances your game exponentially.

Strengthening your chest

A strong chest draws the arms closer together at address and keeps the relationship between the arms consistent throughout the swing, a fundamental that most instructors maintain is critical to generating maximum speed and consistency. The pecs also provide critical balance to the muscles in the upper back that must be strong and active in the swing. A strong chest keeps a strong back properly balanced and allows for all the muscles in the torso to work as a coordinated unit during the swing.

The following exercises allow you to strengthen your chest without fear of becoming stiff or muscle-bound.

✔ **Chest press:** Gyms always have at least one machine devoted to the chest, but golfers who want to develop these muscles need to seek out a particular machine known as an *upright chest press*. This machine is structured so that you sit upright with your back against a backrest, and the grips are directly in front of your chest. Adding a nominal amount of weight, push the handles away from your body until your arms are straight, then slowly return to the start position (see Figure 9-1). Depending on your current fitness level, repeat this exercise 10 to 20 times without pausing.

Figure 9-1:
Laura at the chest press machine.

Many chest press machines are built differently. Some have you lying on your back and pushing the weight upward. That's not the best technique for golfers simply because of the added pressure this lift places on the shoulders. The upright chest press works solely on the *pectoralis majors,* so stick to the upright machines for this exercise.

✔ **Flat chest press:** For a free-weight chest exercise, try the *flat chest press,* a simple lift using light to medium dumbbells and a bench or exercise ball (see Chapter 8). Lying on the ball, hold the dumbbells directly above your head with your palms facing one another. Slowly and symmetrically, lower the weights down and to your sides until your elbows and forearms form 90-degree angles (see Figure 9-2). This combination of moving the weights out and down simultaneously forces the pectoralis major to control and balance the weight while the muscle is contracting. This is a great exercise for development of the chest region.

The flat chest press is one of the few lifts where a continuous motion from start to finish isn't necessary. After you move the dumbbells to the down position with the arms at 90-degree angles, hold the weights in that position for a few seconds before slowly straightening the arms back over your head. You'll feel the sensation of this lift throughout the entire chest. Depending upon your current fitness level, repeat this exercise 10 to 20 times.

Figure 9-2:
Laura on an exercise ball doing a flat chest press.

✔ **Push-ups:** If you aren't in a gym and you don't have dumbbells, you can still strengthen your chest with one of the most basic, exercises of them all: the good old-fashioned push-up. You have a couple different ways to perform this exercise depending on your arm and chest strength.

- The first way is designed for those golfers who aren't as strong in the chest and arms as they once were, or for those just starting their workout programs. You start from a kneeling position with your hands and knees on the floor. Then extend your arms fully and, crossing your ankles, pick your feet off the floor by bending your knees. Now walk your upper body outward with your hands until your back is completely straight. From this position, slowly lower your body toward the floor by bending your arms at the elbows. Without lying your torso fully onto the floor, try lowering your torso until your arms form a right angle before pressing upward and fully extending the arms (see Figure 9-3). Be careful not to lock your elbows when pressing upward. Depending on your current fitness level, repeat this exercise 10 to 20 times without pausing.

- The second and more difficult way to perform this exercise requires you to fully extend your body onto the floor, keeping your legs and back as straight as possible (see Figure 9-4). With your toes firmly on the floor and your hands beside your chest, lower your torso until your arms form a right angle before pressing upward and fully extending the arms. Be careful not to lock the elbows when pressing upward. Depending on your current fitness level, repeat this exercise 10 to 20 times without pausing.

Figure 9-3:
Laura performing a push-up from her knees.

Figure 9-4:
Laura performing a push-up from her toes.

 You can isolate various parts of the chest muscle and control the degree of difficulty of your push-ups by varying your hand positions. Hands closer together focuses the exercise toward the *sternum* (or breastbone) and increases the level of difficulty. The farther away from the body the hands are, the easier the push-up will be as the exercise works more of the entire chest.

 None of the exercises that I describe should hurt your elbows, wrists or shoulders. If you feel any twinge of pain in these joints, stop immediately. These lifts are designed for your chest. Any joint pain may be a sign of a more serious problem and should be examined by a doctor.

Building up your back

A fully developed (taut but flexible) upper, middle, and lower back can carry you a long way in golf. In addition to reducing your chances of injury, back strength is essential in generating clubhead speed and getting the most out of the effort you put into your swing. To get the most out of your back exercises, think of the back as three separate regions:

✔ **The upper back.** Consisting primarily of the trapezius and *sub-scapula,* this region rotates with the shoulders and is the axis on which all upper body turning is based.

✔ **The middle back or latissimus dorsi.** The transition region of the back between the turning upper body and the steady lower body.

✔ **The lower back or lumbar region.** This area absorbs a great deal of pressure from address through impact and follow-through.

Each of these regions has specific needs. In the next few sections, I recommend some strengthening exercises that work each region to give you a maximum golf benefit.

Upper back

Rub your hand across your shoulder and down your back to your shoulder blade, and you can feel the primary muscles of the upper back. These muscles help set the club on the backswing by assisting in the turn. They are also instrumental in generating clubhead speed on the downswing by uncoiling the upper body. The following are a few exercises to help strengthen this critical muscle group:

✔ **Upright rows:** While standing with dumbbells in each hand (palms facing the body), slowly lift the weights straight up toward your chin as if a bar or tether were connecting the dumbbells. To do this exercise properly, keep your elbows out and your hips tucked under slightly to support your low back (see Figure 9-5). Then slowly lower the dumbbells until your arms are straight down, keeping your elbows slightly bent. Depending on your current fitness level, repeat this exercise 10 to 20 times without pausing.

Figure 9-5:
Laura doing upright rows with dumbbells.

Pops or catches in the shoulders are bad signs. If you feel anything painful or unnatural in the joint, stop immediately.

✔ **Shoulder shrugs:** While standing with your arms hanging at your sides holding dumbbells, slowly raise your shoulders. Draw your shoulder blades close together and move in a seamless circular motion as though you were drawing the letter C backwards (see Figure 9-6). Depending on your current fitness level, repeat this exercise 10 to 20 times without pausing.

Figure 9-6:
Laura doing the shoulder shrug.

✔ **Lateral pulldowns:** A machine exercise where, from a seated position, you hold the handles above your head with your palms facing away from you. Pull downward, keeping your head as still as possible. Using your *sub-scapula muscles* (lateral muscles located in the center of your back), slowly pull the weight until your hands reach your shoulders. Then slowly extend the arms upward, returning to the original start position (see Figure 9-7). Do this exercise pulling the bar in front of your face to chest level. You can also increase the intensity of this lift by altering your hand position on the bar, moving your hands closer together or farther apart according to how you feel. Depending on your current fitness level, repeat this exercise 10 to 20 times without pausing.

If you find you must drop your head or roll your back to perform this exercise, you're trying to lift too much weight. Form and fluidity are the keys to gaining maximum benefit from this exercise.

Figure 9-7:
Laura doing
lateral
pulldowns.

Middle back

The next set of exercises strengthens and tones the latissimus dorsi, which is the large muscle in the center of your back below your shoulder blades. The lat is sometimes called the swimmer's muscle because it is so well developed in championship swimmers. The lat is also the first upper body muscle that must change direction when the lower body initiates the downswing. Although most over-40 golfers may never achieve the development of an Olympic swimmer, strengthening the middle back is critical for your health and for your golf game. Consider the following exercises:

✔ **Seated mid row:** This machine lift is one of the best middle back strengthening exercises you can find and one definitely worth incorporating into your normal workout routine. Sitting down with your chest against the upright pad, you do this exercise by holding the grips in front of you and pulling the weight directly toward you, keeping your elbows low to your sides and your back still and straight. Without stopping or pausing, slowly return the weight by extending your arms back to the start position (see Figure 9-8). Depending on your current fitness level, repeat this exercise 10 to 20 times without pausing.

Figure 9-8:
Laura doing
a seated
mid row.

✔ **Rowing:** If your gym has a rowing machine (see Figure 9-9), I recommend using it for a number of reasons. In addition to being a great cardiovascular workout, rowing with resistance develops middle back and leg strength, both of which are critical to good golf. Rowing is one of the most highly recommended strength and conditioning exercises that you can add to your workout program. A good 20 minutes on the rowing machine can do wonders for your back and your heart.

Figure 9-9: Kelly on a rowing machine.

Lower back

It isn't a universal rule that all over-40 golfers have lower back problems; it just seems that way. A disproportionate percentage of over-40 golfers suffer some ailment of the lower back. These ailments can range from fatigue and an occasional twinge, to more serious compression and nerve problems in the lumbar region. The list of pro golfers regularly treated for lower back problems is long and distinguished, and includes such notables as Fred Couples, Davis Love, Ernie Els, Greg Norman, and Larry Mize.

The pros hit hundreds of balls a day and put enormous pressure on their lower backs. Some of their problems are unavoidable, but you don't have to suffer that same fate. Most of the lower back problems amateur golfers face result from poor posture and a lack of strength and conditioning in the lower back. You can cure both those faults. The following are some exercises to help you strengthen the most frequently injured area of the body for golfers.

✔ **Back extensions:** Sitting on the horizontal bench, place the center of your back on the back pad. Then, keeping your back straight and bending at the hip, contract your abdomen and lean backward, slowly lifting the weight in one smooth motion until your body is fully extended (see Figure 9-10). Without pausing, reverse directions, returning to the start position in an equally slow and smooth motion. Depending on your current fitness level, repeat this exercise 10 to 20 times without pausing.

WARNING!

This low back extension is an excellent strengthener for the lower back region. It is also a disaster waiting to happen if you try to lift too much weight, lift too quickly, or try to perform too many repetitions. I certainly recommend adding this lift to your workout, but do so with extreme care. You can easily injure the area you want to strengthen.

Figure 9-10:
Laura
doing back
extensions.

✔ **Low prone lifts:** For a no-frills lower back exercise that isn't likely to cause you any problems or worries, lie flat on your stomach with your legs fully extended, and slowly raise your legs, keeping your hips and upper body firmly on the ground (see Figure 9-11). You can hold this lift for several seconds, then slowly return your legs to the ground. Depending on your current fitness level, repeat this exercise 10 to 20 times without pausing.

Figure 9-11:
Laura
engaging in
low prone
lifts.

WARNING!

None of these exercises should hurt. If you feel any pain or discomfort in your lower back, stop lifting immediately and consult a physician. The possible problems in the lower back are many and varied, and you don't need to take any unnecessary chances.

Energizing your abdominals

When you think of athletes with washboard abs, golfers aren't the first people who come to mind, and for good reason: Many golfers look pudgy. But today's golfers, especially those over-40 trying to extend their playing careers, understand how imperative keeping the abs strong and flexible is. In addition to insuring good posture throughout the swing, the abs are the balancing muscle group to the lower back, which means that they are as instrumental in preventing injury as any muscle group in the body.

As a Hall of Fame athlete and full-time mom, Nancy Lopez was looking for ways to extend her winning career after her 40th birthday. Like many LPGA professionals, Nancy hired a personal trainer to develop a health and fitness program that suited her body and her game. One of the first areas her trainer focused on was the abdominal region. Nancy started on a healthy regimen of sit-ups, crunches, and ab stretches to strengthen her midsection and protect her lower back. "At one point I was doing 700 sit-ups a day," Lopez said.

The regimen worked. Now in her twenty-third season as a professional, Nancy is still one of the most competitive players in women's golf.

And by doing the same kind of exercises Nancy did, you can keep your abdominals fit (and improve your golf game) long after the age of 40. For example, try the following:

- ✓ **Crunches for strength:** The most common exercise for the abdominal region is the crunch. A few years ago the crunch replaced the full sit-up as the exercise of choice for most athletes simply because the crunch isolates the abdominal muscle group without jeopardizing the back. The crunch is also an easy exercise to perform. Simply lie on your back with your knees bent so that your feet are flat on the ground. With your hands behind your head, crunch your torso by lifting your shoulders off the ground and pulling your chest toward your thighs. Do this while keeping your neck completely straight, your feet firmly on the ground and lifting your chin toward the ceiling (see Figure 9-12). After several repetitions, you'll feel this exercise in the upper and middle abdominal region. Depending on your current fitness level, repeat this exercise 10 to 20 times without pausing.

- ✓ **Side obliques:** Although crunches are great for the upper and middle abdominals, they do little for the obliques, a hard-to-reach muscle group that runs along your side just above your belt. To strengthen this muscle, a modified (or side) crunch is required. Lying on your back with your knees up as if preparing for regular crunches, drop both knees to one side, keeping your shoulders and torso steady. Then, with the knees firmly to one side, lift your torso upward (see Figure 9-13). This move is very small, but one you can instantly feel in your obliques. Depending on your current fitness level, repeat this exercise 10 to 20 times without pausing. Do the same for the opposite side.

Figure 9-12: Laura doing crunches.

Figure 9-13: Laura doing side obliques.

✔ **Lower ab lifts:** The lower abdominal, the muscle group between your groin and your navel, is the toughest midsection muscle to reach. As such, the best exercise to strengthen this muscle is the lower ab lift. This exercise is like a crunch in reverse. Lying on your back in the crunch position with your arms at your sides, lift your hips off the ground, keeping your shoulders and feet firmly planted (see Figure 9-14). After several repetitions you'll feel this exercise in the hard to reach muscle below your belt. Depending on your current fitness level, repeat this exercise 10 to 20 times without pausing.

Figure 9-14: Laura doing lower ab lifts.

✔ **Ab stabilizers:** To bring all the midsection muscles together for the stabilizing strength needed to effectively complete 18 holes of golf, try an exercise called the ab stabilizer. While sitting down with your knees pulled up and your arms crossed in front of you, slowly lean back until you feel tautness in your abs, keeping your torso straight and balanced (see Figure 9-15). Hold your body in that position for few seconds, then bring yourself back to the start position and depending upon your current fitness level, repeat this exercise 10 to 20 times. If you reach the 20 repetition maximum and feel as though you can do more, simply increase your hold time while contracting the abdomen. You'll feel this exercise throughout your torso as all the muscles in your midsection work to keep your body stabilized.

Figure 9-15:
Laura
doing ab
stabilizers.

Staying Limber through Stretching

After every strengthening exercise, you need to stretch the area you just worked. But you should also stretch your torso before a round of golf in order to keep the muscles loose and warm before calling on them to execute golf shots. The following are some on-course and off-course stretches for the torso that can keep you limber and ready to play.

The back

Just as the muscles in your back are sometimes hard to identify when you're lifting, they're equally hard to stretch. But you have to try. Nothing prepares you for golf like a few good back stretches, such as:

✔ **Cat stretch:** The simplest stretch for the back is the cat stretch. With a Golf Fitness Stretch Trainer (a professionally designed stretching aid), a strap, belt, or towel for assistance, stand with your feet together and bend at the waist until your legs and torso form a 90-degree angle. Holding both ends of the Stretch Trainer with the center portion of the strap under your feet, arch your back as high as you can, simulating a mad cat. Pull on the strap for resistance as you round and stretch the upper and middle muscles of the back (see Figure 9-16). Hold this stretch for 15 to 30 seconds.

Figure 9-16:
Laura doing
the cat
stretch.

You can practice a slight variation of this stretch on the course prior to a round. Simply hold a golf club across your knees and focus on rounding your back upward as far as possible (see Figure 9-17).

Figure 9-17:
Laura doing
the cat
stretch with
a club.

✔ **Low trunk stretch:** This stretch requires the assistance of a Golf Fitness Stretch Trainer or similar strap. Lying flat on your back with your legs straight, place the strap beneath the arch of one foot, pulling the leg completely upright with the ends of the strap. Extend the opposite leg downward. Hold both ends of the strap in the opposite hand of the leg that is lifted. (If your right leg is in the air, hold the ends of the strap in your left hand and vice versa.) Extend the other arm away from your body. Then slowly rotate the raised leg across the extended leg as far as possible without your shoulders leaving the floor (see Figure 9-18). After you reach the maximum stretch point, turn your head in the opposite direction of the leg until you're facing the arm extended on the floor. Hold for 15 to 30 seconds and repeat with the opposite leg. This stretch does wonders for your lower back, but be careful: Extending too far in this stretch can cause damage to the sciatic nerve in the lower back. If you feel any pain or discomfort while doing this stretch, stop immediately. A good rule of measure is to drop the right leg across the body to a 10 o'clock position and the left leg to a 2 o'clock position.

This is perhaps the best lower trunk stretch any golfer can practice. You should work this one into your regular daily routine.

Figure 9-18: Laura doing a low trunk stretch.

✔ **Lower back stretch:** To stretch those hard-to-reach muscles in the lower lumbar region, once again lie on your back with your knees up and your feet flat. Then wrap the Stretch Trainer around your hamstring and pull your leg as close to your chest as possible without lifting the other foot, hip, or your shoulders off the floor (see Figure 9-19). Finding this stretch may take a few seconds, but after you do hold it for 15 to 30 seconds with each leg.

Figures 9-19: Laura doing a lower back stretch.

The midsection

You may not normally think of your abs as an area that needs stretching, but after a good workout you will find that nothing feels better than a good abdominal stretch. Consider the following choices:

✔ **Abdominal stretch:** You can stretch your upper, middle, and lower abdominal muscles with one simple exercise. Lying flat on your front side with your leg fully extended, bring your hands to your sides as if you were preparing for a push-up. Slowly straighten your arms and push your chest and head upward, but keep your hips firmly on the ground (see Figure 9-20). You can feel this stretch throughout the abdominal region. To intensify the stretch, tilt your head back and look to the sky. Hold this stretch for 15 to 30 seconds. You'll feel better for the rest of the day.

Figure 9-20:
Laura doing the abdominal stretch.

✔ **Lateral oblique stretch:** It may have been a tough muscle to find in the crunch exercise (See the section "Energizing the abdominals" earlier in this chapter), but stretching the lateral oblique is easy and it feels great. You can perform this stretch anywhere, and especially before every round. Simply hold a club over your head with your left hand on the hosel (clubhead) and your right hand near the grip. Then, with your feet shoulder-width apart and your knees slightly flexed, lean your torso to one side, keeping your head between your extended arms throughout. After you lean as far as you can (and stretch the lateral oblique for a full 30 seconds) slowly straighten up and repeat this action on the other side (see Figure 9-21).

When you hit 40 and gravity begins its mischief on your torso, your golf game will suffer if you don't stem the tide. The exercises in this chapter can set you on your way to better golf as you age. Plus, you'll feel better than you have in 20 years.

Figure 9-21:
Laura doing
a lateral
oblique
stretch.

Chapter 10

Developing Strong Roots: Lower Body Strength

"Jack Nicklaus was the first player to really overpower golf courses with his length. He had tremendously strong legs and hit the ball long and high. At the time he came out, nobody else could do that."

— Ken Venturi

The importance of the lower body in golf is absolutely unquestionable. It is the firm foundation on which the swing is developed, and the initiator of power and speed in the downswing (see Chapter 6). A coiling effect is created by turning the shoulders around a sturdy base (see Chapter 5). These fundamentals are the root of golf. You can't overemphasize the importance of the lower body in every aspect of the swing.

Most professionals who were playing in the 1960s and 1970s agree with Venturi's statement that Jack Nicklaus had the strongest lower body in golf and that his powerful legs were one of the factors that made him such an imposing force. When this fact became apparent, golfers around the world began working to strengthen and stretch their lower bodies to gain a Nicklaus-type advantage.

One of the first things I do with my Senior Tour clients is measure their lower body strength and flexibility. Most clients are shocked by how stiff they have become and how much strength they have lost with age. I tell them that these changes are common. The loss of strength and flexibility in the lower body is so subtle that most golfers don't realize it's happening.

But its effects on the golf game are dramatic. Loss of lower body strength and flexibility creates reduced distance and accuracy as swing planes change and you call upon your upper body to do more than it should. Clubhead speed diminishes as the legs lose their spring and the hands and arms take over. I put more than 90 percent of my clients on some form of strength and flexibility program for the lower body to stop these problems. The exercises and stretches that I explain in this chapter can help you incorporate similar workouts into your routine as well.

Working the Lower Body in Your Golf Swing

At address, the hips, thighs, hamstrings, calf muscles, and ankle flexors, along with all the ligaments and tendons below the waist, combine to provide a solid base on which the rest of the golf swing can develop. The *gluteus* muscles (your buttocks) help position the body as the torso tilts at the *hip girdle* (the area of the hip that bends), while the hamstrings allow the knees to flex and the body's weight to be positioned for a strong athletic move. See Chapter 5 for more details on the lower body's role through the swing.) The calf muscles keep the body sturdy and ready for the action of the golf swing.

After you initiate the *takeaway* (or backswing), the hips and legs go to work. You place tension on your hip flexor as you turn your shoulders around a relatively steady lower body. At that point, your quadriceps and hamstrings are taut as the momentum of the backswing shifts your body's weight to the back foot, and the calf muscles are actively keeping you in balance, properly centered with the feet active.

At the top of the backswing, your lower body is called into action, as the *hip flexors, abductors,* and *adductors* explode into the shot, rotating and shifting, pulling the upper body into the downswing and moving the club along the *swing plane* toward the ball (see Chapter 6). The calf muscles also drive your legs through the shot, initiating the push off the back foot and absorbing the weight shift in your front leg. As shown in Figure 10-1, this action continues into the follow-through where your left leg acts as a brace on which the entire body turns. The hips, thighs, and lower legs are all active as the club continues on plane after the ball is well on its way toward the target.

Figure 10-1:
The lower body swing sequence.

The will to play

There are those who try to discount the importance of the lower body by pointing to trick-shot artists who dazzle crowds by hitting balls while sitting on stools or kneeling on their knees, but these gimmicks are just that: circus stunts that have no bearing on the reality of your golf game. Even the most famous trick-shot artists would agree that the lower body is crucial to consistently good play.

One of golf's most heartwarming stories is that of trick-shot artist and motivational speaker Dennis Walters. Walters was a burgeoning amateur with a bright future that seemed to be shattered by a devastating car accident in 1975. "I loved golf and dreamed about playing professional golf for a living," Walters says. "But 25 years ago I was in an accident and I became paralyzed from the waist down. I can't use my legs and can't feel my legs. There are a lot of other things I can't do as well, but one thing I knew that I would always do was play golf."

Soon after his accident, Walters wheeled himself out to the driving range where he starting taking swings. At first he wasn't very successful. He whiffed a few shots, topped others. But soon he was able to make consistent contact. A friend of Walters' was inspired by his dedication and designed a swivel seat for a golf cart so that Dennis could wheel himself into position to hit shots. "25 years later, I still love golf, and I'm still playing," he says.

Walters is able to hit balls off enlarged tees, and hit shots with goofy golf clubs, including one with several swiveling universal joints in the shaft. But what he isn't able to do, and what he knows he will never be able to do, is play top-notch competitive golf again. His swing, although great for a man in a wheelchair, can't create the clubhead speed needed to compete professionally. He is certainly among the best paraplegic golfers in the world, a testament to his will and determination, but even Dennis admits that a strong and active lower body is a crucial component in championship-caliber golf.

Strengthening the Lower Body

You can do a number of strengthening drills to help you develop your lower body in a way that enhances your setup, your backswing, and the movement of your lower body through the downswing. Because the muscles below the waist are the largest in the body, you can likely lift more weight when going through the exercises in this chapter. But don't overdo it. Fitness is not a footrace. Take your time and work at a pace that works for you. Your body is a great machine — listen to it.

Leg press

Strong glutes help place your body in the proper position at setup, and they assist in the hip rotation on both the backswing and the downswing. The leg press is a machine exercise that primarily focuses on the gluteus but also works the *quadriceps,* another critical muscle group in the setup and the turn. Like most machines, the *leg press* is reasonably self-explanatory. Sitting in the provided seat, place your feet firmly and flatly against the platform with your knees flexed and reasonably close together (see Figure 10-2). You don't want your legs to flare to the sides during this exercise. Press the platform with your feet until your legs are fully extended, then slowly return to the start position. Depending on your current fitness level, do 10 to 20 repetitions of this exercise. Select a weight for which you can complete the recommended reps.

Figure 10-2: Laura using the leg press machine.

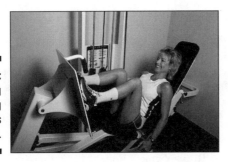 

Your back and bottom should stay on the seat during the leg press exercise. If doing that is difficult, you're trying to lift too much weight. This exercise is not a back workout. If you can't extend your legs while keeping your torso relatively still, choose a lighter weight. Poor form can result in injury. Lifting a lighter weight using good technique is better than risking an injury trying to lift a heavier weight.

Calf press

Calf muscles are power generators during the downswing. In addition to providing balance as the shoulders turn around your sturdy lower body during the backswing (see Chapter 5), the calves push off and propel your lower body through the downswing. With the leg press machine, you can also work these critical calf muscles. Sitting in the same position as you did for the previous exercise with the balls of your feet on the platform, fully extend your legs, lifting the weight by pushing the platform away from you. After you fully extend your legs with your feet flat on the platform, you're in the start position for this calf exercise. Now, slowly work the calf muscles by rising onto your toes, extending the weight slightly (see Figure 10-3). Repeating this action — rising onto your toes then returning the platform to the balls of your feet — strengthens the calf muscles while the glutes and quadriceps remain taut. Depending on your current fitness level, do 10 to 20 repetitions of this exercise. Select a weight for which you can complete the recommended reps.

Figure 10-3:
Laura doing
calf presses
on the
leg press
machine.

Quadricep leg extension

Your *quadriceps* — the large thigh muscles you use to bounce a child on your lap — support the *lateral shifting* of your lower body, which moves weight from your right side to your left side during the golf swing. The most effective exercise for isolating and strengthening the quadriceps is another machine exercise.

Sitting on the provided seat with your knees bent at a 90-degree angle and your shins against the crossbar that runs along the front of the machine, do this lift by flexing your feet (opposite of pointing) straightening your legs, and pressing the crossbar upward (see Figure 10-4). You'll quickly feel this exercise in your thighs, but that doesn't mean that you should speed up the lift. Depending on your current fitness level, repeat this exercise for 10 to 20 repetitions. Select a weight for which you can complete the recommended reps.

A slow, steady lift with a smooth transition from the ascent to the decent maximizes the benefit to the muscles.

Figure 10-4:
Laura
completing
quadricep
leg
extensions
with both
legs.

This lift isolates both the quadriceps, but Figure 10-5 shows that you can also use it to work one leg at a time. Doing so makes sense in certain circumstances. If, for example, you have suffered injury or atrophy in one leg and that leg is considerably weaker, you can isolate it and attempt to regain balance in the strength of both thighs.

Figure 10-5:
Laura
performing
the
quadriceps
lift with
each leg.

Although this lift is often used in rehabilitation after knee surgeries, you should not feel any pain or have any catches in your knees while doing it. If you feel any discomfort in your knees, stop lifting immediately. The only time that you should perform this exercise with bad knees is on the advice of a physician, and only then under strict monitoring.

Hamstring press

The *hamstrings,* which are the muscles the run down the back of the thigh between the glute and the pits of the knees, provide stability and consistency to the setup, and drive the right leg through the shot on the downswing and follow-through. Strengthening these muscles is important to keeping the head and upper body still during the swing.

The most effective way to isolate and strengthen the hamstrings is on a machine specifically designed to work this muscle. In this exercise, you sit on the seat with your legs fully extended and your calf muscles resting on the crossbar on the front of the machine. After adjusting the weight, slowly bend your legs at the knees, pushing the crossbar down until the legs form 90-degree angles (see Figure 10-6). Without stopping or jerking, you smoothly finish this exercise by returning the legs to the start position. Depending on your current fitness level, repeat this exercise for 10 to 20 repetitions. Select a weight for which you can complete the recommended reps.

Figure 10-6:
Laura executing hamstring presses.

You may be shocked by the impact this exercise can have on your golf game. In a matter of weeks after incorporating this exercise into your routine, you'll find that your lower body action through impact has improved dramatically and that your upper body is more stable during the swing.

Free-weight lunge

Because the lower body works in such a synchronized and coordinated way during the golf swing, adding some strengthening drills to your workout that require all the leg and hip muscles to work together is a good idea. One such exercise is the *lunge* — a free-weight exercise where you hold dumbbells with your arms hanging at your sides. You do this exercise by taking a larger-than-normal step forward onto a step and slowly dropping the knee of the trailing leg to a point close to but not touching the ground (see Figure 10-7). Your head and torso naturally dip as you drop the trailing knee and bend your front leg. Finishing the exercise, push off the step and stand erect, then repeat the process with the other leg. Depending on your current fitness level, repeat this exercise for 10 to 20 repetitions. Select a weight for which you can complete the recommended reps.

Your arms are at your side throughout this lift. All the tension is in your legs.

Calf raise

If the other calf strengthening exercises in this chapter don't appeal to you, try the *free-weight calf raise.* This exercise requires you to hold dumbbells with your arms hanging at your sides. Then, standing on the bottom of a stair with your heels hanging off the back of the step and the weights at your sides, lower and raise your heels off the back of the step (see Figure 10-8). Depending on your current fitness level, repeat this exercise for 10 to 20 repetitions. Select a weight for which you can complete the recommended reps.

Figure 10-7: Kelly demonstrating the free-weight lunge.

Figure 10-8: Larry demonstrating the calf raise.

Ball squats

Another exercise that tones the entire lower body requires the assistance of an exercise ball, but doesn't involve weights. Standing near a wall with the exercise ball wedged between your back and the wall and keeping your weight properly centered, slowly bend your knees, lowering your entire body but keeping your back straight using the ball as a lever (see Figure 10-9). This exercise doesn't have to be continuous. You can (and should) stop and start this squat, holding various positions for several seconds to fully exercise different muscles of the lower body. Depending on your current fitness level, repeat this exercise for 10 to 20 repetitions.

Against all odds

Many cynics looking for evidence (or excuses) to prove that a strong lower body isn't really that important in golf always seem to cite, and subsequently distort, one of the most heroic stories in sports: the improbable success of Casey Martin. Stricken by a congenital bone disease that left his right leg weak and atrophied, Martin successfully earned the right to play on the PGA Tour and successfully won the right to ride in a golf cart while playing because of his handicap.

Many people misconstrue Casey's success to mean that the lower body isn't that important.

How could it be? Casey can barely walk, and he's among the best in the game. The legs can't be that important. Nothing could be farther from the truth. Casey has made some exceptional swing modifications to offset his handicap, and his hip action and strong left leg allow him to drive his lower body through his shots without relying on his atrophied right leg. He is talented and courageous, but Casey is a bad example for those who want to somehow discount the importance of the lower body in golf.

Figure 10-9:
Laura demonstrating the ball squat.

Although the motion of this exercise is a full one, never squat so far that your bottom drops below your knees. Your legs should form 90-degree angles at the bottom of the squat. Anything deeper and you risk injuring your knees.

You may notice that several lower body exercises that you may have seen in the past weren't included in these recommendations. Among them are:

✔ Full squats with a bar and free weights on your shoulders

✔ Jerking a bar of weights off the floor

✔ Any lift where the legs bend beyond a 90-degree angle

Not only are these exercises bad for your golf game, they can cause serious damage to your back, knees, shoulders, and neck. Some exercises you simply need to avoid. These three are among them.

Stretching the Lower Body

In addition to the lower body warm-up stretches that you need to incorporate into your routine before every round (see Chapter 7), you should spend an ample amount of time at home or in the gym stretching the large muscles of your lower body. Here are some stretches that limber the lower body and make the moves required in the golf swing much easier.

- ✓ **Hamstring and glute stretch:** Sitting on the floor with your legs fully extended and spread slightly wider than shoulder-width apart, place a measuring stick between your legs, and, in a smooth motion, lean forward, extending your arms and keeping your back as straight as possible (see Figure 10-10). Note on the measuring stick how far you can stretch.

Figure 10-10: Laura sitting on floor and stretching.

As you make this stretch a part of your daily routine, measure your improvement. You may be surprised at how quickly and effectively this stretch loosens the glutes, hamstrings, and areas of the lower back.

- ✓ **Glute stretch:** For a deeper, assisted stretch (one that requires the aid of a stretching tool) that adds a great deal of flexibility to your glute and hip flexors, lie on your back with your feet on the floor and your knees up. Pick up one foot and place your ankle on the opposite knee. Then with both hands, or with the assistance of a Golf Fitness Stretch Trainer (a professional designed strap), lift both legs off the floor (see Figure 10-11). You'll feel a deep stretch in the glute and hip flexor. Hold that stretch for 15 to 30 seconds, and repeat the process on the other side. You'll feel great, not just during this stretch, but during your setup on the golf course afterward.

Figure 10-11: Laura stretching her glutes.

✓ **Quadriceps stretch:** One of the best assisted stretches for your quadriceps involves the Stretch Trainer, belt, or other strap. With the Stretch Trainer wrapped around the bottom of one foot, lie on your opposite side and let the strap slip to the top of your foot. Take the ends of the Stretch Trainer behind your head with both hands and pull your leg back, stretching the quadriceps, abductor, and hip flexor (see Figure 10-12). Hold for 15 to 30 seconds and repeat to the opposite side.

Figure 10-12: Laura stretching her quads with a Stretch Trainer.

✓ **Assisted hamstring stretch:** While you have your strap handy, from a sitting position, wrap it around the bottom of one foot, then lie on your back and pull the leg straight into the air using the strap (see Figure 10-13). By pulling on the strap or Stretch Trainer, you can quickly find this stretch in your hamstring. Hold it for 15 to 30 seconds, then repeat the process with the opposite leg.

Figure 10-13:
Laura lying down for assisted hamstring stretch.

✔ **Assisted calf stretch:** Wrap your belt or Stretch Trainer around the ball of one foot while sitting with your legs straight out in front of you. Keeping your back and legs straight, pull on the Stretch Trainer until you feel the stretch in your calf (see Figure 10-14). Hold for 15 to 30 seconds and repeat with both legs.

Figure 10-14:
Laura doing the assisted calf stretch.

You can cut corners in a few areas of golf, but stretching and strengthening the lower body is not one of them. As you age, your lower body isn't as supple or strong as when you were younger, and that shows up in your golf game with diminished distance and accuracy. If you do nothing else to stem the tide of age in your golf game, you *must* incorporate some lower body strengthening and stretch training into your routine. Your golf game depends on it.

Part IV
Improving Balance and Endurance

The 5th Wave By Rich Tennant

"What? It helps me with my balance."

In this part . . .

Good golf is like a ballet; the motion is beautiful and seemingly effortless. This doesn't occur by accident. Like any athletic move, the golf swing requires precision and, more than anything else, balance. In this part, discover how to improve your balance and conditioning after 40, and how balance and conditioning can help lower your scores. The drills and exercises that I outline in this part can not only help your golf game by improving your overall balance and fitness, but they can also improve your general health and well-being. Who knows, you may even become a better dancer.

Chapter 11

Restoring Balance, Timing, and Rhythm as You Age

"Whether they naturally swing with a fast, medium, or slow tempo, I think a lot of golfers miss out with their spread or distribution of speed — their rhythm — within their overall tempo. The better the rhythm of the swing, the better the swing is likely to work, irrespective of whether its overall tempo is slow, medium, or fast."

— Jack Nicklaus

*I*f you're over 40 and have teenage children, chances are pretty good that your timing and rhythm have been called into question. And if you've been challenged to ride a roller coaster or other carnival ride in recent months, you've probably questioned your own balance and equilibrium. The simple fact is that as you grow older your balance changes, your rhythm changes, and activities that require exact timing don't come as easily and naturally as they once did.

Some of these changes come from muscle deterioration and slowing reactions caused by the hardening of tendons, general inactivity, a redistribution of the body's weight, and general loss of strength and speed. Balance is strictly a function of the inner ear. That's why ear infections often lead to dizziness. Age also has an effect on your inner ear. Bones weaken, cartilage deteriorates, fluid and debris build up, and hair follicles grow and change. All these factors combine to change the dynamics of the inner ear and, however slightly, alter your balance as you grow older.

Human mechanics and body positions aside, the golf swing is, at its core, a dance — a ballet — with you as the only dancer on stage and the ball and club as the only essential props. Like all dances, the importance of body position is secondary to the rhythm and timing of the movements. Properly executed golf swings are rhythmic actions — smooth and consistent. Some swings are faster than others, even among the greatest players in the world. Ben Hogan had what many called a slashing swing, lightning quick in both directions, but no one ever questioned Hogan's timing or rhythm. Ernie Els has one of the most fluid, silky swings in golf, a smooth, slow, and equally rhythmic action.

Week in and week out on the PGA Tour, the Senior PGA Tour, and the LPGA Tour, spectators consistently marvel at how far professional golfers hit the ball with seemingly slow, effortless swings. This weekly phenomenon has nothing to do with arm position, hand position, shoulder turn, hip rotation or weight shift; the spectators who ooh and ah at Larry Nelson and Laura Baugh are spellbound by these players' timing, rhythm, and balance. This is also one of the reasons golf has become so popular on television. In addition to watching the competition, many viewers tune in to see the artistic fluidity with which professionals swing. Most amateurs aren't nearly as balanced and rhythmic in their own swings, and they hope to pick up some tip or hint to this sweet-swinging secret.

The Golf Swing: A Major Balancing Act

Smooth golf swings are pretty, but the only reason they attract such awe is because of the results they produce. If a rhythmic, balanced swing resulted in a shot that traveled only a few yards and was less accurate than an off-balanced whack, everyone would watch the thrasher. The fact is, good rhythm can (and more often than not does) result in good golf shots. Never, ever do off-balance, poorly timed swings produce consistently good shots.

In this regard golf isn't much different than any other sport. All good athletic moves require balance. A quarterback throws touchdown passes from a balanced posture. An NBA star shoots free throws, jump shots, and fast-break dunks from a balanced position. Even when these athletes appear out of control, flying through the air and executing miraculous feats, they are, for the most part, balanced. Like gymnasts who can flip, spin, and contort themselves in ways that seem inhuman, athletes in various sports make complex actions look easy because of the rhythm, timing, and balance that they display.

The entire purpose of the golf swing is to hit a ball as far and as straight as possible with the implements provided. To accomplish that goal you need to manipulate your body to create maximum clubhead speed at the exact millisecond the club comes into contact with the ball. You also need to manipulate your body so that the clubface is square to the target line at that same moment of impact.

Excess clubhead speed at the top of the backswing, or as you turn the shoulders on the backswing is useless and wasted. If anything, the excess clubhead speed at those moments detracts from the clubhead speed at impact.

A properly balanced and properly timed swing generates maximum speed and consistency at the moment of impact. Rhythm comes from proper timing, and timing is a function of good swing mechanics and proper balance. It all comes together to produce a smooth, seemingly effortless action that results in long, straight golf shots.

Unfortunately, many over-40 amateurs have trouble with timing, rhythm, and balance for the following reasons:

✔ As older muscles stiffen, golf swings get shorter. This *shortening of the swing* (where the shoulders don't turn as far as they once did and the arms aren't as fully extended as they once were) throws off your timing and causes you to speed things up. Your balance and rhythm are adversely affected by these subtle changes in your swing.

✔ Modifying basic swing mechanics as you age also throws off your timing. Any change can disrupt your timing, which has an adverse effect on your rhythm.

✔ Weaker hands, no matter how subtle the change in strength, tend to grip the club tighter, and the extra grip pressure leads to a shorter, quicker action in the swing.

But all is not lost. In this chapter, I explain some things you can do to improve your balance and rhythm, even as you age.

Developing Better Balance, Timing, and Rhythm

Even if you can't dance, shoot a free throw, or tap your feet in time with a jukebox, you can do some simple drills to increase your balance, rhythm, and timing in golf. In many cases the benefits of these drills aren't as immediate or straightforward as the benefits you can feel from the strengthening and stretching drills that I present in other chapters of this book. But they are no less important.

Drills that improve your balance and timing improve the likelihood that you'll hit the ball squarely on the clubface with the clubhead moving at its maximum pace at impact. Doing so is crucial to good golf, just as important, in fact, as strength and flexibility.

Using some fancy footwork

A great drill to improve your balance and insure that your swing tempo is smooth and consistent is the *feet together drill,* where you take full swings with your feet together. This drill is simple. You set up, then adjust your stance until your feet are touching (see Figure 11-1). If, in this position, you take a viciously quick swing, you may fall down. If your balance is in question, you'll lose your footing, and if your swing is too slow in spots and too fast in others, you'll feel instability in your feet and legs.

In some instances you can hit balls with your feet together, but I recommend doing so only after you've adequately practiced swinging with your feet together *without* hitting balls for several days or weeks.

Figure 11-1:
Steve
swinging
with feet
together.

Feeling the weight of the club

You can perform a number of exercises with a *weighted club,* a club that is five to ten times heavier than the ones you carry in your bag, to enhance your balance, timing, and rhythm. For example, the Momentus Swing Trainer, a patented, weighted club that has the weight perfectly balanced in the shaft, is pictured in Figures 11-2 through 11-6, and I recommend the Momentus or a similarly balanced, weighted club for the following drills.

If you don't have access to a weighted club, holding two clubs instead of one is sufficient. But, a weighted club is well worth the investment and is something that I highly recommend regardless of your skill level.

Never take a full swing at full speed with a weighted golf club. The chances of injury if you do are far greater than any benefits you may gain.

Momentum to ¼ back

To get a feel for the rhythm and timing of the release of the golf club through impact, start with a ¼ swing. This swing is different from the one you use in a pitch or chip shot, because those shots may involve a different setup or other variations in the swing. The ¼ swing is the same as a normal full swing except that it's shorter. Your setup is the same, your hand position and ball position are the same. You simply take the club back ¼ of the way that you normally would on a full shot.

For this drill, lift the club a few inches off the ground (so as not to make contact with the ground or floor), then slowly and rhythmically push the club into a position in front of the ball. All swings with a weighted club should start with this move to protect the integrity of the shoulders and to avoid injury. For these purposes this starting move is called *momentum*. After moving the club to the momentum position, slowly and rhythmically take the club ¼ way into your backswing, hold that position for two counts, then slowly return the club to address (see Figure 11-2). Repeat this action 8 to 10 repetitions, getting a feel for the timing and rhythm of moving the club from momentum to the ¼ back position, holding the club there for two counts, before slowly — very slowly — returning the club back to address. After several swings with the heavy club you will be on your way to improving your rhythm.

Momentum to ½ back

This move is almost identical to the momentum to ¼ swing, but instead of moving the club from the momentum position to ¼ back, start at address, push the club forward to momentum, then take a ½ backswing with the clubhead positioned at 12 o'clock. Hold that backswing for two complete counts — one one-thousand, two one-thousand — before slowly returning the club back to the address position (see Figure 11-3). Repeat 8 to 10 repetitions.

Momentum to full back

If you can handle the previous two drills, this one will likely be easy. Repeat the same action — moving the club from address to momentum — but this time go back to a full backswing (see Figure 11-4). Hold that position for two full counts, then slowly, taking a minimum of three full counts, return the club to address and repeat 8 to 10 repetitions until you feel comfortable with the balance, rhythm, and timing of the full swing.

Figure 11-2: Kelly going from address to momentum to ¼ back and then back to address.

Figure 11-3: Kelly going from address to momentum to ½ back and then back to address.

Figure 11-4:
Kelly going from address to momentum to full backswing and then back to address.

Momentum to ½ back and swing

The three previous slow procedures can give you a better feel for the balance, timing, and rhythm of the swing. They can also prepare you for the next two drills, which involve actually swinging the club through the shot. Holding the weighted club a few inches above the ground (so as to avoid hitting the ground or the floor and causing injury), push the club to momentum then take it ½ back and hold it there for two counts. But rather than slowly returning the club to address, go ahead and swing through the shot, holding the finish position for a minimum of three full counts before slowly returning to address (see Figure 11-5). Repeat 8 to 10 repetitions.

Momentum to full back and swing

Once again, holding the weighted club a few inches above the ground (so as to avoid hitting the ground or the floor and causing injury), push the club to momentum then take it to full back and hold it there for two counts. Swing through the shot, holding the finish position for a minimum of three full counts before slowly returning to address (see Figure 11-6). Repeat 8 to 10 repetitions.

Figure 11-5:
Kelly moving from momentum to ½ back and swinging through.

Figure 11-6:
Kelly from momentum to full back and swinging through.

The momentum to full back and swing drill is probably the best balance and rhythm exercise that you can practice. It gives you a feel for the slow, accelerated movements of the golf swing with all parts of the body working in concert to create maximum speed during that millisecond when club meets ball at the bottom of the downswing.

Balance and rhythm aren't genetic gifts or accidents of birth; everyone discovers and practices balance and rhythm just like other aspects of the golf swing. By working through the drills in this chapter, you can go a long way toward developing a swing that looks just as smooth, silky, easy, and flowing as those you see on Sunday afternoons on the PGA, LPGA, and PGA Senior tours.

Chapter 12

Endurance and Over-40 Golf

- -

In This Chapter

▶ Impacting your over-40 golf game with better cardiovascular endurance

▶ Trying out different types of endurance training

▶ Working out to improve endurance for a better golf game

- -

"We compete, we keep score, we take risks, we get stuck in a trap, we scramble back, we recover. But most of all, we play to win. And nothing increases our chances of victory like being in sound physical and mental condition."

— Ernie Els

*H*ere's a news flash: Cardiovascular exercise is good for you! I'm sure you've heard that pronouncement before, probably from your spouse or your doctor or the thousands of fitness and health experts that litter the airwaves with advice on living longer and feeling better. In fact, you're probably sick of being told about the importance of getting out there and sweating, raising your heart rate through aerobics, biking, or running, or spending your spare time on simulated stair and cross-country skiing machines. All you want to do is to play better golf, and these get-in-shape exercises couldn't have any bearing on that, right?

Wrong. Cardiovascular exercise is essential to good golf. In addition to improving your general health, being in better shape improves your energy levels, increases your stamina, allows you to focus better before, during, and after a round, and enables your body to work more efficiently by burning fat at a better rate and providing more oxygen to your muscles.

Not only does being in better cardiovascular condition improve the way you feel after a round of golf, it also improves the quality and consistency of your swing, allowing you to remain competitive and fresh for an entire 18, 27, or 36 holes. You can walk around the course more effectively, hit better shots, and gain greater confidence in your competitive skills simply because of enhanced conditioning.

Given all those facts you would think that everyone would engage in cardio-vascular conditioning. But they don't. The problem is that cardiovascular exercises are difficult. Getting your heart rate up, and sustaining that elevated heart rate long enough to gain substantial benefit is tough. Such exercise can also be drudgery. Many of the exercises people associate with cardiovascular conditioning — biking, running, and so forth — are generally considered boring, painful, and about as much fun as root canal surgery. Given the option of hanging out in the clubhouse and having another beer or adjourning to the gym for an hour on the exercise bike, many opt for the easy way out. Eventually their golf games show this choice.

Discovering Why Cardiovascular Training Matters

Doctors and healthcare providers frequently recommend exercises, such as speed walking, biking, cross-country skiing, and other activities that accelerate your heart rate for many reasons including:

- Cardio exercises burn fat and help lower cholesterol in your blood-stream. In other words, they're good for you.

- They also oxygenate the bloodstream — increase the amount of oxygen in the blood — in a way that helps muscular development.

- They improve the flow of blood to the brain, thus helping to reduce the risk of strokes and other debilitating diseases.

- They increase the efficiency with which your body burns fat and calories, even at rest, so that your body still burns excess fat long after you stop exercising.

- They reduce the risk of heart disease.

These are all noble and admirable reasons to exercise and elevate your cardiovascular conditioning, but they don't specifically deal with your golf game. If living longer isn't a big deal for you as long as you're shooting better scores in your Saturday afternoon foursome, you still have ample reasons to incorporate cardiovascular conditioning into your routine.

For example, golfers who are in good cardiovascular shape:

- **Have fewer timing problems.** Because their heart rates don't fluctuate as greatly during a round, and because their muscles are properly oxygenated, they can maintain a consistent rhythm for the entire round.

- **Are stronger in the late holes of closely contested matches.** Out-of-shape golfers hit what's known at the *13th hole wall* when, however slightly, they begin to fatigue in the closing five holes of a round. Golfers in good cardiovascular condition don't have that problem.

✔ **Can concentrate better, especially in the latter holes of a round because of increased oxygen flow to the brain.**

✔ **Recover quickly from taxing circumstances.** After walking up a hill to an elevated green where you have a 15-foot putt for birdie, the last thing you want is to be winded as you stand over your next shot.

✔ **Have less fat in their bodies.** So, their muscles tend to respond to stimuli better than those of golfers in poor cardiovascular condition.

Getting Started on Cardio Conditioning

You need to consider these four variables when implementing a cardiovascular conditioning program for golf:

✔ **Intensity,** which is the effort used during exercise. Intensity is the single most important factor in developing aerobic fitness. You can measure intensity by calories burned per hour, your perceived exertion, or measuring your heart rate during exercise.

✔ **Frequency,** which is the number of cardio workout sessions you do per week. Building cardiovascular capacity takes a minimum of 3 sessions weekly unless you're walking the course three times a week, and then two sessions is usually sufficient.

✔ **Duration,** which is the number of minutes spent per cardio workout. A 20- to 30-minute training session in your target heart rate zone increases aerobic fitness. A direct relationship exists between intensity and duration. In other words, if you decrease the intensity, you can increase duration and so forth.

✔ **Mode,** which is the type of exercise you choose to do. Try to mix a number of cardio exercise activities into your workouts. Doing so keeps your body from getting too used to the same exercise and prevents you from becoming bored.

If you're a beginner in the workout world, the low-intensity workout is the place for you. These workouts are less than 20 minutes long and consist of activities, such as a brisk, steady walk or a stroll on a treadmill. These walking exercises simulate what you may experience if you walked 18 holes of golf. Try to elevate your heart rate during these cardio workouts to a sustained level that increases cardiovascular capacity. I also recommend low-intensity workouts for golfers who are overweight or who have been diagnosed with heart or blood pressure problems. Even then, however, a physician, trainer, or other specialist should monitor these exercises.

After you feel comfortable with your initial cardio workout, you can slowly progress into the higher-intensity realm of aerobic workouts where you get winded and sweaty and your heart rate jumps up. If you have ever undergone a stress test as part of a physical, you know what an aerobic workout is. Your body is challenged through vigorous activity — speed walking, rowing, or riding an exercise bike — until your heart rate increases to well more than half its full capacity, and you maintain that rate for several minutes. This type of workout oxygenates your blood and exercises your heart in a way that is beneficial to your whole body.

Measuring Your Cardio Zone

One of the objections to labeling exercises is the eye-of-the-beholder argument. What is low-intensity for you may be a pretty healthy exercise regimen for your overweight neighbor, and what you consider a good hearty workout may be a light jog in the park for the 17-year-old down the street. Aerobic workouts are individually measured by monitoring your heart rate.

Whether an exercise is increasing aerobic capacity depends on the heart rate of the person doing the exercise. If your heart rate exceeds a certain beat-per-minute level, you're engaging in aerobic exercise. But before you can determine whether or not your workouts are enhancing your cardiovascular capacity, you must first calculate your maximum heart rate and find out what percentage of that maximum you need to reach for a good workout.

Calculating maximum heart rate

Your age is the determining variable in what constitutes your *maximum heart rate* or the rate at which your heart can process oxygen into the bloodstream. If you're 100 pounds overweight and a heavy smoker, you may take issue with having the same maximum heart rate as someone your age who runs a couple marathons a year, but that's the way it is. Just because your maximum heart rate is the same as someone who's in better or worse shape than you are doesn't mean your respective hearts beat at the same rate. It means only that your maximum heart rate is the same based on your ages.

The formula for calculating your maximum heart rate is:

Maximum heart rate in beats per minute (bpm) = 220 – your age.

The number 220 is the constant in this formula with your age as the variable that affects the outcome. So, for example, if you're 45 years old, your maximum heart rate is 220 – 45, or 175 beats per minute. If you are 50 years old, your maximum heart rate is 170 beats per minute (bpm), and if you are 39, your maximum heart rate is 181 bpm.

This calculation makes no judgement as to your physical conditioning, but it is the formula physicians use to determine what kind of shape you're in. If you're a 40-year-old with a maximum heart rate of 180 bpm, and your heart, at rest, beats at 90 bpm or 50 percent of your maximum heart rate, the doctor is likely to chastise you mightily for being alarmingly out of shape. If, under that same premise, a 5-minute brisk walk elevates your heart rate to only 75 bpm, 42 percent of your maximum heart rate, you'll be given a hearty congratulations and asked how many miles you run every day. Either way, the basis on which your fitness and training are measured is your maximum heart rate.

Determining heart rate

You can measure how fast or slow your heart beats in a number of ways, each with varying degrees of accuracy. For example,

- ✔ The most reliable and effective measurement is a heart rate monitor. These devices are sold at sporting goods stores and are no more intrusive than a sweatband or bracelet that you wear on your wrist. They monitor your heart rate at all times and give you a running beats per minute (bpm) measurement that changes as your activity level increases and decreases.

- ✔ Many workout machines — bikes, rowing machines, as well as stair-climbing and cross-country-ski simulators — have heart rate monitors built into the handles. These monitors give you a running bpm measurement and are great for gauging how close you are to your maximum heart rate as you work out.

- ✔ The low-tech method of calculating heart rate is the 10-second measurement. Using a clock or watch with a second hand, simply find your pulse at your wrist or at the side of your neck and count the number of heartbeats in a 10-second timeframe. By multiplying that number by six, you can effectively calculate your bpm. For example, if your heart beats 20 times in a 10-second period, your bpm is 120.

Calculating your heart rate is an important part of designing and maintaining a good cardiovascular workout program. Take a few minutes now to practice calculating your heart rate with a watch or clock. After you establish your current heart rate in beats per minute (bpm), calculate what percentage your current bpm is to your maximum heart rate.

The answer is your bpm divided by your maximum heart rate. So, if your current bpm is 80 and your maximum heart rate is 180, your heart is currently beating at 44.4 percent of its capacity (80 ÷ 180). That is an important calculation, and you should practice counting and calculating it several times. You'll see why as you read on.

Maximizing Your Cardio Training

As you exercise your heart rate goes up as your body needs more oxygen to keep up with the activity that you require from the muscles. Blood pumped through the heart carries oxygen to the muscles. So it stands to reason that as your body needs more oxygen, your heart rate goes up to accommodate the body's request.

After your heart rate hits 60 percent of its maximum, you're working *aerobically,* which means you're effectively utilizing oxygen and burning fat as your primary fuel source. Aerobic actually means the consumption of oxygen, not a class of people doing choreographed dance moves. Sustaining an aerobic state of exercise for an extended period of time — a minimum of 20 minutes and a maximum of 45 minutes — can do wonders for your body in terms of burning fat and calories and oxygenating the blood, which helps your mind, your muscles, your veins, arteries, and heart.

If you are a 50-year-old woman, for example, a moderately brisk walk can elevate your heart rate to 102 bpm, which is 60 percent of your maximum heart rate (see the section "Calculating maximum heart rate" earlier in this chapter). If you sustain that rate for only a minute or two, you didn't accomplish much in the way of benefits, but if you keep that heart rate up for 20 minutes and walk one-and-a-half miles in the process, you can burn a substantial number of calories and a good bit of fat.

Low-intensity workouts

The lower end of the aerobic heart rate zone is the *low-intensity, fat-burning workout zone.* It ranges from 60 to 70 percent of your maximum heart rate. For a 50-year old, that is 102 bpm (maximum heart rate of 170 × 60 percent) to 119 bpm (maximum heart rate of 170 × 70 percent). In that heart rate zone, your body experiences the benefits of a low-intensity aerobic exercise. This feeling is similar to what you may experience if you walk briskly uphill to the elevated green on a par three, or trot to your ball after hitting it within inches of the hole. If you sustain that pace for 20 to 30 minutes, breaking a good sweat along the way, you are in the fat-burning workout zone where your body is using fat as its primary fuel to sustain this pace. If you are in relatively good shape, you may have to work harder to reach this low-intensity target heart zone. This occurs because a well-conditioned heart processes oxygen more efficiently, even during exercise. Whatever activities are required to reach this zone, the benefits are the same. A good low-intensity workout effectively burns fat if you maintain it for a reasonable period of time. Figure 12-1 shows you more about heart rate training zones.

HEART RATE TRAINING ZONE

Beats per 10 Seconds	AGE				
	20-29	30-39	40-49	50-59	60-69
Minimum THR	20	19	18	17	16
Mid-Zone THR	23	22	21	20	19
Maximum THR	28	27	26	24	23

Figure 12-1: Cardio zone chart.

High-intensity workouts

After your heart rate increases beyond 70 percent of its maximum capacity, you're in the *cardio-intensive aerobic zone.* This is great for your respiratory system and heart because it means you're relying more heavily on oxygen to drive your actions, and your body is burning carbohydrates as well as calories and fat.

As a beginner, you won't be able to sustain this level of intensity for an extended period of time, but as you improve your cardiovascular conditioning you can push yourself to work out longer. A sustained heart rate of 65 percent of maximum capacity is the optimum zone to substantially improve your cardio conditioning while burning fat and calories.

Any intense cardiovascular workout program that you undertake should always be monitored. If you aren't in a setting where you have access to a professional trainer, at least work out with a friend. If you feel any discomfort or lightheadedness from your workouts, seek the advice of a healthcare professional. These types of workouts are great for your body and your golf game, but only if properly executed and monitored.

Exercising for the Heart and Soul of Golf

One of the reasons more golfers don't engage in cardiovascular exercises is because, like most adults in their thirties, forties, or fifties, golfers can't seem to find the time, nor can they find the motivation. What most won't admit (but what is in fact the truth) is that they're intimidated by the prospects of taking on a new exercise regimen, especially one that requires an activity that they may not be familiar with, such as biking, rowing, or even the dreaded aerobics class.

Some golfers aren't even comfortable watching most of these activities, much less engaging in them. But those who understand the value of good cardiovascular conditioning to their golf games eventually bite the bullet. They start off slowly, spending only a few minutes on the exercise bike or treadmill, but they slowly improve, working their way into more diverse exercises and even, occasionally, into an aerobics class.

Boredom is another factor that discourages people from their needed cardiovascular workouts. Running or riding a bike isn't stimulating enough to keep their interest. They become bored and soon quit working out altogether.

To avoid that pitfall, mix up your workouts. Include rowing, biking, stair climbing, and skiing with your walking or treadmill exercises. Throw an aerobics class or two into the mix. Listen to music as you work out, or play games with yourself where you race an imaginary opponent or a clock. The type and mix of activity is unimportant, as long as you do something to improve your cardiovascular conditioning.

So, stop procrastinating and try some of the following exercises and see if your body and golf game don't improve in the process.

Trying the treadmill

What could be more boring that walking on a treadmill? Not only are you just walking, you're not getting anywhere! Your feet are moving, but you're not advancing. How inane!

But the treadmill can be a great tool for cardiovascular training (see Figure 12-2). Not only can you stabilize and maintain a steady, brisk pace for a good fat-burning aerobic workout, you can mix up your workout and even throw in some higher intensity training. If, for example, you start out with a three-mile-per-hour pace at an even level on the treadmill, it won't take long for you to work up a sweat and begin breathing deeply. If, after 5 minutes of this pace, you add to your speed so that now you must walk at 3.3 miles per hour, it becomes a little more challenging. If, 5 minutes later, you add an incline to your walk, you can quickly test your cardiovascular conditioning. If you repeat this process until you're speed walking at 3.5 miles per hour on a healthy incline, you could easily reach maximum aerobic conditioning

If you try this type of exercise, be sure to measure your heart rate at various intervals throughout your workout. You want to maintain a good aerobic workout without overdoing it.

Figure 12-2:
The
treadmill.

Taking a ride on the bike

Most everyone has seen a stationary bike. They're a common sight in almost all gyms and in quite a few private homes. In many homes, these bikes are used as coat racks or laundry piles, while in others dust mites may have accumulated on the gears and the spinning mechanisms may have rusted to a halt. The reason that these bikes have fallen into disuse is the same reason that treadmills are looked upon with such inordinate disdain: boredom. Riding a bike without getting anywhere is almost as bad as walking without moving forward; it seems a wholly silly exercise. But stationary bikes can be wonderful harbingers of health, with expanded cardiovascular capacity as the result (see Figure 12-3).

Figure 12-3:
The
stationary
bike.

Aerobics: Dreaded nightmare or helpful fun?

Most male golfers would rather four-putt a green from eight feet for double bogey than set foot in an aerobics class. Images of ballet classes with men in tights and slippers bounce around in their heads, and when they mentally transport themselves into that arena, with other perfectly coordinated people executing flawlessly choreographed moves as they stumble and bumble under the lights while the entire room laughs at their pathetic motions, they can't get away from the area fast enough. It is as though the aerobics room were a Level Five biohazard container, and going near it could result in contamination.

The truth is that these classes aren't that bad, and no matter how spastic you are, nobody will laugh at you. Nobody cares. They're all too busy trying to keep up with the instructor themselves to worry about the steps you miss. After you take the monumental leap of faith and actually spend time in an aerobics class, you may find that the cardiovascular workout is second to none, and boredom is never an issue.

In fact, classes specifically tailored for golfers — with swing training, strength drills and golf-specific cardiovascular endurance exercises incorporated into the workout — are now available. People in the fitness industry are beginning to understand that sports-specific classes attract new members to gyms, and anything that broadens the base of people working out is good for their business. Golfers have specific needs. Gym owners are realizing that and offering programs that fit those needs.

Climbing the stairs

Stair machines (see Figure 12-4) are what you make of them. If you methodically push one foot down after the other, you will, indeed, eventually reach an aerobic zone and burn fat if you do it long enough. But wouldn't it be more fun to mix up your workout a little bit?

Figure 12-4:
The stairs.

In the old days as part of their team workouts, the Chicago Bears used to run the stairs at Soldier Field — up one side and down the other — hitting every step along the way. This was a great conditioning drill to get the team in good cardiovascular shape. But long before the physiological benefits of interval training were known, the Bears' coaching staff inserted a little wrinkle into their drill. Periodically during the running of the stairs, a coach would blow a whistle, and when the whistle sounded, all the players had to sprint to the top of the stadium, regardless of where they were. If they had kept a good leading pace throughout the run, they probably weren't far from the top when the whistle blew. If they had taken a slightly slower pace, they had farther to sprint, and if they had been lackluster during their run, they were usually at the bottom and had to sprint up every step in Soldier Field.

Take a hint from those Bears' coaches and add a few whistles to your step workout. Increase your intensity for a minute while on the stairs, then back off the pace and resume your normal stepping. Do five to ten intervals with adequate cooling-down periods in between, and you will have designed yourself a world-class stair-stepping workout.

I didn't offer running as a preferred aerobic exercise for good reason. If you haven't been a regular runner, your 40th birthday is no time to start. Running puts enormous pressure on the knees, ankles, and hips — pressure that can ultimately lead to bursitis, swelling, bone fatigue, shin splints, tendonitis, and other unpleasantness that golfers over 40 should avoid if possible. You have no reason to include running in a cardiovascular program when so many other low-impact options are available with fewer downsides and much greater benefits.

The truth is that you don't have to start your cardiovascular workout with a 100-mile bike ride, a 2-mile swim, and a mini-marathon every Saturday with occasional rock climbs and cross-country ski races thrown in for fun. A walk around your block will do. Any activity that elevates your heart rate into a fat-burning aerobic area and sustains that target heart zone for a minimum of 20 minutes is a good start. That could be a brisk walk, or a bike ride, a stint on the stair machine, or a hearty speed walk on the treadmill. Any aerobic work is better than no aerobic work.

You can always tell the golfers who are in good cardiovascular shape. They're the first ones walking onto the green, ready to play no matter what the circumstances. They're the ones who show no signs of fatigue, and in fact seem to grow stronger as the round progresses. They march purposefully up hills, onto greens, into bunkers, and onto tees, never huffing, puffing, or manipulating their swings because they can't catch their breath. They're also usually the ones who are shaking their disheveled opponents' hands after the round is over. There is rarely any doubt who won these hotly contested matches.

Part V

Golf Isn't a Contact Sport: Avoiding Injury

The 5th Wave — By Rich Tennant

"Don't laugh - it's added 30 yards to his drive."

In this part . . .

Golf participation is on the rise in America because as the baby-boomer population ages, sports such as softball, recreational basketball, flag football, and rugby — activities where serious injury is not only possible, but likely — are diminishing in popularity. Although you don't have to worry about the bumps, bruises, sprains, tears, and broken bones that are a part of everyday life on the football field, baseball diamond, and hockey rink, golf isn't completely safe. A number of injuries can directly result from your golf game.

Knowing how to recognize those injuries and head them off at the pass is a great benefit, especially after you turn 40. Prevention is far better than rehabilitation, but you must be aware of both. If you have a golf-related injury, you need to have a general idea of the steps you can take to correct the problem, and if you don't have any injuries you need to know how to maintain your health. This part gives it all to you, including injury recognition and prevention.

Chapter 13

Oh, My Achin' Back

. . . .

In This Chapter

▶ Discovering why back injuries are so common among golfers

▶ Exploring the physiology of the golfer's back

▶ Preventing back injuries before they happen

▶ Treating injuries after they occur

. . . .

"Golfers these days play year-round, which means more air travel, more sitting, riding, meeting, and practicing than ever before. It's not the golf swing that's ruining these guys' backs, it's the 'Too much' that's doing it. I try to restore function. It's no different than what might happen with a knee or a shoulder. After surgery on those joints, the first thing we try to do is rehabilitate and restore the function. The same is true with the back."

— Tom Boers, back specialist to the pros

The PGA cites lower back pain as the number-one golf-related ailment, which isn't surprising given the number of amateurs and professionals who complain of back pain. Sometimes this pain is simply a result of overexertion — a few too many swings with a back that isn't quite ready — but this pain can also be a sign of a far more serious problem. Many things can (and often do) go wrong with golfers' backs, in part because the back is one of the most vulnerable parts of the body during golf, and it is often unprepared for the pressures and manipulations added by the golf swing.

The parts of the back (see Figure 13-1) that have to withstand the pressures of the swing are:

✔ The *disks* (sometimes called intervertebral disks) which are, as the name implies, small, round, cushioning plates of cartilage between the vertebrae

✔ The *facet joints,* which are the joints that connect the vertebrae

✔ The *ligaments* of the facet joints

✔ The *muscles* that surround the spine

✔ The *vertebrae* themselves

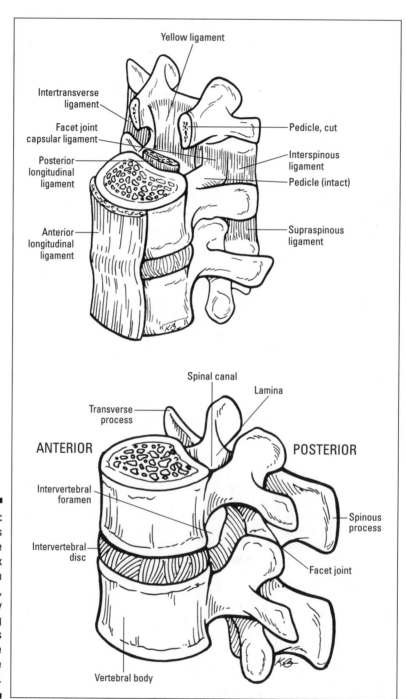

All these parts in your back work together during the golf swing and all are in jeopardy as a result of the pressures placed on them during that swing.

Targeting the Pain in Your Back and Neck

The vast majority of golf-related back injuries occur in the lower back or *lumbar* region, but other parts of the back and spine are also susceptible to problems. Some of the more common back ailments include muscle strains, herniated disks, and inflamed joints and ligaments. (Broken vertebrae and cracked ribs are rare, but definitely possible among golfers, especially those over 40, who substantially increase their practice and playing time.)

When discussing back problems, you can think of the spine (see Figure 13-2) in three different regions.

- ✔ The *lumbar,* or lower back, which extends from the tailbone upward through the lower curve of your back, and includes 5 vertebrae.

- ✔ The *thoracic* or middle back region, which is the area in the center of your back between the shoulder blades consisting of 12 vertebrae.

- ✔ The *cervical* region, which encompasses the upper back and neck, contains 7 vertebrae.

One of the most overlooked injuries relating to the spine is also one of the most avoidable: the injured neck. More than 90 percent of neck problems stem from poor posture and an unnatural bending in the cervical curve of the spine (see Figure 13-3). These problems usually occur when you try to accentuate a particular head position — head down to keep your eye on the ball or head up to allow the shoulders to turn — but in so doing you put the neck in a vulnerable position. Neck problems can be devastating to your game. I recommend checking your setup (see Chapter 4) to see if you can avoid those problems before they arise.

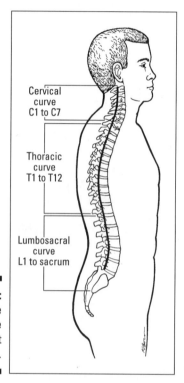

Figure 13-2:
The spine
has three
distinct
regions.

Figure 13-3:
The good,
the bad, and
the ugly of
the setup.

Keeping your head down like this can end in trouble for your neck.

Forcing your head up isn't much better.

Keeping your neck in line with the rest of your spine prevents potential problems.

Examining Back Pain by the Numbers

Among the 20 million amateur golfers in America, almost seven million complain of back pain or experience back injury on an annual basis. In fact, as a percentage, lower back problems lead the way on the ailment list of amateurs, with 36 percent of all male amateur golfers and 27.4 percent of all female amateur golfers experiencing some form of back problem in their golfing careers. The numbers are slightly lower for professionals, with 25 percent of all male professional golfers and 22.4 percent of all female professionals experiencing back problems.

If you're over 40, your chances of having back problems go up 10 percent. Over-40 golfers tend to play more often while exercising less than golfers under 40. Golfers over 40 are also more apt to carry a few extra pounds in their midsections, which puts additional stresses on the back region.

According to extensive medical research, 25 percent of amateurs who play an average of two rounds of golf a week develop back problems because of overuse of the muscles, tendons, bones, and joints in the back. Twenty-one percent are injured because of a trauma, such as hitting a tree root or rock during the golf swing or *hitting a shot fat* (hitting the turf behind the ball) and sticking the club in the ground. *Overswinging,* which means flailing away with a swing that is too hard and too fast, accounts for 19 percent of the back problems amateurs experience. The remaining 35 percent of problems result from poor form, poor posture, poor conditioning, and a lack of proper warm-up and stretching.

In professional golfers, overuse accounts for 80 percent of problems, while trauma accounts for only 12 percent. The remaining 8 percent can be traced to chronic or genetic disorders in the back region that are worsened by the amount of stress professional golfers place on their backs.

Identifying the Sources of Back Stress

Even if you have perfect posture, perfect form, and a well-conditioned trunk, golf still puts your back in jeopardy. The golf swing isn't a natural act, and the pushes and pulls that the setup and swing place on the back region create problems for even the best players. To avoid problems in the back region you must first understand the *forces* (those unnatural influences that add stress and strain) imposed on the lower back during the golf swing.

✔ A *shear force* occurs during the setup when the spine is tilted at address. Even when played correctly, golf puts the spine in an unnatural position. To get a feel for this, take your stance, move one hand to your lower back, and feel the taut muscles that hold your spine in place. This force causes strain when combined with other forces over extended periods of time.

✔ A *compression force* occurs as you initiate the downswing and compact the spine. This force is similar to the compression you may experience if you plop into a hard chair from a distance of about six to eight inches.

- A *rotation force* occurs on the axis of the spine as the shoulders turn around steady hips during the backswing and again as the hips unwind to initiate the downswing. This is the coiling and uncoiling action that I talk more about in Chapters 5 and 6, and it produces an enormous amount of pressure on the lumbar region.

- A *lateral bending force* occurs at impact and in the early moments of the follow-through when the head is still and behind the ball, but the hips and hands have moved to the left side. This awkward side-bend in the spine isn't natural, and, again, creates abnormal compressions in the lumbar area.

Individually these forces may not seem like any big deal, but their cumulative effect is pretty dramatic.

The peak shear forces that amateurs place on their spines during the golf swing is more than half as intense as the forces that rowers place on their backs during races, and 65 percent as intense as the force experienced during isometric torso lifts by weight lifters. The compression force on the spine during the golf swing is about eight times your body weight. It isn't unusual given the magnitude of these forces to actually find fractures in the vertebrae of some older golfers, especially those who present early symptoms of osteoporosis. (Stress fractures in the ribs near the lower thoracic vertebrae are also found in golfers over 50.)

TOUR TALK

Bouncing back from injury

Fred Couples, who at age 41 remains one of the most popular professionals on tour, experienced the worst nightmare a golfer can encounter just 45 minutes prior to his tee time at the Doral Ryder Open in 1994. While warming up with an 8-iron, Fred experienced what he called "an explosion" in his lower back. "I looked at my coach and told him I was in trouble," Fred said. A cart was dispatched to transport Fred to the rehabilitation trailer for an exam. After about 20 minutes of massage therapy, Fred thought he was ready. But when he stood, he realized he was still in pain.

On the advice of his friend and fellow tour player Don Pooley, Fred sought the help of physical therapist Tom Boers. Tom didn't take long to pinpoint Fred's problems. Years of hitting balls with his long, sweet swing had put undue pressure on certain disks and joints in Fred's back. The "explosion" that Fred felt on the driving range at Doral wasn't caused by some instantaneous trauma. It was simply the cumulative effect of years of practice, playing, and placing too much pressure on his spine. Tom knew this and prescribed rest, strength exercises, stretching exercises, cardiovascular training, and regular physical therapy.

Fred sees Tom three or four times a year for therapy, and he sticks to a structured warm-up and post-round exercise format to keep his back in good playing shape. Without that program, Fred wouldn't be able to play. With it, he is one of most competitive over-40 players in the game.

Understanding Different Kinds of Back Pain

Sometimes you can easily recognize a back problem. You wake up, put your feet on the floor, attempt to stand, and fall back onto your bed in agony. Other times you take a swing with a club, and a pain shoots through your back, shoulders, legs, and hips. In those instances you clearly have a problem. But, other problems aren't so easy to recognize. Sometimes back problems can present themselves with pain in the leg or hip region. Other problems mask themselves as temporary conditions, an occasional twinge that goes away after a day or so but returns later.

The duration and quality of pain that you experience in your lower back is a good indication of exactly what kind of problem you're dealing with. Doctors commonly diagnose sudden *unilateral* (one side of the spine) and *bilateral* (both sides of the spine) lower back pain that radiates or pulses and is accompanied by muscle spasms as a *lumbar muscle strain* or a *pulled muscle.* Although the pain from these muscle injuries can be intense, it is often localized and no better or worse when you move.

Pain that radiates down through the leg and hip region, or that starts as leg or hip pain alone may not be a hip problem at all, but a back problem. *Lumbar disk degeneration* or a *herniated disk* may not show up in the form of back pain, but as leg pain, hip pain, or even foot pain. The onset of this pain can be gradual, or it may come in one big explosive episode. Usually prolonged sitting, leaning forward from a standing or seated position, or coughing or sneezing aggravates pain from these conditions.

Facet joint problems (irritation in the area where the disks connect) are usually *localized,* meaning that you feel the pain where the problem is located instead of being disguised in the hips or legs. The problem with facet joint injuries is that the pain often comes and goes, which lulls you into a false sense of believing that nothing is wrong. Left untreated, these problems can lead to major difficulties that can require surgery.

Because so many problems in the back are similar in the symptoms they present, having all back problems checked out by a qualified physician is imperative. Just letting it go can lead to disastrous consequences.

TOUR TALK

Back on track

It seemed like such a vexing problem. European star Jose Maria Olazabal, former Masters champion and Ryder Cup hero, was, for practical purposes, bedridden with a mysterious pain in his feet that doctors from around the world had unsuccessfully attempted to cure. By late 1995 the pain in his feet had become so unbearable that Olazabal was forced to literally crawl from his bed to the bathroom. The prognosis was grim. Many doctors said that Olazabal had been stricken with rheumatoid arthritis, and his chances of playing golf competitively again were severely limited. It appeared as though Spain's golfing hero would be sidelined, a promising golf career cut interminably short.

Then Olazabal got a call from a German doctor who wanted to test a theory he had been considering. This doctor believed that Olazabal didn't suffer from arthritis, and in fact didn't suffer from foot problems at all. He believed the problem originated and emanated from the lower back. That diagnosis proved to be correct. After 18 months of crippling misdiagnoses and excruciating pain, Olazabal finally had relief. The treatment on the lumbar region of his back did the trick. In 1997, he once again assumed the role of Ryder Cup leader as the Europeans retained the cup in his homeland of Spain, and in 1999, Olazabal entered the elite realm of multiple-major winner when he captured his second Masters title.

What could have been a career ending foot injury turned out to be a very treatable back ailment, and rather than watching golf on television from the confines of his bed, Olazabal is once again a competitive force in championship golf.

Preventing Problems before They Start

Although some back problems are unavoidable, you can head the vast majority of them off at the pass through proper fitness training, good technique, and few common-sense steps that protect your back from stress and strain.

Strengthening your abs

Weak abdominals and added weight in the midsection combine to create major unwanted strains on your lower back. Too much weight in the midsection adds more stress to the back because the lumbar muscles must support that additional weight. Weak abdominal muscles also lead to poor posture at address, which puts even more strain on the lower back.

Because the abdominals are opposing muscles to the lumbar muscles of the back, you must be sure to give equal weight to strengthening both your front and your back. Crunches and other abdominal exercises that I outline in Chapter 9 are very useful for preventing back problems.

Anything that strengthens the trunk lowers your chances of injury. A solid abdomen goes a long way toward keeping the back doctor at bay.

Stretching for protection

Just because you aren't playing golf today doesn't mean you shouldn't stretch your back. Regular stretching exercises for the back, abdomen, and sides protect the back from injury, and should be done on a daily basis regardless of your future golf plans. It's easy to forget about stretching in the middle of the winter when golf is the last thing on your mind, but winter is exactly the time when you need to stretch. By keeping the back strong and flexible in the off season, you dramatically reduce the risk of injury when you do return to the course.

The stretching exercises that I outline in Chapter 9 are invaluable when it comes to protecting your back. I recommend making them a part of your daily routine, no less important than brushing your teeth or combing your hair. Other benefits to stretching every day include:

- ✔ **You feel better no matter what you're doing.** Sitting in the office, driving the kids to school, or just relaxing at home all feel better if you have taken a few minutes out of the day to stretch.

- ✔ **The rust from a golf layoff won't show quite as quickly or dramatically if you have kept up with your stretching.** A couple of weeks without swinging a club won't kill your game as long as your back is still limber from exercise.

- ✔ **The risk of non-golf-related back problems goes down when you stretch every day.** Feeling confident on the golf course because of the precautions you're taking is wonderful, but knowing that you can reach the can of peaches on the top shelf of the pantry without fear of injury is equally comforting.

Back stretches should take no more than 10 minutes a day. For example, Laura Baugh does her daily stretches in the shower so that the pulsating hot water can add to the experience. When and where you stretch is irrelevant. The point is to do it every day. Your back, your golf game, and your life will be better for it.

Taking a professional lesson

Poor form is a major cause of back problems in amateurs, and no amount of strengthening or stretching can help your back if your posture and swing are putting you in a dangerous position. The best way to insure that your form isn't potentially damaging your back is to see a golf professional and take a lesson.

When you get to the practice tee with your teaching pro, be an active participant in the teaching process and do the following:

✔ **Explain your health concerns to your instructor.** If you explain your desire to minimize pressure on your back, your pro will know what to look for and what recommendations to make.

✔ **Talk with your pro about your practice and playing schedule.** If your teacher recommends changes that require three-day-a-week practice sessions and you practice only one hour a week, the lesson hasn't done either of you any good. By being up front with your pro about your goals and the amount of time you can devote to your game, both of you come out winners.

✔ **Ask for a video lesson if your club or driving range provides it.** Videotaping has become such an integral part of teaching these days that most facilities offer video as an option. When it comes to proper form and the pressures you place on your back, nothing works better than seeing yourself on tape.

✔ **Explain your off-course workout plans to your instructor.** It's always good for teachers to know what their students do away from the course to prepare themselves. Your strengthening, stretching, and cardio endurance regimen are important factors to share with your golf instructor.

Most people take golf lessons to improve their golf games, but an added benefit to game improvement is injury prevention. If you enter the lesson with injury prevention as your primary objective, improving your game can be a welcome byproduct.

Warming up well

Warming up your back prior to practice or play is one of the best preventative measures you can take to protect yourself from injury. The back is vulnerable enough. You don't need to add to the potential problems by jumping out of the car on a cool afternoon and heading straight to the first tee after sitting at your desk all day. You can do plenty of things to warm up quickly and protect your back without delaying your round. A little extra time on the front end may prevent a debilitating injury in the long run. With that idea in mind, carefully run through the following basic warm-up drills before charging off to the first tee:

✔ **Spend at least five minutes going through the stretching drills that I outline in Chapter 9, as well as the warm-up drills in Chapter 5.** Even if it means hitting fewer practice balls before you play, these warm-up exercises are invaluable to your health and your game. You will actually play better if you hit no balls and warm up effectively than if you hit a full bucket of balls with no warm-up.

- ✔ **After going through your stretches and warm-ups, hit a few pitch shots before taking any full swings.** Don't let your first shot of the day be a full-throttle, out-of-your-shoes rip with a driver. If you do, it may be your last swing of the day, week, month, or year. Work yourself slowly into a full swing, saving the driver until you are warm and ready.

- ✔ **Take a few swings from the opposite side.** If you are a right handed player, turn the club over and take a few left-handed practice swings, and if you are left-handed, try swinging a few times from the right side. Doing so promotes balance in the muscles and gets the muscles on both sides of your back ready to perform.

Not mimicking what you see on TV

Golf professionals are well-conditioned athletes who hit hundreds of balls a day. They have honed their skills and toned their bodies to make highly effective golf swings. Unless you put countless hours and unlimited effort into your game, mimicking what you see on TV is foolhardy. Not only are you unlikely to succeed, you may hurt yourself in the process.

Gary McCord, who is an outstanding Senior Tour player (and author of _Golf For Dummies,_ 2nd Edition, Hungry Minds, Inc.), said of Tiger Woods, "If I tried to swing like that, not only would I hurt myself, I would probably screw myself into the ground!" If Gary can't do it, you can't either. These men and women are professionals. Copying certain aspects of their swings can do serious damage to your back.

Lifting your bag carefully

The list of players who have injured their backs by lifting their golf bags out of car trunks or off luggage racks at airports is astonishing. Davis Love, Calvin Peete, and David Toms are just a few of the professionals who have either injured or aggravated existing back problems by carelessly lifting their golf bags. Even a light golf bag can cause damage to your back if you lift it incorrectly.

Just as you have to pay attention to your form when lifting weights during strength training, you also need to watch your form as you lift your bag out of your car, off your golf cart, or out of storage. Haste leads to injury when lifting your clubs. Never jerk your bag up.

Dressing warmly in cool weather

Cold muscles are tighter than warm muscles, and without adequate cold weather clothing, you may be putting your back at risk. If you've ever worked outside in cold weather — shoveling snow, raking leaves, or stacking firewood, for example — you understand how quickly your back muscles can fatigue.

That same fatigue occurs on the golf course, which leads to tension in your back muscles. Tension leads to stress, which could lead to injury. A warm sweater, padded vest, or extra insulating layer around your midsection can prevent potential problems. Like the Boy Scouts always say, be prepared.

Avoiding hillsides

Not everyone hits the golf ball into the middle of every fairway (except in their dreams!). Even the best players misfire and find themselves with awkward side-hill lies. When that happens, taking extra precautions to protect your back is vitally important. Simply walking along a hillside with one foot higher than the other can lead to back problems. Always try to walk straight up and straight down hills, and take special care to keep your footing secure when standing or hitting a shot from a hillside.

Getting a double-strapped golf bag

The days of the single-strapped golf bag are over. Bag technology has advanced to the point where balanced, double-strapped bags (see Figure 13-4) are a must. You carry these bags like hiking backpacks, with straps on both shoulders instead of just one. This duel strap system distributes the weight of the bag over both shoulders and eliminates unbalanced pressure on the muscles of the lower back. Given the cost of the therapy and prescription drugs you may need if you injure your back, the cost of a new double-strapped golf bag is a bargain.

Checking your shoes

Shoe support is a much bigger deal than most people think. Bad golf shoes, or good golf shoes with worn spikes, have caused countless back injuries over the years. But just as golf bag technology has advanced, shoe technology is light-years ahead of where it was only a decade or so ago. A good pair of shoes can save your back. Talk to your local pro or sporting goods specialist about the features and benefits of the newest footwear on the market.

Figure 13-4:
A double-strapped golf bag is a must to protect your back.

Handling Back Injuries

Sometimes back injuries happen no matter how much prevention you apply. When they do, the first order of business is to stop what you're doing and rest your back. Of all the injuries that you can possibly sustain in your back, none is improved by simply working through the pain. All you do when you try to gut it out is further aggravate the injury and possibly prolong your recovery.

All backs are different, and the problems that can arise are many and varied. But here are some universal steps to take if you have back pain or if you feel as though you may have an injury in the back region. Consider the following:

✔ **See a doctor:** Self-diagnosis when it comes to back pain is impractical at best and, more often than not, foolish. Too often, ailments in the lumbar and thoracic region mask themselves with other conflicting symptoms. Only a doctor can effectively analyze the state of your back and determine an effective course of treatment.

✔ **Take an aspirin:** Over-the-counter non-steroid anti-inflammatory drugs, such as aspirin or ibuprofen can't hurt an ailing back, and they could definitely help your problem. When you use these products as directed, these anti-inflammatory medicines can tide you over until you see your doctor.

✔ **Follow the R.I.S.E. prescription:** Dr. Cindy Chang, M.D. at the U.C. Berkeley Health Center devised a prescription that is both simple and effective for treatment of muscle-related back pain due to golf. She calls it the R.I.S.E. prescription, and it stands for:

- **Rest:** Cut back on the frequency and intensity of the action that caused the pain in the first place, and if the problem is serious, spend some time becoming reacquainted with a firm mattress. Complete bed rest probably isn't the answer to your back problems unless a physician says so, but ample rest is important to any recovery process.

- **Ice/heat:** In the first 48 hours after an injury, apply ice to reduce swelling and inflammation. After 48 hours, heat in the form of warm baths or showers works as an effective treatment.

- **Support:** Consider a brace or wrap to provide you with support and mobility.

- **Exercise:** You eventually have to get back into action. With the guidance of a physician, walking, and a slow reentry into the golf game complete your treatment.

Trying to come back too soon from a back problem can only lead to more trouble. In 1998, Ernie Els injured his back two weeks before the U.S. Open. He immediately flew to Georgia to meet with Tom Boers, and the two of them tried to get Ernie's back into condition for the second major of the year. Tom advised Ernie to get off his feet for a while, which Els did, but not long enough. Ernie's back wasn't ready when he arrived in San Francisco for the championship, and he played terribly. It was another two months before he was back in shape again, a time that perhaps could have been shortened if he had gotten plenty of rest up front.

You shouldn't walk around in fear of injuring your back, but don't ignore the potential dangers inherent in the golf game either. Preparation, precaution, and prevention can prevent back problems. And a solid plan for recovery can minimize the effects of an injury if it occurs. Take your back seriously, and look after it.

Chapter 14

What's Up with My Rotator Cuff?

"A lot of people think a shoulder injury is no big deal. Well, I'm living proof that for a golfer a shoulder injury is a huge deal, a devastating deal."

— Jerry Pate, 1976 U.S. Open Champion

*B*ecause your shoulders are such a critical part of the golf swing, shoulder strength, and shoulder health are major concerns for golfers of all ages, but particularly for those golfers over 40 who are losing muscle mass with age. Older golfers are 15 percent more likely to sustain rotator cuff injuries than golfers in their teens, twenties, and thirties because older shoulders are more susceptible to trauma and more vulnerable to repetitive motion injury.

Without strong, healthy shoulders the other mechanics of the golf swing don't mean much. Strong legs and hips, for example, are no good if your shoulders can't turn (see Chapter 5). A strong back and a strong abdominal region are meaningless in terms of your golf swing if your shoulders aren't able to support the *swing plane* (see Chapter 6) and uncoil in a manner that generates maximum clubhead speed at impact.

Without a proper shoulder turn around an axis, you have no golf swing. The only option left for a player with limited or restricted shoulder mobility is to pick the club straight up in the air with the hands and arms and throw it at the ball with the biceps, triceps, and forearms. Not only is such a motion impossible to control and repeat, it creates no leverage and generates little clubhead speed. The result is a short, off-line shot. In this chapter, I explain how the rotator cuff works and give you some strength and flexibility exercises that are a must in preventing potentially devastating injuries.

Gender and shoulder strength

A striking disparity exists among genders when it comes to shoulder injury. Only 11 percent of male amateurs and professionals experience shoulder problems. But 16.1 percent of female amateurs experience problems with the rotator cuff. The discrepancy between amateur women and professional women is even more pronounced. Only 7.5 percent of female pros have shoulder problems, less than half the number of female amateurs who have trouble, and 3.5 percent less than all male golfers.

So, why are amateur women more likely to have shoulder problems than men and female professionals? The only logical answer is technique.

Female professionals hit more balls and play more rounds than amateurs, so professionals are actually more likely to suffer injuries from repetition than their amateur counterparts. But professionals, both men and women, have sound swing mechanics and aren't putting undue stress and strain on their shoulders because of poor technique. The same cannot be said of amateurs who put enormous strains on their shoulders by swinging the club in all sorts of odd ways.

But that doesn't explain why both professional and amateur men have the same percentage of shoulder injuries while women amateurs are more than twice as likely as female professionals to have shoulder problems. Women amateurs don't swing the golf club any worse than average or poor playing men. Why is there such a big difference between professional and amateur women when a similar difference doesn't exist between male amateurs and professionals?

The answer to that one is strength. Men are (for the most part) physically more powerful than women, which means the male shoulder can get away with making goofy swings better than the female shoulder. The good news for women is that as their form and technique improve to the point where they are considered in the top echelon of amateurs or on par with club pros, their chances of having a shoulder injury decrease below that of men. This provides another great argument for taking golf lessons from a qualified professional. Not only can women who practice good technique eventually beat their male playing partners on the course, they will stay healthier and more injury-free.

Your Shoulder: A Real Hoppin' Joint

You have four muscles that run over the top of the shoulder, around the sides, and up from the arm to hold the shoulder in place and give the joint its full range of motion. The ends of those four muscles form tendons that fuse together where the *humerus* (the large bone of the upper arm) meets the *glenoid* (the bone structure at the end of the scapula that acts as a socket for the ball of the shoulder). These fusing tendons form what is known as the *rotator cuff,* the Grand Central Station of the shoulder (see Figure 14-1).

Think of the shoulder as a universal joint. It allows your arm to roll in a circular fashion like a windmill, to reach across your chest and grab your opposite arm, to reach up, out and back, and to rotate your arm in both directions. To gain a feel for all the motions your shoulder goes through in golf, try the following:

1. **Stretch your arm in front of you as far as you can, as if you were reaching for an object just outside your grasp.**

2. **Make that same move over your head, reaching as high as possible and stretching the shoulder upward as far as you can.**

3. **Now, reach across your chest, grabbing your opposite shoulder and pulling, as if you're giving yourself a one-armed hug.**

4. **After a few seconds of holding that hug, reach behind your back and touch one of the *thoracic vertebrae* between your shoulder blades.**

5. **Finally, place your elbow on a table with your hand in the air and rotate your forearm like a windshield wiper, palm touching the table on one sweep and the back of your hand touching the table on the other sweep.**

That full range of motion illustrates the extremes your shoulders go through during the golf swing. Your muscles are called upon to pull, push, twist, and rotate, all in one fluid and repeatable motion.

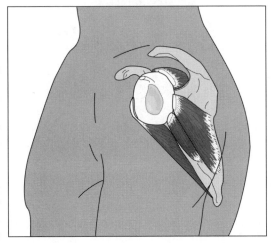

Figure 14-1:
The rotator cuff is the center of the shoulder universe, where all its muscles ultimately converge.

Shouldering a Proper Golf Swing

During the golf swing the lead shoulder rotates internally — just like the windshield wiper action in the exercise earlier in the chapter. It also moves laterally across the chest. The shoulder lifts the arm as you bring the club back on plane. All these motions are reversed on the downswing with a little added pressure. As the hips initiate the downswing and pull the shoulders behind them, the lead shoulder rotates externally, again just like the windshield-wiper drill. It also moves laterally back across the chest, only this time it has more force behind it because the lower body is pulling the shoulders down (see Chapter 6 for more on the mechanics of the downswing). You got this feeling when you gave yourself the one-armed hug in the example exercise earlier in the chapter.

The trailing (or non-target) shoulder is also called upon to make a series of complex motions during the swing. As the trunk rotates and turns the shoulders on the backswing, the trailing shoulder rotates, setting the right arm at the top of the swing and keeping the club on plane. This puts enormous pressure on the rotator cuff. That pressure increases as the hips initiate the downswing and the trailing shoulder is pulled into the action. The elbow and wrist of the trailing arm generate a great deal of the club's speed through impact, and the trailing shoulder rotates across the chest as the upper body drives through impact and follow-through (see Figure 14-2).

Figure 14-2:
Swing
sequence
from
takeaway to
impact.

The complex action with the shoulders requires synchronized and balanced movements between all the muscles in and around the rotator cuff. Anything that throws off that synchronization, such as poor form, bad timing, or weakness and tightness in one or more of the essential muscle groups, creates a potential crisis in the rotator cuff as the other muscles compensate for your miscue.

Recognizing the Causes of Rotator Cuff Injuries

Regardless of the sport, two primary causes of injury exist for the rotator cuff: repetition and trauma. Take baseball, for example. Overhand throwing of a baseball is not, in and of itself, a dangerous action. Children and adults do it every day. But major league pitchers must be extremely cautious about the frequency of their pitching. You rarely see a starting pitcher throw more than once every four or five days. On those occasions when a pitcher does pitch on three days of rest, coaches monitor his pitch count very closely to make sure that he doesn't overdo it. A hundred or so pitches and a starter who is working on three days rest is normally removed from the game regardless of how well he is throwing.

Golfers don't have the support of coaches, teammates, middle-relievers, and closing pitchers. Nor do most amateur golfers have a team of orthopedists standing by after every round to monitor the condition of their bones and joints. Golfers are, for the most part, on their own, and like any other athletes, they sometimes overdo it.

Repetition: Getting too much of a good thing

Even if you swing the golf club perfectly every time you hit a ball in practice or during a round (a golfing impossibility, but a nice thought nonetheless), you put repetitive strain on your rotator cuffs. As you age this strain becomes more of a problem because 40-year-old tendons are naturally harder and tighter than 20-year-old tendons. You may not practice any more or less than you did 10 years ago, but certain body parts (like your rotator cuffs) now respond differently to that practice. Repetitive motions such as hitting 50 to 100 balls before or after play create problems in the shoulder.

No magic number of repetitions pushes you over the edge and causes injury to your rotator cuff. Some people have no trouble hitting hundreds of balls a day, while others start to fatigue after only 20 or 30 balls. That's why strengthening and stretching the entire shoulder region is such a critical component to injury prevention. But you also need to take a look at how and how often you practice and what effect that practice has on your shoulder health.

Golf is like any other athletic endeavor: Gradually working yourself into shape is much better than overdoing it in grand but sporadic sessions. You wouldn't run a marathon if you hadn't run at all in several months, nor would you be likely to embark on an eight-hour power-lifting strength training session if you hadn't lifted weights in more than a year.

You know better than to embark on such foolish and fanciful endeavors, but that logic often escapes your noggin when it comes to golf. If you're like most amateurs, you think nothing of riding out to the driving range on the first pretty day of spring after a month or more of golf-less solitude. When on the practice tee you proceed to hit a mountain of range balls, as if hundreds of swings in one mammoth session will expel all the cobwebs that winter left on your game.

The same is true of preparing to play in your club championship, for example. Too many people rush out to the range the week before the tournament in an attempt to cram an entire summer's worth of practice into six days. As a result they usually play worse than if they had simply maintained their normal practice and playing routines, and there is a better than average chance that they will sustain some injury as a result of these overzealous sessions.

Here are some other steps you can take to protect over-40 shoulders from repetition-induced injury:

- ✔ **Always warm up your shoulders before taking any swings, even if you don't plan to hit many balls.**

- ✔ **Stretch your shoulders before and after your practice and play. Limber muscles and stretched tendons are less prone to injury.**

- ✔ **Be aware of the temperature.** Cold muscles tend to stiffen quicker than warm muscles, and stiffer muscles are more prone to repetition injuries. You may feel completely comfortable hitting balls in 40-degree temperatures, but your shoulders are working twice as hard as normal to swing the club and stay warm. An extra layer of clothing — either a vest, sweater, or jacket — in moderate to cool temperatures will insulate your vulnerable muscles and reduce the risk of injury.

- ✔ **Have a practice plan and stick to it.** Beating balls simply for the sake of being on the practice tee isn't doing your game any good, and may harm your health. Always arrive on the range with a plan and stick to that plan. If you're working on your wedge game, don't stay on the range an extra hour to hit drivers. You're not doing your body or your game any good.

✔ **Spend as much time stretching and strengthening your shoulders as you spend practicing your swing.** Stronger and more flexible rotator cuffs are less likely to sustain injury. The more time you spend strengthening and stretching the shoulders, the less time you will spend away from the game due to injury.

Acute *tendonitis,* or inflammation in the tendons of the rotator cuff, is the most common self-inflicted shoulder injury that comes from overdoing it. But tearing of the tendons can also occur from this sort of repetition. That tearing can be devastating. You could lose your ability to lift your arms above your head, or even pick up a glass of water. In those extreme circumstances, surgery is the most likely course of corrective action. It doesn't have to be that way, however. By changing your habits, you can minimize the chances of that gloomy prognosis, and keep the surgeon away.

Here are some things to keep in mind:

✔ **Never resume a full practice and playing schedule immediately after a long layoff.** Gradually work yourself back into full-blown practice sessions without taking on too much too quickly.

✔ **Play a few nine-hole rounds in the early days of the season.** It's tempting to take advantage of a pretty day by playing as much golf as you can in the time that you have, but doing so can lead to serious problems. A more disciplined approach is to leave a little daylight for others and play only nine holes the first few times out.

✔ **Try swinging a club in slow motion at home to keep your muscles tuned and toned without adding to any potential repetition problems.** Going through your swing as slowly as possible provides some strength to the shoulders while keeping the muscles warm and attuned to the actions of the swing.

✔ **Stop practicing and playing the moment you feel any fatigue or soreness in your shoulders.** It doesn't matter if you have hit only 10 shots; if your shoulders say it's time to quit, you need to pack up and save your shoulders for another day.

Trauma: Not what you see on ER

Rotator cuff injures are pretty evenly divided between those caused by repetition and those that result from some trauma. When you say trauma, people usually conjure up images of an emergency room with teams of doctors swarming around a critical patient. Although things like broken bones, heart attacks, and gunshot wounds are definitely traumatic, they aren't the kinds of traumas many over-40 golfers have to worry about.

A new approach

With his 41st birthday looming and his game at an all-time low, Payne Stewart wasn't sure how to mount the career comeback he knew he had in him. He loved to practice his game, but he couldn't spend hours on the range beating balls any more. His shoulders were already showing signs of age and the last thing he needed was a debilitating tear in his rotator cuff. Shoulder surgery would all but end any chances he had of making a comeback. He knew he needed to change his routine, but adding more practice time wasn't necessarily the answer.

Instead of spending more time on the range, Payne took a different route. He hired a personal trainer, installed a gym in his Orlando home, and began an intensive workout regimen to strengthen, among other things, his weakening shoulders. Rather than spend hours on the driving range after a round when he was out on tour, Payne would hit a few balls to work out any kinks that may have crept into his swing, and then adjourn to the tour's fitness trailer for a full workout focusing on strength and flexibility in the shoulder region with particular emphasis on the rotator cuff.

The strategy paid off. Payne finished second at the 1998 U.S. Open in San Francisco, then came back with two wins in 1999 at the AT&T Pebble Beach Pro-Am and the 1999 U.S. Open at Pinehurst. He was also a member of the victorious U.S. Ryder Cup team. During this revitalization of his game, Payne spent no more time on the driving range than he had in previous seasons. He simply prepared his body, including his shoulders, better for the course.

The kind of trauma that adversely affects your rotator cuff can be anything from banging your shoulder against a doorframe to hitting a root or a rock on your downswing. It doesn't take much to create a minor injury in an older rotator cuff because the tendons aren't as flexible, and they are more prone to strains or tears. Some of the minor traumas that can lead to rotator cuff injuries in golfers include:

- ✔ **Hitting the ground before the ball during the swing, which is commonly referred to as *hitting it fat.*** This seems like a minor incident, but if you think about it, your club is traveling between 80 and 100 miles per hour during the downswing. Sticking the clubhead in the ground while the shoulders continue to turn through the swing is like a mini car wreck. It can easily tear the vulnerable tendons of the rotator cuff.

- ✔ **Hitting an object other than the ball such as a tree root, rock, or hardpan surface.** If your body is prepared for the impact of club against ball, anything that disrupts that preparation or adds to the event is considered a mild trauma. You may feel what's known as a *stinger,* where a jolt of pain shoots up your hands and arms but dissipates after a few minutes, or it could result in something far worse, such as a strain or tear in a muscle or tendon.

✔ **Changing or modifying your swing to suit specific circumstances on the course.** For example, you make a punch swing around a tree or a swing designed to curve the ball one way or the other or maybe you just make a bad swing. Whatever the cause, this sort of change can result in enough trauma to cause injury.

✔ **Playing hurt.** As I allude to in an earlier analogy in this book, a small injury to the rotator cuff is like a small pothole in the highway. Another way to think of it is like a cassette or VHS tape. A small scratch on the tape can go unnoticed or simply be a minor annoyance in the early going. But the more times you play the tape, the more pronounced the problem becomes until the tape is unusable. If you continue to practice and play with a slight shoulder injury, it could easily become a big shoulder injury that requires dramatic treatment to repair.

Some of these traumas are accidents that cannot be avoided while others are created solely by the golfer. Either way, the following are some things you need to do immediately upon experiencing a trauma in the rotator cuff:

✔ **Stop playing or practicing.** Further aggravating an injury by continuing to play is counterproductive and foolish.

✔ **Check the range of motion and degrees of pain in the shoulder.** If you have full mobility and no pain, you're probably safe. But if you can't move your shoulder in a particular direction (like lifting your arm above your head), or you experience a stabbing pain when you move your shoulder, you have a problem.

✔ **Immobilize and rest your shoulder immediately, adding ice in the first 48 hours if you experience any swelling.** Doing so may not completely remedy the problem, but it won't hurt it either. It's a good precaution until you can have your shoulder checked out by a specialist.

✔ **See a doctor.** Even if you haven't torn your rotator cuff, your doctor may prescribe some specific exercises or treatments to strengthen and protect that area for the future.

Strengthening Your Rotator Cuff

All shoulder-strengthening exercises are important for better golf as you get older, and I recommend incorporating various shoulder exercises into your regular workout routine (see Chapter 8). But, in this section I explain some strengthening drills specifically designed for the rotator cuff. Look at them as preventative medicine, a protective tune-up for a vulnerable body part. If you've experienced rotator cuff problems in the past, these lifts are also great rehab exercises.

Of course, always seek the advice of a physician or physical therapist before embarking on any rehabilitation program, but if your doctor clears you to work out, these exercises can go to the top of your list.

Side-lateral deltoid lift

This specific machine exercise strengthens the major muscles of the shoulder that protect the rotator cuff. Sitting in the provided seat and facing the stack of weights, place the outsides of your arms on the pads and grab the handles. Then in a singular, fluid, lifting motion, slowly raise your elbows and forearms like a bird raising its wings before flight (see Figure 14-3). You'll feel this exercise in the center of your shoulders. After fully raising your arms, slowly lower them back to the start position without dropping the weight or rushing the return. Depending on your current fitness level, repeat 10 to 20 repetitions. Select a weight that allows you to complete the recommended number of reps.

Figure 14-3: The side-lateral deltoid lift protects the rotator cuff from injury.

External rotation

The king of all rotator cuff exercises is a lift called *external rotation*. This is a free-weight exercise in which you lie on your side with your bottom arm extended directly above you as if you were using your biceps as a pillow. Then bending the top arm, place your elbow against your side. Holding a dumbbell in your top hand (palm down) lift the weight, keeping your elbow against your side and the triceps against your body (see Figure 14-4). Repeat this lift 10 to 20 times with each arm, depending on your fitness level.

The external rotator lift is not a large move. Your rotator cuff may not have a great range of motion in this direction, and you shouldn't force it farther than is comfortable. Never lift the weight so far that your arm extends behind your body. A small lift is more beneficial than a big one with this exercise.

Figure 14-4:
Kelly strengthens the rotator cuff through external rotation.

Internal rotators

The *internal rotation* strengthens the rotator cuff by working the shoulder in the opposite direction of the external rotators. This exercise is critical for balance in strengthening all parts of the rotator cuff.

For this exercise you lie on your side, but instead of extending your bottom arm outward like a pillow, prop your head up with a firm pillow or a rolled towel and tuck your bottom arm close to your body, bending it at the elbow. Keeping your triceps against your body and holding a dumbbell in your bottom hand (palm up), lift the weight to your chest with a rotating motion that keeps the elbow planted on the floor (see Figure 14-5). Repeat the action slowly and fluidly for 10 to 20 reps, depending on your fitness level and then repeat to the opposite side.

Figure 14-5:
Kelly working the internal rotation.

You'll likely feel a tendency to jerk the weight up from this position by lifting the elbow and arm off the floor. That is the natural tendency your body has to let larger, stronger muscles take over. In order for this exercise to be effective you need to pay close attention to form. If you need a lighter weight, by all means use whatever weight you can comfortably and effectively lift. Like the external rotator, this is not a big motion. Don't overdo it.

No injuries are good, but rotator cuff injuries can be particularly devastating, and sometimes, as in the case of Jerry Pate, career ending! As you age, you should do whatever it takes to strengthen and protect your rotator cuffs.

Chapter 15

Avoiding Hand and Elbow Injuries

In This Chapter

▶ Understanding golfers' elbow and how to prevent it

▶ Recognizing and preventing some other common hand injuries

▶ Using strength and flexibility drills for your hands, wrists, and elbows

> *"If you use anything other than an ideal grip, then the compensations you make will probably lead to inconsistencies and unnecessary injuries. I've noticed in tennis, for instance, that a weak grip puts strain on the elbow and can lead to tennis elbow. You have to factor that into any changes you consider in golf."*
>
> — Nick Price

*B*ecause the only real link you have with the golf club is through your hands, it's not a big surprise that golfers' hands and wrists are prone to injury. These injuries can range from mildly annoying soreness in the thumb to swelling, immobility, and pain in the fingers and wrists. Sometimes rest is all that you need to cure these ailments, but golfers are also prone to more serious hand and wrist injuries that could require rest, and even surgery to correct.

The same idea holds true with your elbows. The muscles in your forearms along with your biceps and triceps form tendons at the elbow, and you occasionally strain those tendons by repetitive use. These repetitive use injuries are common among older amateurs and they can lead to painful problems.

More than 30 percent of all amateurs experience some pain or injury in their hands, wrists, elbows, or all of the above. Hand and wrist ailments are the leading injuries among all professionals, substantially greater in terms of total numbers and percentages than back problems (see Chapter 13) or shoulder pain (see Chapter 14). The large hand-and-wrist-injury disparity between professionals and top-notch amateurs and those recreational golfers with slightly higher handicaps depends on two factors:

> ✔ Good players generate more clubhead speed; therefore, their hands move faster through impact than most amateurs.
>
> ✔ Professionals and top-notch amateurs hit more golf shots than occasional players, which means the best players are more inclined to suffer the ill effects of *repetition injuries* (injuries that result from making the same motion over and over).

But a reverse disparity exists with elbow injuries. Amateurs are far more likely than professionals to have elbow problems, which warrants a closer look.

Golf Elbow and the Over-40 Game

The term, *golf elbow* isn't as openly used in today's vernacular as the term *tennis elbow*, but the two afflictions are very similar. Tennis elbow, medically known as *lateral epicondylitis* occurs in the racquet arm of tennis players, and results from hitting backhand shots where the racket arm is extended during an across-the-chest swing. The *pronation and supination* (turning the palm downward or upward) that go with this shot sometimes lead to small tears or strains in the *exterior* tendons of the elbow. As a result, small motions become so painful that daily life becomes difficult. A tennis elbow sufferer may not be able to open a jar or lift a book off the floor because of the pain. The only way to treat this injury is to rest and immobilize the elbow until the body can heal itself.

These symptoms affect golfers in slightly different spots within the elbow, but for almost exactly the same reasons. With golf elbow, which is technically called *medial epicondylitis,* the lead arm is normally affected. An overwhelming number of cases (more than 90 percent) report pain in the lead arm, which is the left arm for those who play right-handed, and just as is the case in tennis elbow, the tendons in the joint are prone to strain, inflammation, and minor tears. The only difference is that in golf elbow the *inner* tendons are affected. The reason that golf elbow is isolated to the inner part of the joint is that all the *flexor muscles* — the muscles that pull the palm of the hand toward the arm — connect with the inner part of the elbow called the *medial epicondyle.* Inflammation and tenderness occur in the medial epicondyle region from the repeated pronation and supination of arms during the golf swing. Minor traumas, like hitting shots fat, are also a common cause of golf elbow. See Figure 15-1 for a closer look at the elbow.

Understanding what golf elbow is doesn't explain why amateurs are five times more likely to get it than pros. In fact, because golf elbow is a repetition injury, logic would dictate that pros are more likely to suffer its effects than are amateurs. After all, pros hit more balls, but most instances of golf elbow occur in amateurs 35 or older who play more than three rounds a week.

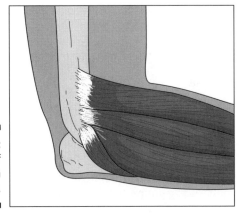

Figure 15-1:
Graphic of the human elbow.

Older amateurs are more likely to suffer from golf elbow than pros who play and practice six days a week for the following reasons:

✔ **Weaker forearm muscles and tighter tendons.** The flexor muscles of the hand and forearm aren't normally high on anyone's stretch list, so as those muscles and tendons become stiffer with age the likelihood of suffering from golf elbow increases dramatically.

✔ **Increased grip pressure.** Strain on the tendons in the elbow is directly linked to the amount of pressure being applied on those tendons. The tighter you grip the golf club, the more stress you place on the medial epicondyle. Pros don't choke their clubs in a death grip; many amateurs do. That's the major difference between the percentages of pros with golf elbow and amateurs who suffer from this injury.

✔ **Higher frequency of common swing mistakes.** Overcocking the wrists and lifting the club with your hands strains the flexor muscles and puts undue pressure on the tendons of your elbow.

Recognizing and treating golf elbow

Sometimes the pain from golf elbow is mild, a small annoyance that goes away after you rest your arm for a day or so, but inevitably returns the next time you play. As the injury progresses a dull pain may become more constant. Shaking hands with someone becomes a painful encounter, and lifting slightly heavy objects, such as a packed suitcase shocks your system. The pain is isolated in the inner elbow, making that area tender to the touch at all times, but the pain shoots through your entire body when you put stress on your elbow joint.

If untreated, golf elbow can become so painful that you won't be able to grip a club. Fortunately, it doesn't have to come to that.

In fact, treating golf elbow is easy, and if you catch it early enough the injury shouldn't disrupt your normal routine. Easy remedies include the following that you can do yourself at home.

- ✓ **Rest:** Like in tennis elbow, the inflamed tendons that cause golf elbow simply need time to heal. A couple of days of complete rest with no lifting and little bending of the injured elbow can allow your body's natural healing agents time to work their magic on these sore tendons.

- ✓ **Ice:** For 10 to 15 minutes at a time, several times a day for the first three to four days of your injury, icing your elbow can reduce swelling and ease the pain.

- ✓ **Heat:** If pain continues after the three-day ice treatment, add wet heat to the mix, soaking your elbow in a bowl of warm water for 10 to 15 minutes at a time several times a day for several days. If the pain persists beyond a couple of weeks, see your doctor.

- ✓ **Anti-inflammatory, non-steroid drugs:** Taken as directed, aspirin and ibuprofen help reduce swelling and pain caused by tendon strain. When used with other treatments, an aspirin a day can go a long way toward curing your sore elbow joints.

You can also do the things on the following list with a doctor's supervision or recommendation.

- ✓ **Ultrasound therapy:** Your doctor may prescribe ultrasound treatments for persistent pain from golf elbow. These treatments are painless and effective, but they require regular office visits to your physician.

- ✓ **Steroid injections:** In severe and persistent cases your doctor may recommend injecting a small dose of steroids, such as cortisone into the injured area. This is a radical step, but one that usually works. No matter how serious your condition, rarely do you need more than two or three injections.

- ✓ **Forearm braces:** You can purchase braces specifically designed to reduce pressure on the elbow tendons at most sporting goods stores or through your doctor. These braces aren't always effective at treating golf elbow, but they do help reduce the pain so that you can enjoy yourself on the course.

Preventing elbow problems before they occur

The good news about golf elbow is that with proper exercise and technique you can dramatically reduce your chances of ever having any problems.

Whether you change your grip, adjust your swing, or work a few preventative exercises into your daily routine, you have plenty of simple ways to lower your odds of experiencing this injury.

Reducing your grip pressure

Many scholarly golf instructors have written endless treatises on the importance of a sound grip in golf, but no matter which method you use in your game or which principles of the grip you believe or disbelieve, two things should not be in dispute:

- ✔ No matter what method you use to hold the golf club (see Chapter 3 for more on the different types of grip), the purpose of the grip is to put your hands on the club so that they work as a unit to generate maximum clubhead speed and consistency at impact.

- ✔ Relaxed hands move faster through the hitting zone than tight, tense hands.

To test this golf adage, hold your arm straight in front of you and flap your hand from side to side as if you were slapping an imaginary troll. Now clinch your fist as tightly as possible and attempt to move your hand the same way. The hand moves much slower when you clinch your fist than it does when the hand is open and relaxed. The same thing is true during the golf swing. A tight death grip on the club slows the hands down through impact, while relaxed hands move quickly and efficiently through the hitting zone.

Lightening your grip pressure allows you to move your hands quickly and freely through impact, and reduces the stress on tendons in your hands, wrists, and elbows. Those facts are indisputable. But the problem with that concept is not in logic and reason; the problem lies in the fact that hitting something with relaxed hands goes against your natural instincts. Any time you prepare to hit something, your body naturally tenses. It's a rudimentary response. Whether you hit a punching bag or a ball, your body's natural response is to brace for impact. Tension in your hands extends up your arms and into your chest and back, throwing your entire motion out of synch and leading to potential injuries throughout the body.

You can overcome these tension-related tendencies, but only by focusing on a relaxed grip pressure and diligently practicing a few key things.

- ✔ **Training with molded grips:** Although the rules of golf do not allow you to play with a grip that has been molded or altered in any way (like form-fitted grips that help you place your hands on the club the right way), you can and should practice with these form-fitted grips. In addition to helping place your hands on the club correctly, these molded grips allow you to reduce the tension in your hands without fear of the club slipping or turning as you swing.

You should take one old club out of circulation and dedicate it solely to practice. Doing so allows you to add a molded grip without running afoul of the rules. You can pick up a molded grip at most golf stores, or order one through any of the thousands of catalog and Internet retailers that specialize in golf merchandise. As long as you don't carry your molded club onto the course, you can practice relaxing your grip pressure with a teaching tool that provides enormous long-term benefits to your game.

✔ **Regularly changing the grips on your clubs:** Touring professionals change the grips on their clubs every four to six weeks. Amateurs sometimes go years without changing their grips. This is a critical flaw among amateurs and one that leads to all kinds of unnecessary complications. The simple fact of the matter is that your grips get dirty and worn as they age. As the rubber or synthetic material wears out, it becomes slick, and you have to grip the club tighter to keep it from slipping during the swing. This tighter grip can lead to bad swings and injury.

All that you need to prevent these problems is a little diligence when it comes to caring for your equipment. For example, here are a few proactive suggestions:

- **Regularly replace your grips, adding new grips at least once every two or three months depending on use.**

- **Clean your grips at least as often as you clean your clubheads.** If you wash your clubs after every round, take the time to wash and dry your grips as well.

- **Wipe your grips with a damp towel before every round.** Doing so removes the dirt and oils from your hands that accumulate on the grips. You always see professional caddies wiping down players' grips before, during and after a round. They know the importance of keeping this part of the club clean.

Stretching the forearms

Regular forearm stretches keep the tendons in the elbow and wrist flexible and ready for action. You can do these stretches at any time — sitting in your office, relaxing at home, or during a round of golf. They should become such a natural part of your routine that you perform them reflexively whenever you have a spare moment.

To do these stretches, simply extend one arm directly in front of your chest and flex the wrist as far back as possible. After you've stretched the hand back as far as it will naturally go, use your other hand to extend the stretch a little farther by applying pressure to your fingers (see Figure 15-2). Hold this stretch 15 to 30 seconds and repeat to the opposite side.

Figure 15-2:
Forearm stretches improve your form and prevent possible joint injuries.

After stretching both hands upward, repeat the same motion flexing the hand downward with your palm facing your chest. After the wrist has stretched the hand as far as it will naturally go, extend the stretch by applying pressure to the back of the hand. Hold that stretch for another 30 seconds and repeat to the opposite side.

This entire exercise takes under four minutes, which is less time than the normal advertisement break in your favorite sitcom. If you repeat this exercise at least once a day, you can substantially improve your form and severely diminish your likelihood of elbow injury.

Doing pronation and supination exercises

Because the repetitive *pronation* (rotation of the arm to a palms-down position) and *supination* (rotation of the arm to a palms-up position) of the arms during the golf swing can inflame the tendons in the elbows and wrists, a simple exercise to strengthen those flexor muscles and prepare them for the swing is in order. This exercise requires only a golf club and a willingness on your part to set aside two minutes of your day.

Sitting or standing with your back perfectly straight, your hips tucked forward, and your arm extended in front of your chest, hold the golf club so that it's pointing straight up in the air. Your wrist should be in a neutral position (no angles). Now, slowly rotate your hand into a palm-up position, stopping the motion when the golf club is parallel to the ground (see Figure 15-3). After the club reaches parallel, smoothly and slowly reverse the motion, bringing the club back into the straight-up position before it rotates over to the other side. Continue rotating until the hand is in a palm-down position and the club is, once again, parallel to the ground. Repeat this exercise for one minute with each arm. Remember to do this exercise in a slow and controlled movement. Rushing through any concentrated exercise wastes your time.

Figure 15-3: Pronation and supination exercises strengthen the flexor muscles and cut down on the chance that you may injure yourself.

 When doing the pronation and supination exercises, never let the club extend below parallel to the ground. Dropping the club beyond that point adds nothing to the exercise and seriously increases your chances of injuring your forearm or your rotator cuff. See Chapter 14 for more on the rotator cuff. Also, as is the case with all stretches, take it slowly. This isn't a race. The slower you rotate the club back and forth through these exercises, the more benefit you gain.

It's All in the Thumbs

 The vast majority of golf-related hand problems are actually thumb problems, because the thumb of the lead hand is the most injured digit and the area of the hand most susceptible to injury during the golf swing. Strain and tendonitis are the most common thumb ailments. These injuries have complicated medical names like *De Quervain's tenosynovitis*, which is tendon inflammation in the joint where the thumb meets the wrist, and *intersection syndrome*, which is localized bursitis that is created by friction between the wrist extensors and the thumb tendons. When executed properly the swing creates certain angles and forces that put pressure on the joints of the thumb. That pressure (some of which is unavoidable) is what leads to injury. But there are also some common swing flaws that add to the problem.

 In order to understand and remedy any problems you have with your thumb, consider these common mistakes:

✔ **Direction change and the thumb.** If you swing the club correctly, pronating the lead arm on the backswing with the wrist cocking along the way to keep the club on plane, you're setting your thumb up to absorb a great deal of pressure. As you initiate the downswing with the hips, and the shoulders are subsequently pulled into the downswing, the thumb of the left hand takes the brunt of force in this directional change. The thumb holds the club in place at the top of the backswing, and when the club changes directions, the thumb absorbs all the forces of mass and speed that come with stopping the club and reversing its direction. That can be a burden that even strong thumbs can't handle. Rest at the first sign of pain or discomfort is the most effective treatment for this sort of problem.

✔ **Hitting too many balls.** Although you may not feel fatigue in your hands, constant sustained pressure on the thumb can lead to tiring of the tendons in the lead hand. Weakened hands tend to grip the club harder, which compounds the problem and adds a whole host of other potential injuries to the list, but the thumb is still the most vulnerable. If a digit is going to go, the thumb is far and away the most likely candidate. Figure 15-4 illustrates where the thumb is positioned on the backswing and the downswing and how the thumb absorbs the pressures of the swing.

Figure 15-4:
The left
thumb
isolated at
the top
of the
backswing.

✔ **Throwing the club with the lead thumb.** In this swing, you take the club back beautifully only to ruin any chances that you have of hitting a good shot by firming up your grip at the top of the backswing and throwing the club toward the ball (see Figure 15-5). To the observer this swing flaw resembles a flyfisherman casting his line, with the hands whipping at the top of the cast. That's great for fishing. It's a swing killer in golf, and a flaw that can cause serious damage to your thumb. In addition to the normal pressures of the thumb, casting the club in this fashion creates additional pressure on the tendons. It won't take long for your thumb to fatigue with this swing.

Figure 15-5:
The left thumb isolated as the club is being cast from the top.

✔ **Gripping the club too tightly.** Added tension only increases the problems your tendons have during the swing. A relaxed grip generates more clubhead speed, but it also protects certain tendons from injury. Strengthening the grip of your left hand reduces the tension in your grip and eliminates many of these problems (see Chapter 3).

Treating a sore thumb

Rest is the best treatment for most thumb injuries. Because most injuries are tendon-related, with tendonitis or other forms of inflammation being the most common problems, nothing works better than complete inactivity of the thumb. Unfortunately that is easier said than done. You use your thumb in almost everything you do, including typing, picking up the newspaper, or drinking a cup of coffee. To take your thumb completely out of commission is almost impossible.

To effectively rest your thumb and allow time for it to heal, consider bandaging your thumb to your hand for complete immobility, or purchasing an immobilizing glove that protects the thumb and keeps it rigid while allowing you to use other fingers. These gloves are usually available at sporting good stores or through orthopedists.

Anti-inflammatory, non-steroid drugs are also helpful in reducing swelling and inflammation in the joints of the thumb. Aspirin and ibuprofen are the most common forms of these drugs.

If problems persist, you need to see a doctor. Chronic pain could be a sign of something more serious than a strained tendon, and you need to have it checked out by a qualified physician.

Dealing with other common hand ailments

Repetition causes almost all wrist and hand injuries. A few exceptions exist, such as wrist sprains, finger dislocation, or fractures that occur from trauma, but those traumas have to be pretty severe — like hitting a large rock or some other immovable object. For the most part, hand and wrist pain comes from the continuous repetition of gripping the club, cocking and rotating the wrists during the swing, changing directions from backswing to downswing, and the miniscule trauma that occurs when the club contacts the ball.

The best medicine for repetitive use injuries — which can manifest themselves in such symptoms as numbness in your fingers, pain, swelling, and lack of mobility — is rest. Too often golfers think that hitting balls and practicing for hours is the answer to playing better. Sometimes a little time away from the repetition of the golf swing is the best thing for your game.

The truth about magnets and bracelets

A huge cottage industry has sprung up in recent years promoting and selling magnetic therapy for golf-related injuries. Magnets are sown into belts to help golfers who have back problems, and they are added to bracelets to help eliminate pain in the hands and wrists. The manufacturers of these products claim that magnets increase the flow of blood to the injured region of the body, thus improving the body's healing powers. Unfortunately, there is no definitive medical evidence supporting these claims. There are plenty of case studies and lots of anecdotal evidence, but for those who are looking for AMA approval or other qualifying documentation, magnets haven't passed the test yet. That's not to say they are bad for you. In fact, a lot of pros and plenty of experts swear by their healing effects. One thing is certain: Magnets won't hurt you. Whether or not they help is still up for debate, but for those who are up for a little experimentation, it's worth giving them a try.

The same is true with copper bracelets that supposedly provide homeopathic healing to the wrists and hands. Everything from carpal tunnel syndrome to mild forms of arthritis is said to be cured by these magic bracelets. Again, there is plenty of anecdotal evidence to support those claims, but no credible scientific verification that copper bracelets do anything but turn your wrist green. Everyone agrees they won't hurt you. If you think they may help, it's certainly worth a try.

Chapter 16

The Knee Bone's Connected to the Hipbone

"Almost all top players will tell you they begin the downswing with the left hip. When I plant my left foot I feel the weight right up through my left leg and my hips as the backswing transitions into the forward swing."

— Ben Crenshaw

The hips and knees are critical elements in almost every aspect of the golf swing. From the moment you begin your pre-shot routine, planting your feet and preparing your posture for action, until the moment the ball is sailing through the air and you're well into your follow-through, the knees and hips stabilize your base, initiate action in your lower body, and provide support. They're the joints that bear the most weight and, although they don't hinge or rotate like the elbows and shoulders, the hips and knees play an active role in the golf swing.

Because they are so active, knees and hips are susceptible to soreness and injury from wear and tear as well as the added stresses that come with common over-40 swing flaws. Some golfers jiggle their lower bodies so violently during the swing that they look like rumba dancers, while others lock their knees like robots and slash at the ball with their upper bodies. These unique moves may not cause too many problems with younger players, but after your body turns 40, too much motion in joints ill prepared for such funky moves can lead to serious problems.

Unfortunately, of all the joints in the body that golfers protect, the hips and knees are at the bottom of the list. In addition to carrying too much weight on these load-bearing joints, most golfers don't take the time or make the effort to warm up their hips and knees, nor do they know which muscles to stretch in order to prevent problems in these joints. In this chapter, I give you some quick, easy stretches to do at home or on the course to keep your knees and hips healthy. I also tell you how to avoid the common swing flaws that lead to hip and knee injuries.

Shooting from the Hip

Like the shoulder, the hip (see Figure 16-1) is a ball-and-socket joint that connects the *femur,* the large bone of the upper leg with the hipbone. A ball made up of bone and cartilage at the end of the femur is held into a socket in the hipbone by a complex web of tendons. The ball-and-socket nature of this joint allows for universal movement of the leg at the hip joint. In other words, it's what allows you to stand on one foot and move your leg forward, backward, side-to-side and in a circular motion (if you're inclined to engage in such moves).

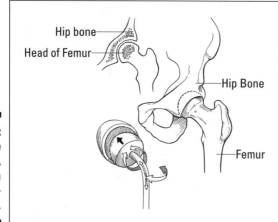

Figure 16-1:
Like the shoulder, the hip is a ball-and-socket joint.

The hip plays a huge role in the golf swing, as does the entire lower body (see Chapter 10), but the motion the hips must undertake during the golf swing doesn't come naturally. There are very few activities in life other than golf where your hips swivel around your right leg and then simultaneously slide and turn, with the left hip absorbing the full brunt of the body's weight as well as the force of the shoulders, arms and, of course, the golf club being pulled through the downswing and follow-through. It's a daunting task for an unprepared hip.

An inflexible hip can't handle all this action. This unnatural motion is why preparing your hip joints as thoroughly as you would any other part of your body before you play is critical.

Discovering healing hip stretches

Fortunately, Mother Nature provided you with a strong hip girdle, so any strengthening exercises that you may want to incorporate into your workout can certainly make you feel better, but they won't do a great deal for your golf game. Flexibility exercises are another matter, however. Few golfers spend any time stretching the muscles in the hip region. As a result, these areas are interminably stiff when you get to the course and sore when you finish playing.

The following are some quick and easy stretches for home and the course that can prepare your hips for the stresses of the golf swing. Spend a minimum of three to five minutes focusing on these stretches before you take your first swing of the day. Your game may improve as a result, and your hips won't hurt afterward.

✔ **Adductor stretches:** There are two primary stretches for the adductor or inner thigh muscles that you can incorporate into your routine:

  • **At home:** Sit on the floor with your back straight and your feet in front of you before slowly spreading your knees apart while bringing the soles of your feet together. Grab your feet with both hands and, while still keeping your back straight, slowly pull your feet closer to you while pressing your knees toward the floor. You can feel this stretch in your inner thighs. Hold the stretch for 15 to 30 seconds, then slowly return to the start position. As illustrated in Figure 16-2, you can also use a Golf Fitness Stretch Trainer (a professionally designed stretching aid) or other strap to assist and intensify this stretch.

Figure 16-2: This adductor stretch can prepare you for your trip to the course.

There is a huge temptation to bounce this stretch. Letting your knees bob up and down as you sit in this position just seems natural. Don't do it! Your adductor muscles are naturally stiff, and any trauma that you create by bouncing a stretch can strain or pull those muscles causing you a great deal of pain.

- **On the course:** Simply spread your feet apart six plus inches wider than shoulder width, turning your feet out like a clown. Place your golf club in front of you with the clubhead facing you for support, bend one knee and slowly shift your weight to one side extending the opposite leg and planting your heel with the toe upward (see Figure 16-3). You can feel this stretch in your right adductor. After holding the stretch for 15 to 30 seconds, slowly move the club and your upper body to the left side and stretch the right adductor for another 15 to 30 seconds.

Figure 16-3: This on-course adductor stretch can be done before and during a round.

Don't rush this stretch, even if your playing partners are razzing you about doing yoga on the golf course. If you properly prepare your adductor muscles for the round, you will be the one who has the last laugh.

✔ **Abductor Stretches:** If you've ever rubbed the outside edge of your hip where your femur meets the hip bone and wondered why that area was sore, you're touching the *abductor muscle,* and it's sore because you probably don't stretch it often enough. Try these stretches to relieve that soreness.

- **At home:** Standing near a wall in your house, you can stretch your abductor muscles by turning so that your right side is facing the wall and you are close enough to the wall to touch it with your right hand without having to fully extend your arm. Cross your left leg over your right leg, keeping both feet on the floor and close to each other. Then push off the wall with your right hand until your arm is fully extended and bend slowly and slightly at the waist toward the wall (see Figure 16-4). You'll feel this stretch in the left abductor. After holding this position for 15 to 30 seconds, return to the start position and repeat the process on the other side.

Figure 16-4:
This at-home abductor stretch keeps your hips supple for the course.

This move will likely throw you off balance. To keep from falling over, move your shoulders over your feet, keeping your left hip extended as far away from the wall as possible.

- **On the course:** At any point before or during a round, you can stretch your abductor muscles with one simple exercise. All you need is a bench, a golf cart, or a club. Hold onto the bench, cart, or club with your right hand and extend your arm away from your body. Cross your left leg over your right leg, keeping both feet on the floor and close to each other. Bend slowly and slightly at the waist toward the object that you have chosen (see Figure 16-5). You'll feel this stretch in the left abductor. After holding this position for 15 to 30 seconds, return to the start position and repeat the process on the other side.

Figure 16-5:
You can stretch your abductor at any time on the course.

✔ **Hip flexor stretches:** You can also stretch the *hip flexor* (the area of the hip that hinges and allows you to sit, squat, and bend over to tie your shoes). Because of the hip flexor's importance in maintaining good posture during the golf swing, you should incorporate these stretches into your daily routine whether or not you plan to play golf. Flexibility isn't something you can turn on and off only on the days you plan to play. Proper flexibility requires a daily commitment.

  • **At home:** In your bedroom or any other carpeted room in your home, start this stretch on your knees with your back straight. From this position, lift one leg and place your foot in front of your body, extending it farther than your knee. Now tuck your hips underneath you and slowly lean forward until you feel the stretch in the opposite hip flexor (see Figure 16-6). Hold this stretch for 15 to 30 seconds and repeat to the opposite side.

Figure 16-6:
At-home hip flexor stretches keep you ready to play.

  • **On the course:** With a club in front of you for balance (with the clubhead turned toward you to prevent the club from slipping), extend one leg behind the other and raise up on the toe of the back foot. Tuck your hips forward and slowly drop into a squat by bending both knees and lowering the trailing knee toward the ground. With your hips tucked underneath, you'll feel this stretch in the hip flexor (see Figure 16-7). Hold the stretch for 15 to 30 seconds and repeat to the opposite leg.

Because gravity is one of the forces at work in this stretch, taking it slowly is extra important. Also, be sure you wear shoes that won't slip and be sure that you perform this stretch on a soft surface like grass. Slipping during the middle of this stretch can be painful.

Figure 16-7:
On-course hip flexor stretches can be done anywhere, anytime.

Fixing damaging swing flaws

Even if you swing the club perfectly, you still place a tremendous amount of pressure on the hip region. In addition, a number of common swing flaws add more pressure to the hips and, if you repeat them often enough, they can lead to serious problems. The mistakes golfers can and do make are many and varied. In this section, I explain some of the most common swing flaws that impede the hip.

Reverse weight shift

Besides being a swing killer, the dreaded reverse weight shift (see Figure 16-8) can do terrible damage to your hip flexor, adductor and abductor muscles, as well as adding strain to the tendons in the hip. In this common swing flaw, your weight moves to the left side during the backswing. Instead of your shoulders turning around a sturdy right hip flexor, the hip overrotates on the backswing, your spine tilts to the left, and your weight shifts to your front foot. From this position, you cannot keep the club on the correct plane, nor can you create the coiling tension that you need to effectively generate clubhead speed through impact. You nullify the energy that you can create by shifting your weight toward the target on the downswing, and it's all you can do to make contact with the ball without falling down.

With all the weight on your left side before the shoulders and arms finish the backswing, you're asking your left hip flexor not only to support all your weight, but also to initiate the downswing and rotate the hips through the shot as well. This is virtually impossible. That's why so many players who suffer through this swing flaw end up falling back onto their right sides during the downswing. The resulting shot is usually a weak *push-slice,* a shot that starts right and goes ever farther right. It's a terrible swing that produces a terrible shot and compounds your likelihood of injury in the process.

Figure 16-8:
The dreaded reverse weight shift, a swing and hip killer.

One drill to help cure this insufferable swing flaw is to stop your swing at the top to see if you can lift your left foot off the ground without falling down. If you can, you're properly positioned. If not, you need to modify your swing until you can make this move.

Hip thrust

Another critical swing flaw that leads to soreness and possible injury in the hip (as well as bad golf shots) is the hip thrust (see Figure 16-9). You can trigger this mistake by an overzealous attempt to shift weight from the right side to the left side without any regard to turning the hips in the process. Instead, you thrust your hips from right to left, moving them laterally without turning them at all.

Figure 16-9:
The hip thrust does nothing to enhance the swing and ultimately damages the hip.

Doing so completely disrupts the downswing and puts the hips in a distressing position. Because you don't turn your hips, your upper body does not pull into the downswing. The club doesn't move. Your weight shifts to the left side, but your hips don't turn. From this position, the only thing you can do is throw the club at the ball and hope for the best. Meanwhile, your hips are thrust into an unnatural position where they must remain as the upper body attempts to recover. The results are usually short, off-line shots and a fair amount of soreness in the left hip after the round.

A common visualization drill that helps this problem is to imagine yourself swinging while standing in a barrel. This mental imagery helps minimize the amount of hip thrust in the swing. Another drill to minimize this affliction can be done at home. Standing in front of a full-length mirror, mark the mirror with a grease pencil one inch outside both your hips, and then try to swing keeping your hips inside the markings. This won't give you the full effect that you would get from actually hitting balls on the range, but you can groove the sensation of this hip action and eliminate a lot of unnecessary problems.

Keeping an Eye on Your Knees

Unlike in other sports, such as football, basketball, baseball, or soccer, knee injuries are not that common in golf. Golfers who suffer from knee troubles can usually trace the root of their problems to some other activity, such as jogging or skiing. Playing golf may aggravate the problem, but is rarely the initial cause.

That doesn't mean that you can't do things to foul up already weakened or injured knees, or increase the likelihood of a knee injury during other activities. Bad swingers of the golf club can hurt just about any body part, and the knee is no exception. The following are the two primary swing flaws that create most the problems with the knees.

✔ **Locked knees:** At no point during the golf swing should your knees lock (see Figure 16-10). If you lock them at address, you can't turn your lower body to initiate the downswing. If you lock your right leg as you take the club back (the most common flaw) you put unnecessary stress on the knee and impede your lower body's ability to turn through the shot. Rarely will you see golfers lock their left knees on the downswing or follow-through, but it does occasionally happen. When it does, these players slap at the ball with their hands and generate very little clubhead speed.

Figure 16-10:
Locked
knees ruin
swings and
create
long-term
problems.

✔ **Sliding knees:** Just as locked knees ruin otherwise good swings, overactive sliding knees (see Figure 16-11) are also a big problem that can
lead to weakening of the joints. The knees are not universal joints. They
are hinges that move your lower legs forward and back. Knees aren't
built to flex sideways. That is why overactive knees that slide outside
your right foot on the backswing and outside your left hip on the follow-
through ruin your shots and hurt after your round. The knees have a
role in the golf swing, but it's a passive role. The more your knees move
laterally, the less likely you are to hit good golf shots, and the more
likely you are to aggravate the tendons and ligaments in your knees.

Figure 16-11:
Sliding
knees hurt
your game
and your
body.

Over-40 players spend a lot of time stretching and strengthening their backs, elbows, shoulders, hands and wrists, but hips and knees shouldn't be ignored. Your lower body is critical to good golf. Paying attention to the joints of the lower body that rotate and slide during the swing will help you prepare your entire body for good golf after your 40th birthday.

Part VI
Taking Golf Fitness to the Next Level

The 5th Wave   By Rich Tennant

"I really have to exercise more. I went from yelling 'Fore' on every shot in my 20's, to yelling 'Wow' in my 30's, to yelling 'Ow' in my 50's."

In this part . . .

Fitness is a must if you want to improve your golf game after 40, but that doesn't mean you have to spend a fortune or join the most chic health club in the country. A few dollars, a few extra minutes a day, and some personal discipline can allow you to take fitness to the next level and move your golf game and your body up a couple of notches. This part helps you discover how to train at home, how to achieve maximum results while exercising, and how to customize your eating habits for better golf and better overall health.

Chapter 17

Getting Fit for Golf in the Gym

· ·

In This Chapter

▶ Analyzing and rating your golf fitness

▶ Consulting a fitness trainer

▶ Building a balanced program

▶ Setting realistic goals

· ·

> *"You want to get ready and fit for golf, but be careful and don't overdo it. You want to be fit enough to walk 18 holes comfortably and give it 100 percent on every shot."*
>
> — Ernie Els

*O*ne of the biggest deterrents to getting fit for golf isn't getting started — most people quite happily trot off to the gym for a trial run at this whole fitness thing — the problem comes the next morning when workout hangover sets in. Golfers are no different than any other newcomers to the fitness scene. You enter the gym with a certain level of anxiety and self-consciousness because it's unfamiliar territory, but you quickly put your inhibitions aside as you lift, run, bike, step, row, and experiment with all the shiny new equipment at your disposal. The next morning, however, you can't move. Every muscle hurts, every joint aches, and you rue the day you ever set foot inside a gym.

This sort of workout is counterproductive, foolish, and, unfortunately, far too common. The entire reason for engaging in the exercises outlined throughout this book, beyond the fact that you may live longer and feel better, is to play better golf. That's difficult when you can't raise the club above your shoulders or take your stance without feeling like you're about to fall over. If your gym experience hinders your golf game instead of helping it, you've defeated the purpose of your workout.

When going to a gym for the first time, or when renewing your commitment to gym life, taking things slowly is important. Good health, like good golf, is a long-term proposition that you shouldn't rush.

This chapter helps you to assess your level of fitness before you even step foot in the gym so that you know what you can handle when you do get there. Plus, I give you some advice about selecting a personal trainer and/or a workout partner as well.

Getting Started: Analyzing Your Fitness

Marching into a gym and going to the first machine that you see is a bad way to begin your journey toward becoming a fit over-40 golfer. In order to create an effective workout program that grows with you, you first need to establish a baseline, a starting point from which to build your fitness. This analysis, which involves evaluating your strength and flexibility, is relatively easy, but not subjective. I designed this analysis to give golfers a fitness baseline. From an objective starting point, you can create a program that works for you.

As you go through the following analysis, keep track of your performance on a piece of paper. The results you log in each of the following tests help you determine your overall fitness level (as you will see at the end of the test). Each test is charted and depending on how you do, you will fall into one of three categories: *eagle* (for expert fitness), *birdie* (for better-than-average), and *par* (for average). There are no bogeys in these tests. The fact that you're making the effort eliminates bogeys and double bogeys from your score.

Test #1: Flexibility

Sit upright on the floor with your legs extended in front of you and your feet slightly apart. Place a yardstick between your feet with the 15-inch mark at your heels. Then place one hand atop the other and lean forward from the waist as far as possible (see Figure 17-1).

Do not bounce or jerk this stretch. The number on the ruler that you can reach with the end of your middle finger indicates your flexibility. Match the number of inches you reach on the yardstick to your age group in Table 17-1 and/or 17-2, to assess your current level of flexibility.

Table 17-1	Men's Score by Age in Years for Flexibility			
	30–39 years	*40–49 years*	*50–59 years*	*60+ years*
Eagle Level	18+ inches	17+ inches	16+ inches	15+ inches
Birdie Level	17+ inches	16+ inches	10–15 inches	9–14 inches
Par Level	12–17 inches	11–16 inches	7–9 inches	6–8 inches

Figure 17-1:
Use a yardstick to test flexibility; extend as far as possible and measure yourself.

Table 17-2	Women's Score by Age in Years for Flexibility			
	30–39 years	*40–49 years*	*50–59 years*	*60 + years*
Eagle Level	21+ inches	20+ inches	19+ inches	18+ inches
Birdie Level	16–20 inches	14–19 inches	12–18 inches	11–17 inches
Par Level	13–15 inches	12–13 inches	9–11 inches	6–10 inches

Test #2: Upper body strength (Men)

Men and women must test their upper body strength in different ways. For men, do as many push-ups as possible from a military position in a 60-second period (see Figure 17-2)

Figure 17-2:
Men should keep their bodies straight while doing push-ups.

Match the number of push-ups you do to your age group in Table 17-3 to assess your current level of upper body strength.

Table 17-3 Men's Score by Age for Upper Body Strength

	30–39 years	40–49 years	50–59 years	60+ years
Eagle Level	37+ push-ups	31+ push-ups	28+ push-ups	27+ push-ups
Birdie Level	25–36 push-ups	21–30 push-ups	18–27 push-ups	17–26 push ups
Par Level	13–24 push ups	11–20 push-ups	9–17 push-ups	6–16 push ups

Test #2: Upper body strength (Women)

Women need to do push-ups from a modified position. Keep your torso straight, balancing on your knees with your feet in the air and do as many push-ups as possible in a 60-second period (see Figure 17-3).

Figure 17-3:
Women take a slightly different position than men when doing push-ups, but the benefits are the same.

Match the number of push-ups you do to your age group in Table 17-4 to assess your current level of upper body strength.

Table 17-4 Women's Score by Age for Upper Body Strength

	30–39 years	40–49 years	50–59 years	60+ years
Eagle Level	34+ push-ups	28+ push-ups	23+ push-ups	21+ push-ups
Birdie Level	22–33 push-ups	18–27 push-ups	15–22 push-ups	13–20 push-ups
Par Level	10–21 push-ups	8–17 push-ups	7–14 push-ups	5–12 push-ups

Test #3: Torso strength

Sitting on the floor with your knees bent and your heels on the floor, place your arms across your chest and slowly lower your torso to a 45-degree angle (see Figure 17-4). Maintain this angle for as long as possible. When you reach your limit, lower to the floor instead of trying to return to the upright position. Doing so is much easier on your back.

Figure 17-4:
This move is tougher than you think. Hold it for a few seconds and you'll see.

Now match the number of seconds you held the angle to Table 17-5 to assess your level of torso strength. Ratings for men and women are the same.

Table 17-5	Rating for Torso Strength Test
Eagle	25+ seconds
Birdie	15–24 seconds
Par	5–14 seconds

Test #4: Lower body strength

Place your back against a wall with your feet approximately 18 inches away from the corner. Bend your knees and lower your torso until your hips are at or slightly above a right angle, and maintain this angle for as long as possible (see Figure 17-5).

Figure 17-5:
Hold your back against the wall to test lower body strength.

Match the number of seconds you hold this position to Table 17-6 to assess your level of lower body strength. Ratings for men and women are the same.

Table 17-6	Rating for Lower Body Strength
Eagle	90+ seconds
Birdie	60–89 seconds
Par	30–59 seconds

Calculating Your Total Fitness

To figure out where you are in the total fitness scheme, grab the piece of paper with your test results from the previous section on it. Now, assign values to your scores based on the following:

- Par = 1 point
- Birdie = 2 points
- Eagle = 3 points

After you assign values to your test results, simply add up your scores from the four fitness tests and compare the total to the following:

- Eagle: 12 (or more) total points
- Birdie: 8–11 total points
- Par: 4–7 total points

For example, Tom a 54-year-old man, reached 12 seconds in Test #1, completed 30 push-ups in one minute during Test #2, held a 45-degree torso angle for 15 seconds in Test #3 and kept a 90-degree lower body angle for 74 seconds in Test #4. Assigning one point for par, two for a birdie and three for an eagle, Tom's scores were 2, 3, 2, and 2 for a total score of 9, or a birdie average.

Putting Your Program into Practice

After you analyze your golf fitness, you can enter the gym with a plan. Use Tables 17-7, 17-8, and 17-9 as a guide in building a workout program.

Because you will likely find both free weights (weights not attached to a specific machine) and machines (weight-lifting machines with stacked weights designed for specific exercises) in the gym, the following programs are designed with both in mind. You must balance free weights while exercising, so you will notice lighter weight recommendations for free-weight lifts. Also, each recommendation is given in terms of a *range,* a suggested bottom and top amount for weight lifting. Any amount of weight within the recommended range is acceptable. The same holds true for recommended repetitions. I give minimum and maximum recommendations for reps. Consider any number of reps in that range to be a good number.

After you become comfortable with a particular weight, a certain number of repetitions, or a certain amount of time on the bike or stair machine, increase your level. Golf fitness, like all fitness, is a growing process. When you hit a plateau, you need to work harder to move yourself to the next level, just as you would if you were stuck at a certain score on the golf course.

Table 17-7	Par Program — 4–7 total fitness points scored
Cardiovascular training and duration	10–20 minutes
Free-weight range	1–5 pounds
Machine or plate-loading weight range	10–50 pounds
Number of repetitions	8–10

Table 17-8	Birdie Program — 8–11 total fitness points scored
Cardiovascular training and duration	20–30 minutes
Free-weight range	5–8 pounds
Machine or plate-loading weight range	20–60 pounds
Number of repetitions	10–15

Table 17-9 Eagle Program — 12 or more total fitness points scored	
Cardiovascular training and duration	30–45 minutes
Free-weight range	8–15 pounds
Machine or plate-loading weight range	30+ pounds
Number of repetitions	15–20

The Par, Birdie, and Eagle programs are year-round fitness regimens that I recommend incorporating into your life at least four days a week. Be sure to include a series of flexibility exercises (see Chapter 21) both before and after you perform these workouts, and wait a minimum of two hours after a work-out before heading to the driving range or the golf course. Hitting balls and playing while your body grows accustomed to these workouts is critical, but not within the first two hours. It's a little like swimming after a big meal — you can do it, if you wait an appropriate amount of time. If you don't continue to play and practice while you work out, you'll be in for a shock when you do return to the course.

Getting Others Involved in Your Workout

Even if you analyze your fitness level and develop a beginning workout pro-gram, consulting with a fitness professional about your individual needs and goals is still a good idea.

In seeking out a personal trainer, remember the following things:

- **Find someone you like.** If you're going to work out with this person one, two, three, or four days a week, you need to get along with them. You wouldn't play a weekly golf match with someone that you couldn't stand. Why should you have any different standard when it comes to the gym?

- **Find someone who understands your sport-specific goals.** A non-golfer can certainly train a golfer in the gym, but someone who understands the game for which you're training is always better. Otherwise your golf-related goals may not translate into language that your trainer understands.

- **Pick a trainer close to your own age, rather than your gender.** The gender of your trainer is less important than finding someone who can relate to the specific ailments that come with your particular age. Men and women often train alike. Teenagers and 40-year-olds may as well be from different planets.

✔ **Check your trainer's certifications.** Anyone can claim to be a personal trainer, just like anyone can offer you a golf tip. The value of the advice you get is normally represented by the training that your trainer has received.

If you're not comfortable with a personal trainer, you may want to consider working out with a partner — another kindred soul looking to become a more fit, healthy over-40 golfer. Plenty of reasons exist for working out with a partner, not the least of which is the pressure you put on each other to be at the gym on time.

Other reasons for working out with a partner include:

✔ **You and your partner can motivate each other to work harder.** You're far more likely to advance to the next level with someone encouraging you every day than if you're trying to motivate yourself.

✔ **Time flies when you work out in pairs.** Having someone around to keep your mind occupied makes working out less like work and more like a social gathering.

✔ **You can always bounce ideas and problems off a peer easier than you can with a personal trainer.** It's good to have a workout partner who understands how much you loathe a particular exercise, but who helps you work through it anyway.

When choosing a workout partner, use the same guidelines you do for picking a personal trainer. Find someone of the same age that you enjoy spending time with and who has golf skills and fitness goals similar to your own.

Key Workout Tips for Golfers

Never forget that you're engaging in a sport-specific workout designed to improve your golf game while you're getting in better physical condition. You're not getting in shape hoping good golf will be a byproduct. Sure, some of the exercises in your golf-specific program are similar to what you see in other non-sport-specific regimens, but individual exercises don't define your workouts — the form, frequency, intensity, and diversity of your exercises do. With that in mind, in this section, I take a look at some key things that you must remember in order to maximize your golf benefits in the gym.

Keep swinging, no matter what

If your gym workout is leaving you so tight and sore that swinging a club the next morning is next to impossible, you're overdoing it. You need to modify your workout, cutting back on the amount of weight you lift or the number of strength exercises you perform, and then add more stretching exercises to your routine. The whole purpose of the program is to improve your swing, not make you so sore that you can't lift the club.

For you to gain the golf benefits of working out, you must keep swinging the golf club. After a workout, your muscles are warm, toned, stretched, and yearning for input. Swinging a club — even if it's in your garage or bedroom for a couple of hours — gives your muscles the feedback they need. Also, as you lose fat and gain muscle, your body changes, which means your swing is likely to change. This isn't necessarily a conscious change, but one that comes from a change in your physical makeup. Either way, you need to keep swinging the club throughout your workout regimen to work through any kinks that may arise as your body gets into golf shape.

If it hurts, it's wrong

Jane Fonda, bless her heart, did tremendous damage to fitness over 40 when she uttered four simple words that blasted out over television speakers around the world for years. "Remember," Fonda said with a perky smile, "no pain, no gain." Sure it was the '80s, and fitness was in its scientific infancy, but pain? In her defense, she got many people off their couches and out of their easy chairs, and she went a long way toward instilling an exercise ethic into the American culture, but pain should have never been a part of the program.

The exercises and stretches that I outline in this book, or in any other program that you may read, see, or otherwise hear about, are not supposed to hurt. They're designed to develop strength, flexibility, coordination, and stamina. Pain is not a requirement.

Of course, that doesn't mean exercise is easy; it's not. Sitting in the locker room or in the *19th Hole* (the clubhouse grillroom or bar) with a drink and a basket of nuts is much easier than changing into gym clothes and running through an hour-long workout. But just because workouts can be hard, doesn't mean they should be painful.

Gym egos hurt your golf game

It's so difficult to walk through a gym with any sense of self-confidence. No matter what time you schedule for your workout, you'll invariably see several perfectly proportioned, hard-bodied athletes working out at the same time. Fate always dictates that these people will choose the bench next to yours, which means you have to watch as they reel off 10 to 12 reps of biceps curls with 75-pound weights, or contort themselves into a yoga master stretch that would certainly cause you to break a bone if you attempted it. These people don't laugh or smirk at you, but they don't have to; the blow to your ego is all your own.

Thinking that way can also cause you to do foolish things like lifting 20 or 30 pounds more than you should or running through two more sets than you had planned. Don't do it! Joe Olympia and Sally Buff don't care that you aren't a sculpted Greek god, and you shouldn't either. Joe and Sally may lift more weight, do more crunches, and glisten more brightly beneath the fluorescent lights of the weight room, but they probably can't hit a high draw over water with a 5-wood. Remember why you're in the gym in the first place, and put those around you out of your mind.

Golf is a game of patience; so is golf fitness

If you remember when you first took up golf, you probably remember the frustrations that you experienced when you went through long stretches of seemingly miniscule improvement. No matter how much you practiced or how hard you tried, you couldn't break through that magical scoring goal you set for yourself (breaking 100, breaking 90, breaking 80, shooting even par). After you finally reached your goal, your improvement seemed limitless. Then you hit another bump and struggled through another period where it looked like you might never improve.

The same idea is true with golf fitness. This isn't a one-day, one-week, one-month, or even one-year process. Fitness is a lifestyle change, the results of which may not become visible for four to six months. You have to remain patient and diligent with your workout regimen. The results will come, eventually. But just like golf, you can't force it.

Set gym times that cannot be changed

Working out has to become a habit, a part of your routine that is no different than eating dinner, going to work, or brushing your teeth in the morning. Habits take time to cultivate. Normally, fitness habits take anywhere from 6 to 16 weeks to become an integral part of your life. During that time, you need to force yourself to stick to a workout schedule that's cast in stone. Pick times and set dates for working out that are fixed and permanent, and don't miss those times for any reason. Anyone can make excuses for missing a workout session. After you start making those excuses they become easier to make a second, third, fourth, and fifth time. Soon you're skipping the gym because you don't want to miss the *M*A*S*H* marathon on cable. By setting workout dates that you can't miss, making fitness a habit you won't break is an easier proposition.

Besides the driving range and putting green, the gym is the most important place for those who are serious about improving their golf games. By analyzing your game and developing a program that suits your individual needs, you set yourself on a path of game improvement as important as the lessons you take in the spring or the balls you hit after a round. It may take a few months, but you will definitely see the benefits of this work in your scores.

Chapter 18

Training at Home

"People just don't get enough exercise through the routine of their daily lives. This shows up with a vengeance in pro-ams, where we are normally playing with professional men and business executives. They sit in offices and cars all week, then ride around the course in golf carts all weekend. I'm often tempted to tell a fellow who is beating at the ball with his hands, or whaling around at it with his shoulders, to get more leg action into his swing. But how can the poor guy use something he hasn't got?"

— Jack Nicklaus

Training for golf isn't something that you do only on the golf course or in the gym. Your home is the perfect place to set up a golf-specific training ground complete with gym equipment, areas where you can work on your swing, and stretching areas. Of course, right now you call these areas the bedroom, bathroom, bonus room (the finished room over your garage), and garage, but that shouldn't stop you from using them for golf.

Finding the time to work out at home may prove more challenging, however. Slipping away once or twice a week to play golf is often more difficult than getting a peace treaty ratified. So how are you supposed to spend *more* time working out when you barely have time to eat, read, and kiss your kids? There are only 24 hours in a day. Where is this workout time going to come from?

The answer is simple: Take a little of the time you spend in front of the television (if you're like most Americans, that adds up to about two or three hours a day) or on the couch and use it instead for a simple, quick, but highly effective golf workout. Even the busiest people have some time they can devote to bettering their bodies and preparing themselves for the game they love.

Building Your Own Home Gym

When you say, *home gym,* many people conjure images of an additional wing on their houses complete with five-figure mirrored walls, special cushioned carpeting, recessed stereo equipment, and an independent heating and cooling system. And, that's even before you purchase the first piece of what's bound to be $100,000 worth of gym equipment. That's a nice fantasy but it's also hogwash. You can outfit your home with all the equipment you need for a full golf-specific workout with less money than you would spend on a new titanium driver.

Obviously you can't purchase all the weight machines and cardio equipment shown in this book, but you can make a few small acquisitions that provide all you need to train for golf in your home. (And, don't worry about finding the space to store all this new equipment. In most cases, you can store everything in a closet or under your bed.)

Home, home on the in-home range

Practicing your golf swing indoors is nothing new. The in-home driving range has taken many forms over the years, including in-home nets into which golfers hit balls, mats that act as teeing areas, foam balls that don't travel very far and are soft and squishy, as well as other contraptions that allow you to work on your swing indoors. Today's models range from extravagant computer-driven virtual-reality suites that allow you to play your favorite courses with nothing more than a screen, a mat, a ball, and a computer projected image, all the way down to balls attached to plastic arms that swivel around like carnival tops when you hit them.

The most common in-home range setup is the prefabricated *golf net,* a dense sheet of nylon netting attached to a PVC frame with a mat of artificial turf nearby. The net allows you to take full swings in your bonus room or garage as long as you're close enough to the net so that off-center shots don't ricochet off the walls. A fair number of professionals have these nets in their homes — usually in their garages — so they can take a few loosening swings at night or on rainy days.

 These nets are also perfect for videotaping your swing. With a net you can shoot video from the comfort and quiet of your own home with little or no help. Simply station the camera so that your mat is in the frame, press the record button, and swing away. A tripod is the most stable way to videotape yourself, but if you don't own a tripod, you can place your camera on a dresser or a bookshelf. As long as you get your swing in the frame, how and where you position the camera is irrelevant. You'll be amazed by the amount of quality analysis that comes from these video sessions.

You can also move the net outdoors. If you don't like the feel of hitting off a mat, take the net into your backyard. Obviously you won't be able to see where the ball would go if you were hitting a shot outdoors, but in some respects that's good. By focusing on the mechanics of your swing and not on the flight of the ball, you're more likely to engrain good habits based on sound fundamentals rather than flimsy quick fixes and gimmicks into your swing.

But even if the net and mat (which can be bought at sporting goods stores or online for less than $100) are too expensive for your tastes, an old sheet, a few feet of rope, and a dozen or so nails will do the trick. By tying the sheet to the rope and suspending it between two trees (with the nails), you can create your own backyard range. If trees are out of the question, nail the sheet to a couple of two-by-fours and prop it up in your garage. With a little ingenuity, setting up an in-home or backyard range is not a big deal. You simply have to make the commitment.

Weighing in with weighted clubs

To continue your swing training at home, you can purchase one of the many *weighted swing trainers* (a club that is upwards of 10 times the weight of a normal club) available on the market. In my opinion, the Momentus Swing Trainer is the best option primarily because it's perfectly balanced, and comes with an instructional video that leads you through the do's and don'ts of indoor swing training. Keeping your muscles warm, loose, and accustomed to the moves you make in golf is vitally important to your game. There are few better tools to keep your swing honed at home than the weighted club.

But like all home-training tools, weighted clubs are useless if they sit in the corner unused. After you purchase a weighted club you should use it every day. In five minutes you can put your body through a systematic swing-training workout that provides as much benefit to your game as any driving range drill.

For more on drilling with a weighted club, see Chapter 11.

Reflecting with grease pencils and a mirror

Most people own a full-length mirror, but if you don't, consider buying one. They're relatively inexpensive and invaluable when it comes to working on your swing. A full-length mirror allows you to make periodic checks of your grip, your stance, your posture, and your head position.

You can also use your mirror to test certain fundamentals, such as how still you keep your head during the swing. To do this you need a grease pencil or some other washable marker to draw various lines, circles and squares on your mirror. In the head drill, for example, you simply draw a box around the reflection of your head and then attempt to swing without moving your head out of the box. Obviously, this tool isn't as effective as video because you aren't hitting a ball in your home, and you have to swing with your head up in order to see your reflection, but as in-home drills go, it's not bad. You can also check things, such as the position of your right knee at the top of your backswing, and how much lateral shift you have with your lower body in the downswing by simply drawing reference lines on your mirror and watching yourself as you swing. Dollar for dollar you won't find many better investments for your golf game than a mirror and a 75-cent marker.

Some people paste photos of professionals near their mirrors so they can see how their setups match up against the best. Doing so is a good idea as long as you are realistic. If you are 5'11" tall and weigh 250 pounds, comparing yourself to a photo of Tiger Woods who is 6'2" and 190 pounds, doesn't make much sense. If you want to establish a model for comparison, pick someone around your own age with whom you share a common body type. Setting up like a pro is a worthy goal, as long as you use some common sense in your comparisons.

Any dumbbell can buy dumbbells

With a couple of sets of dumbbells (handheld weights) you can establish a weight-training center in your home for less than the cost of dinner and a movie.

Many people choose to go a step farther and invest in one of the many home gym systems available through television infomercials (Just dial the toll-free number and have your credit card ready!), which is fine. If the infomercial was attractive enough, and you're enthused enough to devote a corner of your house to the latest and greatest in home fitness technology, by all means make that call. Just understand that in terms of getting your over-40 body ready for golf, it's not necessary. Two sets of dumbbells of varying weights, if you use them properly, provide all the resistance you need to train at home for golf. Any decent sporting goods store has a vast selection of perfectly acceptable and reasonably priced dumbbells. All you have to do is pick the weight you want and make the purchase.

If you travel for business (or pleasure), the newest and niftiest invention in the fitness industry is *water weights* — lightweight pack-and-travel dumbbell bars with inflatable bladders that you fill with water. You simply deflate the bladders, fold them up, pack them in your suitcase, and you have an entire gym in your overnight bag. When you get to your hotel, you simply attach the bladders to the handles and fill them with water. Voilà! The water adds the weight you need, and you never have to miss a workout again.

Stepping up to the challenge

Many in-home exercises are best executed on a step or rise, usually a four- to eight-inch-high riser similar in shape to the professional benches used by aerobics instructors. Of course, you shouldn't go out and purchase a gym-quality step unless you plan to watch a lot of step-class videos in your spare time. What you can do is construct something that will pass as a reasonable alternative to a professional step. You aren't going to be dancing on this thing, so it's not imperative that OSHA sign off on it, but you should build a sturdy, four-inch riser with additional two-inch risers that you feel comfortable standing and sitting on when exercising. It should be long enough so that you can stand on it comfortably, but narrow enough so that you can straddle it without injuring yourself. Four feet long and 18-inches wide is a good model, but not a standard you should feel compelled to stick with. As long as your rise is appropriately sturdy, the dimensions are secondary.

If you aren't the building type, and if asking you to construct a rise for your in-home workout is like asking you to split an atom in your garage, don't fret. You can still perform most exercises using your front-door stoop or the bottom stair of your staircase. The only thing that can stop you from exercising at home is your own lack of motivation.

Powering ahead with Power Balls

The old-style medicine balls that Ronald Reagan and James Cagney used to toss around in the back-lot gym at Warner Brothers have morphed into a smaller, heavier, and more popular workout tool called the *Power Ball*. Because these weighted balls provide resistance for strength training, but can also assist in stretching certain larger, hard-to-reach muscles, many trainers specializing in tennis, golf, and track and field have found Power Balls to be an invaluable tool for strengthening and stretching specific muscle groups.

Golfers can use Power Balls as a replacement for dumbbells in many of the two-handed free-weight strength exercises, such as front deltoid raises, or curls (see Chapter 21), but the balls are also great for working on torso rotations (see Figure 18-1) and oblique exercises (also see Chapter 21). You can purchase a weighted power ball as part of a golf fitness system by calling 1-800-315-2329.

Figure 18-1:
The torso rotation drill using a Power Ball.

Shaping up with stability balls

Stability balls look like oversized toys, the kind of large, soft rubber balls toddlers roll around on when they are learning to walk. But these soft, large balls are actually great workout tools for the home. If you don't have a bench on which to lie or sit when executing certain free-weight lifts like the one shown in Figure 18-2, the stability ball works as a multi-purpose seat, bench, and balancing guide. It forces you to keep your back straight and your feet firmly planted on the floor. If you forget about balance and posture, you're likely to roll off the side of the ball, which can seriously damage your ego (among other things).

Stability balls are not crucial to your home-gym setup, but they're certainly good for a number of uses. If you're looking to consolidate space and maximize your workout experience at home with as little muss and fuss as possible, a stability ball is the way to go. You can purchase a stability ball online at www.spriproducts.com or at your local sporting goods store.

Stretching aids

You can purchase a professionally designed Golf Fitness Stretch Trainer that allows you to measure your flexibility and check your progress, or you can simply dedicate a belt, strip of terry cloth, or some other strap as a stretching aid. The benefits of the Stretch Trainer are the hand grips on each end (which allow you to see your flexibility progress and assist in increasing the stretch itself) and the handles lining the strap. These handles give you a better grip as you perform various stretches, and they also offer a measuring component. If you can move from the second to the third handle, or from the third to the fourth during the course of your program, you know you're becoming more flexible and your workouts are paying off. Figure 18-3 shows Laura Baugh using the Stretch Trainer. You can purchase a stretch trainer as part of a golf fitness system by calling 1-800-315-2329.

Figure 18-2:
Laura lifting
and
stretching
on the
stability ball.

Figure 18-3:
Laura
stretching
her neck
with a Golf
Fitness
Stretch
Trainer.

Setting a Few Ground Rules

Just as you have certain ground rules for working out in the gym, you should stick to a strict set of guidelines in your home gym. Training is training regardless of the location.

You gain just as much benefit from a good workout in your bedroom as you do from an hour in the gym, but you can also hurt yourself just as easily at home as you can in the weight room if you don't adhere to the rules.

Use common sense

The main rule, and the one recurring theme throughout this book, is to use common sense and good judgement every time you exercise. Remember that you aren't training for the Olympics, and the chances of your becoming a world-class over-40 athlete are just as remote now as they were 20 years ago. You can certainly improve your golf game and your general health through working out at home or in the gym, but you shouldn't enter any program with unrealistic expectations, and never push yourself beyond what's reasonable. The purpose of this book is to make you a better golfer, not whip you into shape for the Marine Corps.

Pick a time and stick to it

Setting aside a specific time for golf fitness and sticking to that time is important. It's important in part because your muscles will become accustomed to being stimulated at a particular time. It's also important because you need to establish a routine that becomes as much a part of your home life as drinking a cup of coffee in the morning or watching the evening news.

Good health is a habit. Unfortunately, so is bad health. If you establish a routine — say a half-hour of strength exercises first thing in the morning followed by 15 minutes of stretching in the bathroom — it takes approximately six weeks for this routine to become a habit. You will need an additional three to five more weeks before you see any measurable results on the course. But the habit will become a part of your life, and the health benefits you gain from this sort of routine can help you in golf and everything else you do.

Effective conditioning is a lot like good golf: Practice doesn't make perfect, but it gets you closer. You have to be just as diligent in your home workout as you are in any other aspect of your golf game. If you want to improve your game, you should hit range balls, practice your chipping and putting, and set aside a specific time every day for a few golf-related stretching and strengthening exercises.

Stretch and strengthen equally

A workout that concentrates mostly on strength with little or no time allocated to stretching is counterproductive and can actually hurt your golf game rather than help it. That idea is true whether you're working out in the gym or at home, but because of other distractions, most golfers tend to cut corners at home more readily than in the gym. The first corner they usually cut is flexibility.

For some reason golfers think pumping a dumbbell or running through a few crunches at home is more important than stretching. Nothing could be farther from the truth. No matter how extensive or advanced your workout, you must give equal time at home to both strength and flexibility. One without the other can do more harm than good to your swing.

Pay attention to form

It's easy to become lazy, especially in the comfort of your own home where the television is on and the recliner is within reach. Unlike the gym, where the bright lights, mirrored walls and muscle-bound hard bodies keep you on your toes both literally and figuratively, there aren't many checks and balances in your living room, and sometimes your form slips without your realizing it. That's why you need to pay extra attention to form when working out at home. If possible, perform most of your exercises in front of a mirror so that you have a visual cue. At the very least, paint a mental image of yourself executing a particular exercise with perfect form and try to emulate that image, much the same way you visualize a golf shot before taking your stance.

Don't forget that good form is the key to good results just because you are working out at home.

Listen to your body

Overdoing it when exercising in your bedroom is just as easy as straining or overworking a muscle in the gym. At home, you aren't thinking about the number of repetitions that you're reeling off or the speed with which you're performing a particular exercise. You're thinking about the cobweb that needs dusting in the corner or the lawn you need to mow. Unlike the gym where your primary focus in on exercise, the distractions of home can lead to stresses and strains if you don't pay attention to the signals your body sends.

Whether at home, in the gym, or on the golf course, if an exercise hurts, stop doing it. If your body is fatigued and you feel like you're causing yourself harm, slow down, cut back, or stop altogether. Golf fitness is a long-term proposition. Injuring yourself by overdoing it at home is not the way you want to start your journey to better golf after 40.

Getting Started on the Right Track

This entire book outlines ways to help you build a better golf body as you approach and pass your forties. Of course, as a practical matter, you can't work through every exercise and swing drill in these pages in the first day, week, or even the first month of your exercise regimen. Whether at home or in the gym, you need to establish a plan to attack the aging process as it relates to golf. For the home, start with these three things:

✔ Take the four fitness tests that I outline in Chapter 17 and then calculate your fitness ranking. No matter where you plan to exercise, establishing a baseline for your current fitness is essential to your future.

✔ Consider seeking the advice of a professional trainer. Your body, like your golf game, is unique. Even if you're working out at home, the counsel that a professional trainer can offer is invaluable as you progress in your fitness. Locate a professional trainer by logging on to www.golffitnesscenter.com.

✔ Turn to Chapter 21 and map out a 10-day program for your home gym. After you purchase all the necessary equipment and establish a time and place to work out in your home, all you need to do is follow the instructions. You probably won't set a new course record on the 11th day, but you can be on the right path to better scores and a more enjoyable golf experience.

Age is no excuse for letting yourself get out of shape, but being overweight and out of shape is a surefire way to ruin your golf game. Don't confuse your rising golf scores with your rising age. The two are not linked. It's your body that swings the golf club, and a strong, flexible body can make better golf swings regardless of age. Remember that the next time you nestle comfortably into your recliner with the television remote in one hand and a bag of popcorn in the other. Would you like to shoot a better score during your next round? If so, think about what you can do for your golf game at home.

Chapter 19

Eating, Drinking, and Playing Well after 40

"I had been playing well all year, but just couldn't seem to hold it together for three or four consecutive rounds without becoming fatigued. I wasn't sure what the problem was. Then I went to a nutritionist who ran some tests, and I was stunned. They came back that I was borderline malnourished. After changing my diet, I'm able to stay sharp and focused for longer stretches."

— Larry Nelson

As you have no doubt heard or read, a good diet is essential to good health. The cliché, "You are what you eat," has been around forever because it's true. If you eat well, blending a balanced diet full of vitamins, minerals, proteins, and carbohydrates, your chances of being healthy greatly increase. On the other hand, a diet high in fat and sugars and low in protein and complex carbohydrates leads to muscle deterioration, fatigue, and high cholesterol, and increases your chances of high blood pressure, heart disease, and obesity. Plus, if you live long enough, that sort of eat-what-you-want diet eventually wreaks havoc on your golf game, especially after you turn 40.

Good nutrition improves your strength, endurance, and concentration throughout the day regardless of your activities. Those who eat well present a lower risk of injury than do junk food junkies. Likewise, people who eat well normally heal quicker when they do get injured. This idea holds true for golfers as well as athletes of all shapes, sizes, and ages. Golfers who maintain a properly balanced diet can focus better and stay stronger for longer periods of time than those who dine on candy and beer during their rounds before upgrading to fries and a burger afterward. In this chapter, I explain how shooting better scores after 40 involves taking a different approach to what you put in your body.

The Golfer's Diet: Healthy It's Not

Golfers are habitually bad eaters. Those with morning tee times normally start their days with donuts and coffee, or for those who feel the need for more sustenance, egg and sausage biscuits. That meal usually holds them through nine holes. Between nines, they pick up candy bars or crackers and soft drinks, unless it's after noon when beer may be in the offing. Those calories usually hold them through a few more holes. Then it's another crop of candy, chips, and assorted junk foods topped with cans of liquid sugar or more malt beverages. After the round, it's back to the clubhouse where a smorgasbord of burgers, fries, chips, salted nuts, deep-fried fish, and onion rings awaits. And then these golfers wonder why their scores are so much worse now than just a couple of years ago.

Sound familiar? If you're honest, you'll probably admit to indulging in some (if not all) those food vices.

Fatty foods with empty calories are common fare at golf clubs around the country. Just look at the menus in most clubhouses. They usually include one or two token healthy items, but you must even examine those with great care. A house salad drenched in mayonnaise-based dressing is no healthier than a deep-fried chicken breast on white bread with a pickle. Both are death on a plate, if not literally, then certainly when it comes to your golf game.

Bad diet = Bad scores

Golf is a game of extended endurance. It's not a 100-meter dash where you focus all your energy on one explosive burst, nor can you compare it to a tennis match where you must react quickly in short high-energy spurts with equally short periods of rest between points. Golf is more like a mountainous hike, a steady but slow, taxing journey where focus, rhythm, and consistency are critical elements throughout a four- to five-hour time period.

A good diet provides energy to your body throughout a round, while a bad diet can lead to a loss of energy and endurance before your round is complete. That energy loss is reflected in your scores. So it's not a great leap to say that a bad diet causes bad scores.

No couch potatoes allowed

The number of players — young and old — who have seen their own games revitalized by good diet and exercise continues to grow. "I was determined to play golf professionally and not worry about being in great condition," said Ernie Els. "I was young enough and stupid enough to think that I would never get out of shape and, anyway, playing golf wasn't all that physically demanding. I was lazy, and golf was fun."

Sound familiar? Many amateurs fall into the same trap Ernie did early in his professional career. On the surface golf doesn't seem all that physically taxing. Overweight smokers can still play golf, so getting lulled into the false belief that golf fitness isn't important is easy. But the players who fall into the lazy-golf trap are also the ones who end up fighting injuries and fatigue as they grow older, who wonder why they're losing distance and focus, and who can't understand why their scores aren't as good and their shots aren't as crisp as they once were.

"In 1995 I started having bad rounds toward the end of the year, and I was tired at the wrong times," Els said. "I didn't want to believe it, but I sensed a pattern was beginning to develop, so I decided to get fit. The game was getting more competitive, and the good golfers — the ones who were winning — were in shape. And there was Gary Player, my idol, at age 62 still looking great and playing and winning! He was in shape! I decided it was time to step up and stop kidding myself. I had to get into shape. The game itself had changed — it was a more athletic sport than it had been."

You want the same measure of strength, flexibility, concentration, and physical and emotional steadiness throughout all 18 holes with as little variance as possible. Unfortunately, the golf diet sabotages that objective before you ever set foot on the first tee.

Take the breakfast that I describe earlier in this chapter, for example. Nothing could be worse for someone looking to maintain a steady level of endurance than a dose of complex sugar (donuts) and a jolt of caffeine (coffee). In addition to boosting the body's *metabolism* (the rate at which you burn calories and create energy) by increasing heart rate and adrenaline, the effects of such a meal are short-lived. An elevated sugar level in your bloodstream creates what's known as a *sugar high,* and caffeine temporarily activates your *adrenal gland,* which shoots adrenaline into your bloodstream and gives you a short burst of energy. During activities such as golf, those effects wear off in mere minutes. After three or four holes, you bottom back to earth as the sugar and caffeine are flushed through your bloodstream.

The letdown from a sugar high creates premature fatigue and leaves you craving more sugar. In fact, the molecular makeup of sugar is extremely similar to cocaine, and although the highs and lows for each are quite a bit different, the body's cravings are similar. Just about the time you prepare to tee off on the fourth hole, your metabolism crashes, and your body screams for another pick-me-up.

Things don't improve at the turn when you ingest more sugar and empty calories in the form of candy, soda, or chips. These calories sustain you for about two more holes before you hit your second wall of the round somewhere around the 13th hole. This fall is a little more dramatic because of the number of swings that you have taken and the effort you've exerted.

The final six holes of a round are usually when you want to play your best, but because of what you have ingested, your body rejects you. This is commonly known as the *13th Wall,* the letdown many golfers experience after the 13th hole of a round. More often than not, you construct the 13th Wall long before you reach the 13th tee. The foods you eat before and during a round determine whether or not you can scale that wall and effectively finish your round.

Overcoming the alcohol factor

Nothing tastes better in the middle of a hot round than an ice cold malt beverage. And nothing is worse for your game. Alcohol on the golf course is as common as grass and sand, which is amazing considering the fact that no other sport tolerates such alcohol consumption. Can you imagine playing 15 or 20 minutes of basketball after a drink or two? How about tennis? Do you think you could go an extra set or two if you had a beer? Of course not. But many golfers are convinced that they can play better if they have a drink or two before or during a round.

The common rationale for golfers is the old saw that a drink calms your nerves and steadies your hands, thus improving your touch and feel around the greens. This notion is dangerously untrue. Alcohol impairs your fine motor skills and impedes your balance, which means you actually have less feel around the greens after a beer or two. Alcohol also dehydrates your body and drains essential nutrients from your system. So, although a nice cold adult beverage may taste great on a hot afternoon at the course, drinking it hurts your body and your game in the long run.

Improving Your Diet for Better Golf

All is not doom and gloom when it comes to golfers and their diets. A few changes in what you eat can result in dramatic improvements in your scores. The more you know about what foods are good for you, the better prepared you are to make informed choices about your diet.

Most of the nutrients required for athletic performance fall into one of two categories:

✔ *Macronutrients*. These are the carbohydrates, proteins, fats, and water that your body requires in large quantities to sustain an active, athletic lifestyle.

✔ *Micronutrients*. These are the vitamins and minerals that are important to performance and health. Your body needs small quantities of these nutrients on a daily basis. You can find micronutrients in certain foods or in the form of a supplement.

Macronutrients are the most critical elements in a golfer's diet, especially golfers over 40 who aren't as frisky and energetic as they were 20 years ago. These nutrients drive your energy levels and keep you going for longer periods of time. They sustain your metabolic rate and allow your body to burn calories evenly and efficiently.

In this section, I explain how to change your diet to include the necessary amount of these essential nutrients and help improve your golf game in the process.

Getting the right kind of carbohydrates

There are two distinct types of carbohydrates that have very different effects on your body. Simple carbohydrates are carbs that convert to sugar quickly, while complex carbohydrates break down more slowly. Every diet, whether good or bad, contains a mixture of carbohydrates, sugars, fats, and proteins. Bad diets are high in fat, sugars, and simple carbohydrates that convert quickly to sugar in the bloodstream. Good diets include more complex carbohydrates, such as legumes (beans), fruits lower in sugar like apples and pears, deep green vegetables, whole grain breads, and cereals, pastas, and rice.

For optimum golf performance, you need to eat complex carbohydrates a minimum of two hours before you tee off. A bowl of whole grain cereal or a couple of fruits should do the trick, provided they are eaten in the context of a well-balanced meal. Spinach is another great source of complex carbohydrates and one of the reasons Popeye never seemed to run out of energy.

When on the golf course, forget about the candy bars and chips. If you want to sustain your energy throughout the round and jump over the 13th Wall like it's not even there, eat an apple at the turn, or take a bag of trail mix (nuts and raisins) out on the course with you so that you can snack on the back nine. Ever wonder how trail mix got its name? The complex carbohydrates in this snack keep you going longer on the trail. If your trail is the back nine of your favorite golf course, nibbling on a few nuts and raisins could be the difference between hitting the wall or finishing strong.

Larry's lunch prescription

When Larry Nelson was diagnosed as borderline malnourished, he didn't know what to think. He ate three hearty meals a day, and when he was on the road he was always treated to some of the finest spreads the host clubs could put together. Every golf course on the PGA Tour schedule wants to show off its chefs, so the players enjoy an array of appetizers, entrees, breads, and deserts week-in and week-out. How could anyone who ate in that atmosphere be malnourished? This wasn't a third-world country he was traveling in; they were the finest golf clubs in the world!

The fact is that the quality of the foods at these clubs was second to none. Larry simply didn't eat often enough for the level of activity he was maintaining, and when he did eat, it wasn't the right kind of food for his system. This all came as quite a shock to Larry. In addition to playing the tour for more than 20 years, he is also a Vietnam veteran who knows what it's like to scrounge for food in a less-than-inviting area where nutrition is the last thing on your mind. To be told at age 53 that he didn't know how to eat didn't make any sense.

But like everyone, Larry's metabolism and nutritional needs had changed with age. He was still quite capable of sustaining the same energy levels he had when he was 25 or 30, but to do so he needed to change what he ate, and when he ate. Instead of eating three meals a day, Larry was placed on a six-meal-a-day plan with each meal being small but highly concentrated in complex carbohydrates. He also started carrying small bags of trail mix onto the course with him. From the 10th through the 18th holes each week, Larry could be seen nibbling on nuts and berries between shots, keeping his energy level and his focus high. The results were indisputable. After changing his diet, Larry had the best season of his career and was named the Senior PGA Tour Player of the Year for 2000.

Powering up with proteins

Protein gives you energy and builds and maintains muscle tissue. That's why high protein diets are often recommended for body builders. Meats usually contain complete proteins, while most proteins found in vegetables are incomplete, meaning they lack one or more of the essential chemical ingredients necessary to sustain growth. That's why vegetarians are advised to add soy and other high-protein supplements to their diets.

You need to take in enough protein on a daily basis to build and maintain muscle, but you should also be aware of the fat content in the foods that you consider for protein sources. Beef and pork are high in protein, but they can also be high in fat. The proper intake of protein depends greatly on your activity level and your body weight. Pay attention to your diet as you implement fitness for golf. You'll definitely need extra protein because your activity level will be higher — approximately .6 grams of protein per pound of body weight to function efficiently with your training regimen.

I'm frequently asked what is the ideal golf diet? It's a balance of carbohydrate, protein, and fat. The exact amount of each that you need depends on your training dedication. Implementing the regimen I suggest in this book requires a balance of approximately 25 percent protein, 50 percent carbohydrate, and 25 percent fat. Your doctor can help outline a diet that fits your age, body type, and workout schedule.

Debating water versus sports drinks

Water is one of the most essential ingredients in your body, and staying hydrated is critical to your rhythm, flexibility, strength, and stamina. Research has shown that a drink of water during a round can benefit a player's performance for up to 90 minutes. In fact, some people recommend drinking a cup or more of water on each tee for the first nine holes whether you're thirsty or not. They say ingesting water on a consistent basis throughout the round keeps you fresh and focused.

Although water has great benefits, it still can't provide some nutrients such as carbohydrates and *electrolytes* (compounds that conduct electricity through the body). On particularly hot, humid days when you're out in the sun for more than four hours, your body needs to replenish its electrolytes. That's when sports drinks come in handy. Most of these drinks have high glucose concentrations, along with a healthy dose of carbs and electrolytes to keep your performance standards high in taxing conditions.

But there is a timing consideration when drinking a high-glucose sports drink. Studies have shown that consuming these high-carb drinks 30 minutes prior to playing, while you're still at home or in the clubhouse, can raise your insulin level and could cause *hypoglycemia* (low blood sugar). This can actually decrease your performance and lead to fatigue. In order to gain the full benefit of sports drinks, consume them only when your body needs them, during performance when the blood sugar levels can be maintained.

Any good nutritional program begins with a combination of carbohydrates, proteins, fat, and water to keep you going for long periods of time, but also to keep you on an even keel. You have no artificial highs or lows with this diet, just a steady sustainable energy level that will keep you sharp throughout your entire round.

Their relationship is all wet

If you've ever been to a PGA Tour event, you've probably noticed the large ice chests filled with bottled water on every tee box. And you've probably noticed that players and caddies drink water on almost every hole. That's not an accident. Professionals understand the importance of remaining hydrated throughout a round. They also understand that in the heat of competition drinking water on a regular basis is even more important. If they forget, their caddies are right there to remind them.

One of the best caddies in golf today is Jim McKay. He has carried Phil Mickelson's bag since Phil's rookie season, making their relationship one of the longest in professional golf. In addition to being one of the most conscientious caddies on tour, McKay is also one of the brightest guys in golf. He understands the subtleties of the game, and he does whatever is needed to keep Mickelson sharp during a round.

That includes reminding Phil to drink plenty of water throughout the round, especially when he is in contention. On the final holes of the final round, it's not unusual to see McKay take a couple of extra bottles of water out of the cooler on each tee. Then, without being asked, he will hand a bottle of water to Phil as the two of them are walking down the fairway. Mickelson may not remember to drink if McKay doesn't take the initiative. That's one of the reasons those two men work so well together.

Part VII
The Part of Tens

The 5th Wave   By Rich Tennant

"Betty, you're not going to embarrass me at the club by wearing that hat, are you?"

In this part . . .

This is where the fun starts. As a practical matter, this may be the most productive part of this book, not because the material is any better than any of the other parts, but because this part provides you with quick, useful information that you can immediately put into practice. From discovering the ten mistakes that you're most likely to make when you begin your new life as a fit over-40 golfer to a 10-day workout plan for the home, this part gives you news you can use.

Chapter 20

Ten Questions to Evaluate Your Game

In This Chapter

▶ Evaluating your game, your age, and your health

▶ Being honest with yourself about where you are physically

▶ Thinking about some important questions

In order to establish a program of improvement you must be brutally honest with yourself in evaluating where you are in your game and your fitness. That's not as easy as it sounds. Self-evaluation, especially when it comes to the cold, hard facts of fitness and aging can be tough. You may face some harsh realities about yourself that you never considered. You may have to answer some questions that you never answered before. But the end result is worth it.

After you openly and honestly answer all the questions in this chapter, you'll have a starting point from which to build a new body, a new game, and a new attitude. At the very least, you'll know exactly where you are in your over-40 golf life.

To do this right you need a pen and paper. Some of the answers require calculation, others introspection. You should commit all your answers to paper. Only after you have written down your current status as a golfer can you map a path to improvement. So get your pen and paper ready and answer the following questions. Take your time, be thorough, but most of all, be honest with yourself.

Are You Long Off the Tee for Your Age, Size, and Strength?

No, you aren't going to hit the ball 340 yards unless you're a national long-driving champion. You probably aren't hitting it 250 yards anymore, if you ever did, but that's not the point. The standard you should set is not what you used to do, or what you see others on television do: Your tee-shot standard should factor in how far other people your own age, your own size, and with similar strength and skills hit the ball. Are you the longest or shortest driver in your regular foursome? Do you hit the ball farther than other members at your club who are your age? Compared to the over-40 players you know and with whom you compete, where do you fall on the length scale?

After you write down the answer to this question, test your answer at the course. March off the distance of a few drives the next time you play, and compare that distance to other players you know who are your age, including pros, who have their driving statistics posted in the newspaper and on the Internet for all to see. It may surprise you what you find out about yourself.

How Are Your Scores Compared to 10, 20, or 30 Years Ago?

Are you living in the past? Do you tee off every Saturday morning believing that you can still shoot that mid 70s score you posted on that magical afternoon 15 years ago? There's nothing wrong with positive thinking, and you should certainly have goals and dreams, but you also need to ground yourself in reality in order to make those dreams come true. If you shot in the 70s two decades ago, but haven't broken 85 in a year, make a note of that slip. You can't correct a decline without first recognizing that it exists.

Do You Hit Most of Your Poor Shots Early or Late in Your Rounds?

This question requires a fair amount of introspection and honest analysis of past rounds. But, it also requires some evaluation of your current play. During your next few trips to the course, keep a notebook of your round. After you complete play, log your good shots and your bad shots, what they were, and where they occurred in the round. If most of your poor shots occur late in your rounds, you may have an endurance problem (see Chapter 12). If you hit a lot of bad shots early in your rounds, but get better as the day progresses, you may need to re-evaluate your flexibility, rhythm, and, warm-up exercises (see Chapter 11). Either way, this is great information to have as you work to establish a long-term program for better golf. At the very least, you can be conscious of where and when you're hitting good and bad shots, which gives you something concrete to focus on.

What Parts of Your Body Hurt after Practice?

Most over-40 amateurs have some aches or pains after golf, but few take the time to evaluate the sources of their discomfort. Many times you dismiss these minor ailments as a natural part of getting older, or you block them out because dwelling on a sore thumb or a tender elbow makes you sound like a weenie. That's not a good way to approach your aging body. Sure, minor aches and pains are part of the deal for active over-40 athletes, but you need to know what hurts and why in order to structure an effective training program. You can't completely eliminate your aches and pains, but that shouldn't stop you from recognizing their existence.

Can You Concentrate throughout the Round?

Answering this question requires a great deal of analysis after the fact. Rarely in the middle of a round do you say to yourself, "Gee, I'm just not concentrating the way I'd like". You have to go back after a round and relive the shots in your mind to determine how effective your powers of focus and concentration were. If you can't remember certain shots or holes, you probably weren't as sharp as you need to be. Letting a few easy shots slip away because of bad preparation or laziness signals a slip in concentration as well.

Keep a running journal of how well you concentrate and update it after each round. By reliving the round while it's fresh in your mind, you can hopefully pinpoint the spots where you had mental lapses. After you identify the *when* and *where* of your concentration gaffes, you have a much better chance of determining the *why*.

How Often Do You Exercise Away from the Course?

More than 75 percent of this book is devoted to golf-specific exercises that you can practice away from the golf course. But before you can implement the first one into your daily routine, you need to be honest about where you are in your current golf exercise life. Do you ever swing a weighted club (see Chapter 11) at home? Do you work out in a gym? The only way to design an effective starting program is to know where you are. That means writing down what you do to prepare for golf when you are away from the golf course.

What Is Your Weekly Strength-Training Regimen?

Do you lift weights? Do you do push-ups in the morning? Or are you one of the many Americans who never lifts anything heavier than a 12-ounce aluminum can? Don't be embarrassed if you don't work out regularly. As long as you're prepared to change your lifestyle and engage in regular strength training exercises, your starting point should be viewed as just that: the point at which your journey begins. If you do no strength training now, and you refuse to do any in the future, your prospects of improving your distance, accuracy, and scores on the golf course after 40 fall somewhere between bleak and grim. It's no crime to be a beginner to golf fitness, but to remain a beginner is.

What is Your Conditioning Regimen?

Think about what you do for exercise. Do you walk when you play golf? Do you walk your dog in your neighborhood? Do you ever walk up a flight of stairs? When was the last time you were on a bike or a treadmill (see Chapter 12)? The truth is that you don't have to go to a gym and engage in conventional conditioning exercises, such as stationary bike riding or stair machine workouts in order to be exercising your heart. If you regularly walk, run, swim, bike, row, or engage in any other cardio-intensive activity, you can consider that a part of your regimen. There are hundreds of ways to exercise your heart. You need to search through your daily activities and find one that you like.

How (and How Often) Do You Stretch?

This is another area where saying never doesn't mean you are hopelessly banished to golf purgatory. If you don't stretch regularly, or even if you don't stretch at all, you simply have a more basic starting point from which to begin your program. You need to begin, however. No matter how conditioned you are, or how young you feel, over-40 bodies aren't as flexible as 20-year-old bodies. But they can be if you work at it. Flexibility training requires no talent and very little skill. All you need to become more flexible is the will to perform the exercises and the devotion to work at it every single day.

What Do You Eat and Drink before, during, and after Golf?

Nutrition is just as important in golf as in any other sport. You wouldn't expect to see a starting quarterback drinking a beer and eating a chili dog on the sidelines, and golfers shouldn't abuse their bodies with fatty foods and alcohol while trying to play. A well-balanced diet with the proper blend of proteins and carbohydrates can dramatically improve the concentration and athleticism needed to keep you going late into your round.

Chapter 21

A Ten-Day In-Home Regimen to Better Golf

*T*raining at home is inexpensive, easy, and convenient (see Chapter 18). Comfortably nestled in the confines of your own home you have no legitimate excuse for ignoring your training regimen, even though you may find hundreds of reasons to put it off. The fact is that you have to make the time to work out at home. After you carve an hour out of your day, follow the simple steps that I outline in this chapter for ten straight days. The results will amaze you.

The first step is to test yourself using the Fitness Analyzer tests in Chapter 17. These tests give you a starting guide for how much weight to lift, how many repetitions of each exercise in this chapter to do, and how long to work on cardiovascular training. (See the section "Putting Your Program into Practice" in Chapter 17 for details.)

As you look at the volume of exercises in this chapter, don't panic. As you become familiar with each one, you can quickly move through the workout. The rhythm and flow of the transitions from one exercise to the next will become second nature by the end of the first week, with the entire program lasting no more than an hour.

You can also find a training log (see Figure 21-32) at the end of this chapter. As you work through your ten-day regimen, list each exercise that you perform in the training log along with the amount of weight and number of reps that you accomplish each day. Seeing your results is an important part of the process. Long before you see measurable results in the mirror or on the course, you can see demonstrable results in black and white through this log.

Day One

Put on some loose-fitting clothes, take a few deep breaths, and prepare for your first official golf-specific at-home workout.

Lunge

Standing a comfortable distance from your step platform (see Chapter 18) with a dumbbell in each hand and your arms at your sides, slowly lunge toward the platform. Make sure the entire lead foot lands atop the step. After the foot makes contact with the platform, bend both knees and dip downward, not forward. When the front leg forms a 90-degree angle, slowly return to the start position and repeat with the opposite leg. See Figure 21-1 for an example of how to do a lunge with your step platform.

Figure 21-1: Kelly demonstrates the lunge.

Quad stretch

Sitting with both legs extended and your feet upright, wrap the center of your Golf Fitness Stretch Trainer across the ball of your right foot and hold both ends of the Stretch Trainer (a professionally designed strap used as a stretching aid) in your right hand. Then slowly roll down onto your left side while simultaneously bending the right knee and pulling the right foot toward the buttocks. To accelerate the stretch, grab both ends of the Stretch Trainer behind your head and pull upward. See Figure 21-2 for an example of how to do the quad stretch. Hold this stretch for 30 seconds and repeat to the opposite side.

Figure 21-2:
Laura demonstrating the quad stretch.

Squat

Straddle a step and turn your toes out slightly, holding a dumbbell in each hand with your arms at your sides. With your abdominal muscles taut, squat as though you're sitting in a chair by bending your knees and pushing your buttocks back. Keep your weight in your heels and lower your hips to a level even with or slightly above your knees. Never let your hips drop below your knees in this exercise. Then slowly return to the start position by pushing through your heels. See Figure 21-3 for an example of how to do a squat.

Hamstring stretch

Lying on your back with both knees bent so that your feet are flat on the floor, pull the right leg to your chest and wrap the Stretch Trainer around the arch of your foot. After the Stretch Trainer is in place, slowly straighten your leg holding on to both ends of the Stretch Trainer. When the leg is straight, slowly pull it toward your chest to intensify the stretch, and hold it for 30 seconds. Repeat this process with both legs. See Figure 21-4 for an example of how to do the hamstring stretch.

Figure 21-3: Kelly demonstrates the quad squat.

Figure 21-4: Laura demonstrates the hamstring stretch.

Bent back row

Place one foot atop a step, and place the corresponding hand on your knee for balance. Holding a dumbbell in the opposite hand, extend the arm so that the weight is above your perched foot. Then bending your elbow, draw the weight back in one single motion as if you're pulling weeds from your yard, or pulling the rope on a lawnmower. Slowly return to the start position and repeat the exercise with both arms. See Figure 21-5 for an example of how to do the bent back row.

Cat stretch

Stand on the center of your Golf Fitness Stretch Trainer with your feet together and hold the ends of the strap in your hands. Keeping your arms extended downward, slowly round your back (simulating the bowed back of a mad cat) and tuck your chin to your chest. Hold this stretch for 30 seconds. See Figure 21-6 for an example of how to do the cat stretch.

Figure 21-5:
Kelly demonstrating the bent back row.

Figure 21-6:
Laura demonstrating the cat stretch.

Seated alternate biceps curl

Sitting on a step or bench with your legs together and your torso upright, hold a dumbbell in each hand and extend your arms downward. Rotate your wrists so that the palms are facing your thighs, and slowly lift one arm to your shoulder, using the elbow as a hinge. Slowly return to the start position and repeat with the opposite arm. See Figure 21-7 for an example of how to do the seated alternate biceps curl.

Figure 21-7: Kelly demon-strating the seated alternate biceps curl.

Forearm/Biceps stretch

Standing with your feet shoulder-width apart and your hips rotated forward, place your right hand into the loop of the Stretch Trainer. If you don't have a Golf Fitness Stretch Trainer, loop a belt around the first knuckles of the hand where the fingers meet the palm. Holding your arm straight out in front of you, slowly pull downward on the Stretch Trainer (or belt) until you feel the stretch in your biceps and your forearms. Hold this stretch for 30 seconds and repeat to the opposite side. See Figure 21-8 for an example of how to do the forearm/biceps stretch.

Figure 21-8: Laura demon-strating the forearm/ biceps stretch.

Flat chest press

Lying on your back on a step or bench, place your feet atop the bench holding a dumbbell in each hand. Extend both your arms upward above your chest. Bending your elbows, move the weights away from each other and down until your arms form right angles. Then slowly return to the start position and repeat. See Figure 21-9 for an example of how to do the flat chest press.

Figure 21-9: Kelly demonstrating the flat chest press.

Chest and shoulder stretch

Standing with your feet shoulder-width apart and your hips rotated forward, place the Golf Fitness Stretch Trainer (again, a belt will work, too) parallel to the back with your arms extended downward. Pull on both ends of the Stretch Trainer taking out the slack, and slowly lift the arms upward feeling your chest expand and your shoulders stretch. Hold this stretch for 30 seconds. See Figure 21-10 for an example of how to do the chest and shoulder stretch.

Figure 21-10: Laura demonstrating the chest and shoulder stretch.

Seated front lateral raise

Sitting on the end of a bench with your back straight and your feet on the floor, hold a dumbbell in each hand with your palms down and your hands resting on your knees. From this position, slowly raise the weight to shoulder height, with your arms straight and your palms facing downward, then return the dumbbells to the start position. See Figure 21-11 for an example of how to do the front lateral raise.

Figure 21-11: Kelly demonstrating the front lateral raise.

Shoulder stretches

Repeat the same stretch that you see in Figure 21-10.

Flat cross extension

Lying on your back with your knees bent and your feet flat on a bench, hold a dumbbell in your right hand with your arm extended above your chest. Supporting your right elbow with your left hand, slowly lower the weight to your left shoulder by bending your right elbow, then return the weight to the start position and repeat with both arms. See Figure 21-12 for an example of how to do the flat cross extension.

Figure 21-12:
Kelly demonstrating the flat cross extension.

Triceps stretch

Standing with your feet shoulder-width apart and your hips rotated forward, place the loop of the Stretch Trainer over your right hand and raise your hand over your head with the strap dangling behind you. Place the opposite hand behind your back and grip the Stretch Trainer. Bending the elbow of the extended arm, slowly pull down on the strap, stretching the triceps muscle, and repeat with both arms. Hold for 30 seconds on each side. See Figure 21-13 for an example of how to do the triceps stretch.

Figure 21-13:
Laura demonstrating the triceps stretch.

Assisted abdominal crunch

If you have an ab roller (a training device that holds your head and shoulders in place as you exercise your abdominal region), lie flat on your back with your knees bent and your feet flat on the floor. Grab the ab roller, and crunch your abdominal muscles, rocking forward and tightening your abs. If you don't have an ab roller, placing your hands behind your head and keeping your neck straight while crunching your abdominal muscles achieves the same results. See Figure 21-14 for an example of how to do an assisted abdominal crunch with an ab roller.

Figure 21-14:
Kelly demonstrating the assisted abdominal crunch.

Abdominal stretch

Lying face down with your elbows bent and your hands placed where you can see both thumbs within your peripheral vision, slowly press down, extending your arms upward and arching your back. Hold this stretch for 30 seconds. See Figure 21-15 for an example of how to do the abdominal stretch.

Figure 21-15:
Laura demonstrating the abdominal stretch.

Day Two

Repeat all the stretching exercises from Day One, but do not work on any strength training today. Take a brisk walk or bike ride, periodically checking your heart rate to make sure that you are working aerobically (see Chapter 12).

Day Three

Repeat the following exercises from Day One:

- Lunge
- Quad stretch
- Squat
- Hamstring stretch
- Bent back row
- Cat stretch
- Seated alternate biceps curl
- Forearm/Biceps stretch
- Flat chest press
- Chest and shoulder stretch
- Seated front lateral raise
- Flat cross extension
- Triceps stretch
- Assisted abdominal crunch
- Abdominal stretch

You also need to add the following exercises to your workout.

Upright row

With your feet shoulder-width apart and holding a dumbbell in each hand with your arms extended in front of you, keep the heads of the weights together and slowly lift by bending your elbows, rowing the weights upward toward your chin. After the heads of the weights have reached neck-level, slowly return to the start position and repeat. See Figure 21-16 for an example of how to do the upright row.

Figure 21-16:
Kelly demonstrating the upright row.

Seated simultaneous curl

Sitting on a step with your back straight and your legs together, hold a dumbbell in each hand and place your elbows into your sides with both arms extended downward. Then slowly bend the elbows, simultaneously bringing the dumbbells toward your shoulders; slowly return to the start position and repeat. See Figure 21-17 for an example of how to do the seated simultaneous curl.

Figure 21-17:
Kelly demonstrating the seated simultaneous curl.

Flat chest fly

Lying on a step or bench with your knees bent and your feet flat on the platform, hold a dumbbell in each hand extending both arms upward so that the weights are over your chest. Then move the weights out away from each other and bend your elbows simulating a hugging motion, as if you're wrapping your arms around a large barrel; slowly lower the weights until your arms form a 90-degree angle at the elbows. Then return to the start position and repeat. See Figure 21-18 for an example of how to do the flat chest fly.

Figure 21-18:
Kelly demonstrating the flat chest fly.

Seated side lateral

Sitting at the end of your bench with your back straight, a dumbbell in each hand, and both arms extended at your sides, bend the elbows slightly and lift the weight upward to shoulder height so that your body forms a "T." Then slowly return to the start position and repeat. See Figure 21-19 for an example of how to do the seated side lateral.

Figure 21-19:
Kelly demonstrating the seated side lateral.

Reverse triceps extension

Lying face up on a step or bench with your knees bent and your feet flat on the platform, hold one dumbbell with both hands gripping the *head* of the weight (that's the fat heavy part). Extend your arms so that the dumbbell is over your forehead, then bending your elbows, lower the weight behind your head. Flex the *triceps* (the long rear muscles of the upper arm) to slowly return to the starting position and repeat. See Figure 21-20 for an example of how to do the reverse triceps extension.

Figure 21-20:
Kelly demonstrating the reverse triceps extension.

Day Four

Repeat all the stretching exercises from Day Three, but rather than holding the stretches for one 30-second interval, repeat each stretch three times, holding each for 30 seconds. Do not lift any weights or do any push-ups today.

Day Five

Repeat all the stretching exercises from Day Four, holding each stretch for 30 seconds. In addition, repeat your cardio training exercises from Day Two, but try to increase your speed for the duration of your walk or ride.

Day Six

Repeat the following exercises from Day Three:

- ✔ Lunge
- ✔ Quad stretch
- ✔ Squat
- ✔ Hamstring stretch
- ✔ Bent back row
- ✔ Upright row
- ✔ Cat stretch
- ✔ Seated alternate biceps curl
- ✔ Forearm/Biceps stretch
- ✔ Flat chest press
- ✔ Flat chest fly
- ✔ Chest and shoulder stretch
- ✔ Seated front lateral raise
- ✔ Seated side lateral
- ✔ Flat cross extension
- ✔ Reverse triceps extension
- ✔ Triceps stretch
- ✔ Assisted abdominal crunch
- ✔ Abdominal stretch

You should also add the following exercises to your routine on Day Six.

Adductor squat

With your feet six to twelve inches wider than shoulder-width apart and your toes pointed slightly outward, hold a dumbbell in each hand with your arms extended directly in front of you. Bend your knees and slowly lower your hips, simulating a plié from your favorite ballet. Then slowly return to the start position and repeat. See Figure 21-21 for an example of how to do the adductor squat.

Figure 21-21:
Kelly demonstrating the adductor squat.

Torso rotation

Sit on top a bench with your legs together and a *Power Ball* (a weighted ball, about the size of a basketball, used for strength training drills) extended in front of you just below chest height. Then slowly rotate to one side, keeping your arms extended as if you were placing the ball on the floor beside you without bending your arms and without lifting your buttocks off the bench. Rotate as far as possible, then slowly return to the start position and repeat. Do not use a power ball that is weighted more than eight pounds. See Figure 21-22 for an example of how to do the torso rotation.

Figure 21-22:
Kelly demonstrating the torso rotation.

Seated hammer curls

Sitting on a bench with your legs together and your back straight, hold a dumbbell in each hand and let your arms hang down to your sides. Rotate the wrists so that your palms are facing your thighs, then slowly lift one arm toward your shoulder, bending at the elbow but keeping the wrist firm. Slowly return to the start position and repeat with the opposite arm. See Figure 21-23 for an example of how to do the seated hammer curl.

Figure 21-23: Kelly demonstrating the seated hammer curls.

Assisted oblique crunch

Lying face up on the floor with your knees bent and your feet flat, grab the ab roller (if you have one) and lower your knees to the floor on your right side. Keeping your shoulders and head steady, curl your torso upward until the shoulders raise off the floor, then slowly return to the starting position and repeat. Do the same thing with your knees on the opposite side, giving equal time to both oblique muscles. If you don't have an ab roller, you can do this drill by clasping your hands behind your head and lifting your shoulders off the floor. Any questions about which muscles the obliques are will be answered after five or ten repetitions when you feel the tightening in your sides. See Figure 21-24 for an example of how to do the assisted oblique crunch.

Figure 21-24: Kelly demonstrating the assisted oblique crunch.

Day Seven

Do all the stretching exercises from Day Six in sets of three, holding each stretch for 30 seconds. Repeat the cardio exercise from Day Five, but push yourself a little harder, upping your speed as well as increasing the duration of your walk or ride.

Day Eight

Repeat the following exercises from Day Six:

- Lunge
- Quad stretch
- Squat
- Adductor squat
- Hamstring stretch
- Torso rotation
- Bent back row
- Upright row
- Cat stretch
- Seated alternate biceps curl
- Seated simultaneous curl
- Seated hammer curl
- Forearm/Biceps stretch
- Flat chest press
- Flat chest fly
- Chest and shoulder stretch
- Seated front lateral raise
- Seated side lateral
- Flat cross extensions
- Reverse triceps extension

- ✔ Triceps stretch
- ✔ Assisted abdominal crunch
- ✔ Assisted oblique crunch
- ✔ Abdominal stretch

You should also add the following exercises to your routine for Day Eight.

External rotations

Lying on your side with your bottom arm extended directly above you as if you were using your biceps as a pillow, bend your top arm so that your elbow is planted firmly in your side. Holding a dumbbell in your top hand (palm down) lift the weight upward in a rotating motion, keeping your elbow against your side and the triceps against your body. Slowly return to the starting position and repeat with both arms. See Figure 21-25 for an example of how to do external rotations.

Figure 21-25: Kelly demonstrating external rotations.

Internal rotations

Lying on your side and propping your head up with a firm pillow or a rolled towel, tuck your bottom arm close to your body, bending it at the elbow. Then keeping your triceps against your body and holding a dumbbell in your bottom hand (palm up), slowly lift the weight to your chest in a rotating motion, keeping your elbow planted on the bench or floor. Return to the start position and repeat this action with both arms. See Figure 21-26 for an example of how to do internal rotations.

Overhead triceps press

Sitting on a bench or step with your feet on the floor and your back straight, hold one dumbbell in both hands by cupping one end and extend your arms directly over your head. Then bending at the elbows, lower the weight behind your head, and slowly contract the triceps to return to the starting position and repeat. See Figure 21-27 for an example of how to do the overhead triceps press.

Forearm curls

Sitting on the bench with your feet on the floor, place your forearms on your thighs so that your wrists extend over your knees. With dumbbells in each hand — palms up — slowly curl your wrists, keeping the rest of your body as still as possible. See Figure 21-28 for an example of how to do the forearm curl.

Figure 21-28:
Kelly demonstrating forearm curls.

Wrist curls

Sitting in the same position as you were in the forearm curl exercise with your forearms resting on your thighs, simply turn your hands palms down and slowly curl your wrists upward until the backs of your hands face your chest. Slowly return to the start position and repeat. See Figure 21-29 for an example of how to do the wrist curl.

Figure 21-29:
Kelly demonstrating wrist curls.

Day Nine

Repeat all the stretching exercises from Day Eight in three sets, holding each stretch for 30 seconds. Do not lift any weights today.

Day Ten

Repeat the following exercises from Day Eight:

- ✔ Lunge
- ✔ Quad stretch
- ✔ Squat
- ✔ Adductor stretch
- ✔ Hamstring stretch
- ✔ Torso rotation
- ✔ Bent back row
- ✔ Upright row
- ✔ Cat stretch
- ✔ Seated alternate biceps curl
- ✔ Seated simultaneous curl
- ✔ Seated hammer curl
- ✔ Forearm/Biceps stretch
- ✔ Flat chest press
- ✔ Flat chest fly
- ✔ Chest and shoulder stretch
- ✔ Seated front lateral raise
- ✔ Seated side lateral
- ✔ External rotations
- ✔ Internal rotations
- ✔ Flat cross extension
- ✔ Reverse triceps extension

- ✔ Overhead triceps press
- ✔ Triceps stretch
- ✔ Forearm curls
- ✔ Wrist curls
- ✔ Assisted abdominal crunch
- ✔ Assisted oblique crunch
- ✔ Abdominal stretch

You should also add the following exercises to the final day of your 10-day program.

Hand compressions

This simple exercise involves simply squeezing a small ball, working the muscles in the forearms and the tendons in the hand. You should squeeze the ball as many times as possible with each hand, but exercise each side equally. See Figure 21-30 for an example of how to do the hand compression exercise.

Figure 21-30: Hand compression exercises.

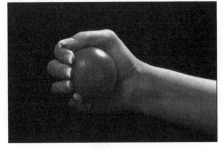 

Digit extensions

Using a common rubber band, wrap one end of the rubber band around your thumb and the other around one finger so that the rubber band is relaxed when your thumb and finger are close together. Then stretch the rubber band by extending the thumb and finger away from each other, and slowly return to the staring position, repeating the exercise as many times as possible with each digit of each hand. See Figure 21-31 for an example of how to do the digit extensions.

Figure 21-31:
Digit
extensions.

Without ever darkening the door of a gym, this program can get you well on your way to golf fitness after 40. After you complete your first 10 days, you can alternate strength training with flexibility and cardiovascular workouts on a regular basis, pushing yourself as you improve in each area. If you keep up with this program, you will see dramatic results.

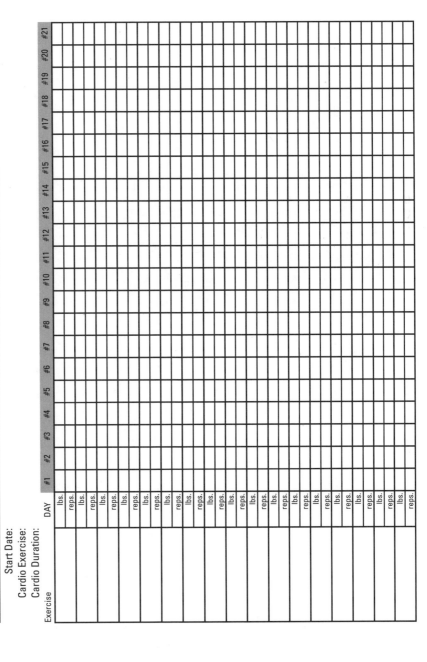

Figure 21-32:
Training log
to use
at home.

Chapter 22

Ten Mistakes of the Weekend Warrior

. . . .

In This Chapter

▶ Explaining the most common mistakes over-40 wishful thinkers make on the golf course

▶ Seeing why practicing doesn't always make you perfect

▶ Defeating the rationalizations that many weekend warriors use

. . . .

Golf's greatest mystery has nothing to do with the swing, the setup, the grip, or any of the mystic hyperbole that Hollywood and certain long-winded golf writers like to heap on the sport. The great, unsolved conundrum of this royal and ancient game isn't how to drive the ball farther or hit it higher, lower, or straighter. And despite what you hear on television every week, the great enigma of golf has nothing to do with putting, either. In fact, it all boils down to one simple, but as yet unscrambled puzzle. The biggest unanswered question facing golfers of all ages for all time is: "What could possibly be going on in that noggin of yours?"

Golf is a thinking person's game. Not only do you have to strategize your way around the golf course, you need to spend a fair amount of time thinking about how you prepare for golf, what you do to your body before, during and after a round, and what kinds of results you can expect from your actions. Like no other game, golf provides you with the perfect cause-and-effect environment. If you hit the ball long and straight and consistently make putts, you play well. If you fight a *hook* (a shot that curves left of your intended target), you're more likely to shoot a big score. And if you abuse your body before you play, your body abuses you right back when it comes time to pencil in your score at the end of the round.

Weekend golfers don't have to be weekend warriors — those silly sweat-drenched people who try to cram seven days' worth of practice and play into five hours on Saturday morning. But the temptations for those who love the game are great. It's hard not to spend as much time on the range and on the course as you can when you have the opportunity. Doing so isn't wrong, as long as you use your head. You can avoid falling prey to the weekend-warrior trap, but first you have to understand exactly what that trap looks like. You have to recognize the biggest mistakes ever made by golf's over-40 weekend warriors.

The Ball-Beating Extravaganza

Letting your overwhelming desire to improve get the best of you is awfully easy. You love the game so much that when you have an extra day off or a few extra hours on a sunny afternoon, you march out to the range with a bushel basket full of balls, ready and eager to solve all the problems the game can throw your way. Two hours later, one of the blisters that you've rubbed on your pinkie finger bursts, your lower back catches, and your arms are so tired that you can barely lift your bag onto your shoulder to march back to the clubhouse. And this is what you call a productive day!

Ball beating in this fashion isn't going to help your game. If anything, it makes you play worse. You have to take a measured and patient approach to every aspect of your game, including practice. Just as you wouldn't jump into a three- or four-hour workout in the gym after laying off for a month, don't run out to the range for a ball-beating extravaganza just because you have a little extra time. Take it easy. Your game will thank you.

The Mind-Is-Willing-But-the-Body-Is-No-Longer-Able Trap

A 60-year-old man faces a shot of 199 yards over water to a flag that is cut in the front right portion of the green with no room for error. He either hits a perfect 200-yard shot, or he goes in the drink. His only other option is to hit a 150-yard shot to a beautiful tuft of land short and to the left of the green. From there he has only 44 yards to the hole with plenty of green to work with and a lie to die for (so to speak). Does this man opt for the lay-up? Of course not! What, are you crazy? Not only does he try to hit the green; he tries to feather a high cut 2-iron into the flag. Then, of course, he's shocked, angered, befuddled, and bemused when his shot squibs along the water like a skipped stone before sinking into the abyss.

Why on earth would a man in his seventh decade of life who plays golf once or twice a week even attempt such a shot? The answer is simple: He did it back in the good old days. He should be able to do it now as well. Unfortunately, your body goes south long before your memory. Good golf is about maximizing what you have, not trying to recreate what's no longer there. The sooner you figure that out, the sooner you can lower your scores.

Over-Stretching and the Dreaded Bounce

Just because you could touch your toes 10 years ago doesn't mean you should bounce your torso (bobbing up and down until gravity and momentum get you there). This is the bigger hammer theory: If a peg doesn't fit in the right hole, you get a bigger hammer. If you're not as flexible as you once were, bounce it until you get there.

Bouncing stretches can cause injury more often than not in golf. Stretches take time, and stretching is a process, not a five-second bouncing session. If you bounce stretches, you're going to get hurt. It's only a matter of when, and how badly.

Out of the Car and onto the Tee

Life is faster and more hectic than ever before, and time is a precious commodity. Your boss wants more of it; your family wants more. You certainly wish you could add a few extra minutes to your days. But trying to cram in that extra phone call before running out to the club for your starting time is eventually going to catch up with you. Nobody can rush out of the office, drive like a maniac to the golf course, jump out of the car, run to the first tee, hit a smooth perfect drive down the center of the fairway, and then play the entire round like nothing is wrong. It doesn't happen.

The few extra minutes that you take to warm up and stretch, hitting a few pitch shots, rolling a few putts, warming up your muscles and joints, and getting your body in a rhythm for golf, pays off in droves on the course. Golf is supposed to be fun. Take a little extra time to make it even more enjoyable.

Hard-Core Practice before a Round

The pre-round practice session isn't a practice session at all: It's a warm-up period, a time to get into a rhythm and put a few positive swing thoughts in your head before heading to the course. Turning the pre-round warm-up into a full-blown practice session, complete with drills and experiments followed by balls, balls, and more balls is a foolish way to spend your day unless you're trying to sabotage your score before you get to the first tee. The only thing you want to do before a round is get your mind and body ready to play. Anything else is wasted effort.

Hard Workouts at Night, Early Play the Next Morning

Playing and working out are not mutually exclusive, as I have tried to impress upon you throughout this book. But what doesn't work is engaging in a hard heavy-lifting workout late in the evening, going to bed shortly afterward, then getting up the next morning and immediately trying to play. Your muscles require a little recovery period after a hard workout. Sometimes that's a half-hour or so of stretching, other times a few minutes in a hot tub does the trick. You need to do whatever it takes to keep your hard-working muscles loose after a workout, even if you're going to bed. If you do, you will thank yourself on the first tee the next morning.

Mistakes on the Course Aren't Always Due to Technique

Many telltale signs illustrate how a golf match is going. One surefire way to know the score of a particular match is to look for the player who's checking his swing plane and the position of his hands at the top of his backswing before and after each shot. That guy is going to lose. You can bet the farm on it.

Many weekend warriors can't leave the swing theory on the driving range or in the clubhouse and simply play the shot that's required for the situation. Pros refer to this affliction as *playing golf swing* instead of playing golf. The course is not the place to worry about the mechanics of your swing. And if you are worrying about where the club is positioned at the top, you're probably going to lose your match.

You Can Work Out the Same Day You Play

Tour pros work out the same days they play. In fact, most of them engage in stretching exercises before the round, while some start their days with a good cardiovascular warm-up like a 15- or 20-minute session on the stationary bike. After their rounds, they hit the weight room for a good dose of strength training before another round of stretching and some additional cardiovascular work.

The truth is that you can and should work out the same day you play. You simply can't be foolish about it. If you do 100 bicep curls an hour before your tee time, you won't swing the club well. But if you spend 30 to 45 minutes stretching before heading to the tee, you have a better than average chance of posting a pretty good score. As long as you use your head, working out can be a normal part of your game-day routine.

Just One Beer to Calm My Putting Nerves

Golf is difficult enough when you have all your wits and faculties about you. When you start impairing your balance, feel, coordination, and timing with alcohol, you're done. Granted the taste of a cold beer can seem like nectar from the gods on a hot day. But if you quench your desire for that nectar on the golf course, you can forget about playing well. You can play golf or you can drink. But you can't do both at the same time.

Just One Pitcher after the Round

You just burned numerous carbohydrates, calories, and electrolytes during an 18-hole round of golf. What's the best thing you can do to replenish those vital nutrients and get your body back in shape for the rest of your day? The answer is certainly not drinking a pitcher of beer. Alcohol saps your body of even more nutrients than golf. A frosty pitcher of your favorite beer isn't something you should give up on completely. You simply need to wait until your body recovers some of what it needs before you treat yourself to something you want.

Chapter 23

Ten Golf Cart Stretches

*E*ven if you take the time to warm up and stretch properly before your round, you may still feel the need to stretch a little more or take a particular golf muscle a little deeper into a stretch. This idea is especially true for those days when you play in less-than-ideal weather conditions and your muscles tense up in a fight to stay warm. At those times, added stretching is a must.

Riding in a cart from shot to shot also gives your back just enough time to stiffen up. That's why I highly recommend walking for golfers of all ages, but especially for those over 40 who need to remain loose and active. But given the fact that you will probably use a golf cart if one is available, here are ten simple exercises to utilize the mechanical beast in ways that may actually improve your game.

Hamstring Stretch

Place your heel atop the wheelbase and place the corresponding hand on the back of the cart for balance and assistance (see Figure 23-1). Pointing your toe in the air and keeping your knee slightly bent, lean forward at the waist until you feel the stretch. Hold this stretch for 15 to 30 seconds before repeating the process with the opposite foot.

Quadriceps Stretch

Facing away from the golf cart, place the top of your foot on the top of the cart's wheelbase, and reach behind your back to hold the cart for balance (see Figure 23-2). Tucking your hips, you should feel this stretch in the front muscle of your leg. After you find the stretch, hold it for 15 to 30 seconds before repeating the process on the other side.

Calf Stretch

Place the ball of one foot on the running board and hold onto the top of the cart for balance. Now point the toe in the air while gently pressing the heel down until you feel the stretch in your calf muscle (see Figure 23-3). Hold that stretch for 15 to 30 seconds and repeat with the other leg.

Figure 23-1:
Hamstring
stretch on
the golf cart.

Figure 23-2:
Quadriceps
stretch for
the golf cart.

Figure 23-3:
Calf stretch
on the golf
cart.

Abductor Stretch

Standing with your side facing the golf cart, reach out with the arm closest to the cart and hang onto the frame for balance. With the arm extended, cross the outside leg over the inside leg and slowly bend toward the cart at the waist until you feel the stretch in your *abductor,* the lower body muscle that moves the hips laterally and allows you to lift your legs out to the sides (see Figure 23-4). Hold that stretch for 15 to 30 seconds before repeating on the other side.

Upper Back Stretch

Face the cart and gently grip the canopy with both hands. Then extend your arms and round your back away from the cart allowing the vehicle's weight to assist in the stretch. Hold that position for 15 to 30 seconds, but repeat the stretch as many times as you need it throughout the round (see Figure 23-5).

Figure 23-4:
Abductor
stretch.

Figure 23-5:
Upper back
stretch on
the golf cart.

Shoulder Stretch

Standing beside the golf cart with your side facing the cart, reach across your body with your outside arm and grab the cart's canopy support bar. Slowly turn your torso away from the cart to accelerate the stretch (see Figure 23-6). Hold for 15 to 30 seconds and repeat the stretch from the other side.

Chest Stretch

Standing to the side of the cart, reach out the arm closest to the cart and grab the canopy support bar. Now move away from the cart until your arm is fully extended and slowly rotate your torso away from the cart until you feel the stretch in your chest (see Figure 23-7). After you find the stretch, hold it for 15 to 30 seconds before repeating with the other side.

Figure 23-6:
Shoulder
stretch with
the cart.

Figure 23-7:
Chest
stretch on
the golf cart.

Low Back Stretches

Sitting in the cart, reach down and hug your arms under your knees, keeping both feet on the floorboard (see Figure 23-8). You feel this stretch in your lower back, but if you want to accelerate it, slowly round your back until you reach your desired stretch. Hold that stretch for 15 to 30 seconds.

Trunk Rotation Stretch

Sitting in the middle of the cart with your back straight and your feet on the floorboard, turn your torso to one side and reach for the bar across the back of the seat. Make this turn with as little hip movement as possible and feel the stretch throughout your torso (see Figure 23-9). Hold the stretch for 15 to 30 seconds and repeat on the other side.

Figure 23-8:
Lower back
stretches.

Figure 23-9:
Trunk rotation stretch in the golf cart.

Forearm Stretch

Sitting on the driver's side of the cart, place the base of your fingers on the bottom of the steering wheel and extend both arms. Then, keeping a slight bend in your elbows, press the heel of your hands downward until you feel the stretch in your forearms (see Figure 23-10). Hold that stretch for 15 to 30 seconds.

Make these stretches a habit during your rounds, and take note of how far you can stretch each time you play. It's not as worthy a goal as making a birdie on the hardest hole on the course, but increasing your stretches each time you play is a challenge that you should set for yourself. You may be surprised by the results that sort of goal ultimately produces.

Figure 23-10:
Forearm
stretch.

Index

• C •

• D •

Notes

Notes

Notes

Notes

Notes

Kelly Blackburn's Golf Fit System

Includes: 1 weighted Swing Trainer, 1 weighted Power Ball, 1 Stretch Trainer, 1 60-minute workout video, and 1 45-minute course warm-up instruction video.

This complete system will maximize your on-course performance. Featuring the MOMENTUS Swing Trainer used by **more than 100 TOUR pros,** the videos show you how to get fit for your game — anywhere! Play better golf for 18 consistent holes and help prevent injuries. **It's fun and easy to use!**

Order the complete system by calling 1-800-315-2329 (refer to item **#GO40–GFS1**). You will receive a $10.00 discount with this coupon.